Windows Debugging Notebook

Essential User Space WinDbg Commands

Roberto Alexis Farah
Dmitry Vostokov
Mario Hewardt
(Foreword)

OpenTask

Published by OpenTask, Republic of Ireland

Troubleshooting and Debugging Notebooks series editor: Dmitry Vostokov

OpenTask books are available through booksellers and distributors worldwide. For further information or comments send requests to press@opentask.com.

A CIP catalogue record for this book is available from the British Library.

ISBN-13: 978-1-906717-00-1 (Paperback)

ISBN-13: 978-0-9558328-5-7 (Hardcover)

First printing, 2011

"Debugging is twice as hard as writing the code in the first place. Therefore, if you write the code as cleverly as possible, you are, by definition, not smart enough to debug it."

Brian Kernighan

0n4 0x04 0000 0100 ***!ready*** *Shows threads in a READY state* ***(KA)***

Table of Contents

Series Editor's Preface

An idea to have a debugging notebook to open and browse when looking for specific debugger commands or hints came to me when I was reading a book Why Programs Fail: A Guide to Systematic Debugging (ISBN: 978-1558608665) written by Andreas Zeller. The author emphasized the importance to keep such notebooks to keep a track of progress and accounts of past debugging sessions. To such a purpose any good notebook with blank pages would suffice but I thought that a specific notebook summarizing experience of a professional engineer would also be very beneficial. Having a list of a debugger commands to browse for debugging ideas would also help here.

That's why I proposed that Roberto would summarize his accumulated debugging experience troubleshooting and debugging complex issues on Windows platforms and extend it with additional tips.

Initially we thought of combining essential and debugging concepts, debugger commands and tools into one volume but later recognized that the notebook would be very heavy. So we split the title into User Space, Kernel Space, Managed Space (.NET), and Concepts and Tools.

Dmitry Vostokov
Memory Dump Analysis Services
Director of Research/Founder
www.DumpAnalysis.com

[This page is intentionally left blank]

Foreword

I remember back in "the good old days" when my applications where either written in C with a bit of assembly or entirely in assembly going directly against the hardware. While the power of direct hardware access was important (and sometimes the only way of accomplishing a specific task) the code quickly became difficult to maintain and troubleshoot due to having to support different types of hardware. This form of development led me to have to rely heavily on a tool known as a debugger. In those days, I made heavy use of debug.com (not the URL, the actual executable) to quickly troubleshoot problems in my applications. Over the years, operating systems have evolved quite dramatically and we no longer have to worry about direct hardware interaction due to an increased layer of abstraction isolating us from the that tedious task. It would stand to reason that with this abstraction layer our task as developers becomes easier. Not quite. With the number of abstractions now sitting between us and the hardware, arguably, debugging has become even more important. While abstractions have evolved in a rapid paste so has our need to rely on effective troubleshooting techniques and tools. Over the last 15 years I have dedicated a large part of my career researching how to make applications more reliable and robust in the face of an ever-changing landscape. As part of this research, I have used debuggers extensively to delve into the details of various platforms (such as Windows and the CLR) focusing on how that particular platform works to better understand why applications fail running on those platforms. After all, with all the benefits that an abstraction brings it is just that – an abstraction. Misuse of the abstraction can lead to devastating results and only by having a solid understanding of how the abstraction actually works under the covers can you effectively troubleshoot problems and make sure that you write the best software possible.

In an effort to educate the community on the importance of debugging I have authored two books (Advanced Windows Debugging and Advanced .NET Debugging) and I am glad to see Windows Debugging Notebook: Essential User Space WinDbg Commands added to the short list books on this very important topic. It is written by Roberto Farah and Dmitry Vostokov with lots of combined experience in the troubleshooting process and provides good descriptions with pragmatic examples of how to effectively debug using some of the most powerful debuggers out there - Debugging Tools for Windows.

I hope you enjoy the book and happy debugging.

Mario Hewardt
CEO/Founder
The High-Tech Avenue ™
www.thehightechavenue.com

Acknowledgements

Thousands of people reviewed Debugging Toolbox blog content and I would like to thank all of them for providing their comments, suggestions and encouragement.

[This page is intentionally left blank]

About the Author

Roberto Alexis Farah, Senior Premier Field Engineer at Microsoft Corporation has been professionally debugging and troubleshooting applications for 10 years. Roberto is the author of Debugging Toolbox:

http://blogs.msdn.com/b/debuggingtoolbox/

[This page is intentionally left blank]

A Note about Heap

Excellent description of process heap and associated issues like heap corruption can be found in Advanced Windows Debugging book (Hewardt & Pravat, 2008). Here is the corresponding UML static structure diagram for Windows XP/2003 heap implementation (reengineered using **dt** WinDbg command) where only the details useful to understand heap structure and its navigation are included:

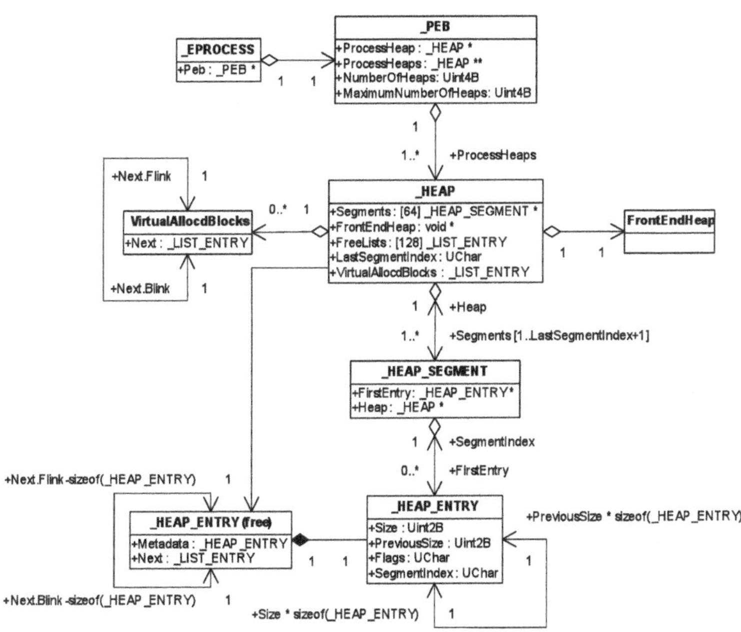

Large heap allocations beyond the certain threshold go directly to virtual memory manager.

There are also minor changes in Vista and Windows Server 2008. The most noticeable of them is the fact that heap segments and free lists are now doubly-linked lists instead of fixed arrays. The first heap segment is at the beginning of the _HEAP structure and additional heap segments are linked through _HEAP_SEGMENT.SegmentListEntry:

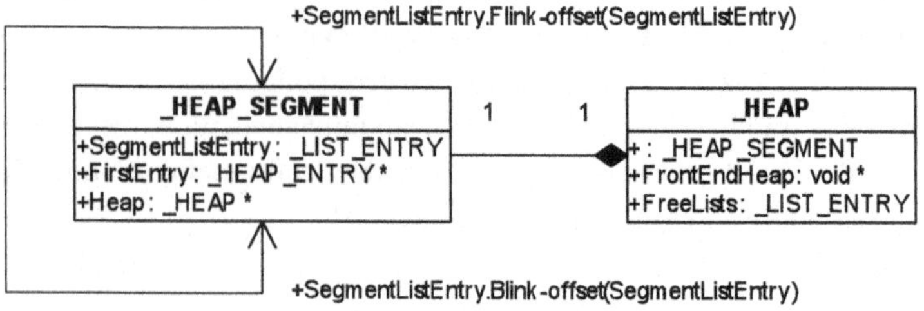

.dump/.dumpcab

Using WinDbg we can create a dump file from a running application, for instance, in a production server. After collecting the dump file we can load the dump file on another machine and analyze it to debug the problem. However, to be effective during our debugging session we need symbols. Thus, here is a trick to get both, the dump and symbols.

First, to get a dump file with all information we use this command:

```
0:000> .dump /mfht c:\Test.dmp

Creating c:\Test.dmp - mini user dump

Dump successfully written
```

.dump command has several options, but if we want a minidump with all information we just need to use **/mfht** where it saves full memory (accessible committed pages), data about handles and additional thread times for **!runaway** and **.ttime** commands.

After collecting the dump file we open it on the production server using WinDbg and reload the symbols again. Then we use the **.dumpcab** command. The arguments are **-a** (force all symbols) and the file name.

```
0:003> .dumpcab -a c:\fulldump

Creating a cab file can take a VERY VERY long time

.Ctrl-C can only interrupt the command after a file has been added
to the cab.

  Adding C:\test.dmp - added

  Adding
c:\publicsymbols\wntdll.pdb\E06BEA155E9748BEA818E2D0DD2FED952\wntd
ll.pdb - added

Wrote c:\downloads\fulldump
```

The file fulldump.cab now has the dump file and all related symbols so we can copy it to another machine, unpack, load the dumps/symbols and start a debugging session.

.writemem

This command allows us to save memory into a disk file. The cool thing about it is that we can save modules too, because they are just raw memory.

Here is an example:

```
0:026> lm
start    end        module name
00400000 00427000   mtgdi      (deferred)
5a700000 5acaf000   mfc90d     (deferred)
63df0000 63f13000   MSVCR90D   (deferred)
71270000 71283000   dwmapi     (deferred)
72cf0000 72d70000   UxTheme    (deferred)
73470000 73475000   MSIMG32    (deferred)
73b90000 73b9d000   MFC90ENU   (deferred)
74fd0000 75053000   COMCTL32   (deferred)
751d0000 751dc000   CRYPTBASE   (deferred)
751e0000 75240000   SspiCli    (deferred)
75240000 75259000   sechost    (deferred)
75260000 75ea6000   SHELL32    (deferred)
75ee0000 75f8c000   msvcrt     (deferred)
75fd0000 76060000   GDI32      (deferred)
76150000 76250000   kernel32   (deferred)
76250000 762ed000   USP10      (deferred)
763b0000 76410000   IMM32      (deferred)
76410000 7649f000   OLEAUT32   (deferred)
764a0000 764e4000   KERNELBASE   (deferred)
765c0000 766b0000   RPCRT4     (deferred)
766b0000 76733000   CLBCatQ    (deferred)
76a00000 76aa0000   ADVAPI32   (deferred)
```

```
76ce0000 76d37000   SHLWAPI    (deferred)
76f40000 77040000   USER32     (deferred)
77040000 7710c000   MSCTF      (deferred)
77110000 7726b000   ole32      (deferred)
77640000 7764a000   LPK        (deferred)
```

Now let's save MFC90ENU.DLL from the list above:

```
0:026> .writemem c:\downloads\MFC90ENU.dll 73b90000 (73b9d000 - 0x1)
Writing d000 bytes.........................
```

Note the "`- 0x1`" above. If we don't do that the command will fail because the debugger will try to write from the base address to the end address inclusive.

Another approach we can use is to get the size of the module and use it as one of the parameters:

```
0:026> ? 73b9d000 - 73b90000
Evaluate expression: 53248 = 0000d000
```

```
0:026> .writemem c:\downloads\MFC90ENU.dll 73b90000 L 0000d000
Writing d000 bytes.........................
```

!runaway

This is one of our favorite commands. It displays information about the time consumed by each thread in User and Kernel Modes. **!runaway** is one of those commands we execute when we think an application is hung with low or high CPU or has some kind of a performance issue. The output is sorted from a thread consuming most CPU time to a thread consuming least CPU time.

Example of displaying just the User Time for each thread (no command parameters):

```
0:000> !runaway
 User Mode Time
  Thread       Time
  52:33b4      0 days 0:00:01.435
 317:2834      0 days 0:00:00.982
  93:2d60      0 days 0:00:00.936
 479:3858      0 days 0:00:00.842
 266:33b0      0 days 0:00:00.842
 658:23d8      0 days 0:00:00.826
 559:1acc      0 days 0:00:00.826
 299:357c      0 days 0:00:00.826
 279:bf8       0 days 0:00:00.826
 719:39c0      0 days 0:00:00.811
 509:38d0      0 days 0:00:00.811
 376:19a0      0 days 0:00:00.811
 314:3700      0 days 0:00:00.811
  84:338c      0 days 0:00:00.811
 731:2fa0      0 days 0:00:00.795
 691:2070      0 days 0:00:00.795
  24:1b88      0 days 0:00:00.795
 800:3ca4      0 days 0:00:00.780
```

```
761:3c08      0 days 0:00:00.780
720:3968      0 days 0:00:00.780
. . .
. . .
. . .
```

!lmi

Like its cousin **!dh** the **!lmi** extension displays the PE header information from a specified module. However, it gives us less details than **!dh**.

Examples:

```
0:532> !lmi mtgdi
Loaded Module Info: [mtgdi]
         Module: mtgdi
   Base Address: 00400000
     Image Name: mtgdi.exe
   Machine Type: 332 (I386)
     Time Stamp: 48785a80 Sat Jul 12 00:17:20 2008
           Size: 27000
       CheckSum: 0
Characteristics: 103
Debug Data Dirs: Type  Size     VA  Pointer
             CODEVIEW    3b, 200dc,    e8dc RSDS - GUID: {EC1B3DB2-25C1-
4337-8676-DFB3C5B1C8C9}
               Age: 3, Pdb: c:\DOWNLOADS\mtgdi\Debug\mtgdi.pdb
     Image Type: FILE     - Image read successfully from debugger.
                 C:\development\My Tools\Book\mtgdi\Debug\MtGdi.exe
    Symbol Type: PDB      - Symbols loaded successfully from image path.
                 C:\development\My Tools\Book\mtgdi\Debug\mtgdi.pdb
       Compiler: Resource - front end [0.0 bld 0] - back end [9.0 bld 21022]
    Load Report: private symbols & lines, not source indexed
                 C:\development\My Tools\Book\mtgdi\Debug\mtgdi.pdb


0:532> !lmi ole32
Loaded Module Info: [ole32]
         Module: ole32
   Base Address: 77110000
     Image Name: C:\Windows\syswow64\ole32.dll
   Machine Type: 332 (I386)
```

```
     Time Stamp: 49eea66c Tue Apr 21 22:09:00 2009
           Size: 15b000
       CheckSum: 1607b7
Characteristics: 2102  perf
Debug Data Dirs: Type  Size     VA  Pointer
             CODEVIEW    22, 138b1c,  13831c RSDS - GUID: {D66D525C-3DF2-
47C7-AB77-594C4E5E2325}
               Age: 2, Pdb: ole32.pdb
                CLSID     4, 138b18,  138318 [Data not mapped]
     Image Type: FILE     - Image read successfully from debugger.
                 C:\Windows\syswow64\ole32.dll
    Symbol Type: PDB      - Symbols loaded successfully from symbol server.

c:\publicsymbols\ole32.pdb\D66D525C3DF247C7AB77594C4E5E23252\ole32.pdb
    Load Report: public symbols , not source indexed

c:\publicsymbols\ole32.pdb\D66D525C3DF247C7AB77594C4E5E23252\ole32.pdb
```

Note the `Base Address` field above. We can get the base address from a module using different commands like **lm** or even **dd**. The latter command is an abbreviation of **D**isplay **D**WORDs but it resolves module names too:

```
0:532> dd ole32 L1
77110000  00905a4d

0:532> dd mtgdi L1
00400000  00905a4d
```

!dlls

!dlls extension shows the table entries of all loaded modules. Also we can use it to see all modules that a thread or process are currently using. The WinDbg help file describes all parameters. Here we are going to describe the most common usage.

- To display file headers and section headers:

```
0:801> !dlls -a

0x00543598: C:\development\My Tools\Book\mtgdi\Debug\MtGdi.exe
      Base   0x00400000  EntryPoint  0x00411929  Size        0x00027000
      Flags  0x00004000  LoadCount   0x0000ffff  TlsIndex    0x00000000
             LDRP_ENTRY_PROCESSED

File Type: EXECUTABLE IMAGE
FILE HEADER VALUES
     14C machine (i386)
       6 number of sections
48785A80 time date stamp Sat Jul 12 00:17:20 2008

       0 file pointer to symbol table
       0 number of symbols
      E0 size of optional header
     103 characteristics
            Relocations stripped
            Executable
            32 bit word machine

OPTIONAL HEADER VALUES
     10B magic #
    9.00 linker version
    C400 size of code
    7C00 size of initialized data
```

```
       0 size of uninitialized data
   11929 address of entry point
    1000 base of code
    1000 base of data
         ----- new -----
00400000 image base
    1000 section alignment
     200 file alignment
       2 subsystem (Windows GUI)
    5.00 operating system version
    0.00 image version
    5.00 subsystem version
   27000 size of image
     400 size of headers
       0 checksum
00100000 size of stack reserve
00001000 size of stack commit
00100000 size of heap reserve
00001000 size of heap commit
00400100 Opt Hdr
       0 [       0] address [size] of Export Directory
   23000 [      8C] address [size] of Import Directory
   25000 [    1E7C] address [size] of Resource Directory
       0 [       0] address [size] of Exception Directory
       0 [       0] address [size] of Security Directory
       0 [     101] address [size] of Base Relocation Directory
   1E940 [      1C] address [size] of Debug Directory
       0 [       0] address [size] of Description Directory
       0 [       0] address [size] of Special Directory
       0 [       0] address [size] of Thread Storage Directory
       0 [       0] address [size] of Load Configuration Directory
       0 [       0] address [size] of Bound Import Directory
   23884 [     7F8] address [size] of Import Address Table Directory
       0 [       0] address [size] of Reserved Directory
```

0n26 0x1A 0001 1010 **!arbiter** *Shows resource arbiters and their ranges*

```
        0 [       0] address [size] of Reserved Directory
        0 [       0] address [size] of Reserved Directory

SECTION HEADER #1
          name
        0 virtual size
        0 virtual address
        0 size of raw data
        0 file pointer to raw data
        0 file pointer to relocation table
        0 file pointer to line numbers
        0 number of relocations
        0 number of line numbers
        0 flags
          (no align specified)

SECTION HEADER #2
          name
        0 virtual size
        0 virtual address
        0 size of raw data
        0 file pointer to raw data
        0 file pointer to relocation table
        0 file pointer to line numbers
        0 number of relocations
        0 number of line numbers
        0 flags
          (no align specified)

SECTION HEADER #3
          name
        0 virtual size
        0 virtual address
```

```
       0 size of raw data
       0 file pointer to raw data
       0 file pointer to relocation table
       0 file pointer to line numbers
       0 number of relocations
       0 number of line numbers
       0 flags
         (no align specified)

SECTION HEADER #4
         name
       0 virtual size
       0 virtual address
       0 size of raw data
       0 file pointer to raw data
       0 file pointer to relocation table
       0 file pointer to line numbers
       0 number of relocations
       0 number of line numbers
       0 flags
         (no align specified)

SECTION HEADER #5
         name
       0 virtual size
       0 virtual address
       0 size of raw data
       0 file pointer to raw data
       0 file pointer to relocation table
       0 file pointer to line numbers
       0 number of relocations
       0 number of line numbers
       0 flags
         (no align specified)
```

```
SECTION HEADER #6
         name
       0 virtual size
       0 virtual address
       0 size of raw data
       0 file pointer to raw data
       0 file pointer to relocation table
       0 file pointer to line numbers
       0 number of relocations
       0 number of line numbers
       0 flags
         (no align specified)
```

- To display version numbers:

```
0:801> !dlls -v

0x00543598: C:\development\My Tools\Book\mtgdi\Debug\MtGdi.exe
      Base   0x00400000  EntryPoint  0x00411929  Size        0x00027000
      Flags  0x00004000  LoadCount   0x0000ffff  TlsIndex    0x00000000
             LDRP_ENTRY_PROCESSED
      Product Name        MTGDI Application
      Product Version     1, 0, 0, 1
      Original Filename   MTGDI.EXE
      File Description    MTGDI MFC Application
      File Version        1, 0, 0, 1

0x00543628: C:\Windows\SysWOW64\ntdll.dll
      Base   0x77630000  EntryPoint  0x00000000  Size        0x00180000
      Flags  0x80004004  LoadCount   0x0000ffff  TlsIndex    0x00000000
             LDRP_IMAGE_DLL
             LDRP_ENTRY_PROCESSED
      Company Name        Microsoft Corporation
```

(S) .catch *If an error occurs prevents termination* *0n29 0x1D 0001 1101*

```
    Product Name         Microsoft® Windows® Operating System
    Product Version      6.1.7100.0
    Original Filename    ntdll.dll
    File Description     NT Layer DLL
    File Version         6.1.7100.0 (winmain_win7rc.090421-1700)

0x005439a8: C:\Windows\syswow64\kernel32.dll
    Base   0x769d0000  EntryPoint  0x769e3e8a  Size        0x00100000
    Flags  0x80084004  LoadCount   0x0000ffff  TlsIndex    0x00000000
           LDRP_IMAGE_DLL
           LDRP_ENTRY_PROCESSED
           LDRP_PROCESS_ATTACH_CALLED
    Company Name         Microsoft Corporation
    Product Name         Microsoft® Windows® Operating System
    Product Version      6.1.7100.0
    Original Filename    kernel32
    File Description     Windows NT BASE API Client DLL
    File Version         6.1.7100.0 (winmain_win7rc.090421-1700)

0x00543ac0: C:\Windows\syswow64\KERNELBASE.dll
    Base   0x76ad0000  EntryPoint  0x76ad563f  Size        0x00044000
    Flags  0x80084004  LoadCount   0x0000ffff  TlsIndex    0x00000000
           LDRP_IMAGE_DLL
           LDRP_ENTRY_PROCESSED
           LDRP_PROCESS_ATTACH_CALLED
    Company Name         Microsoft Corporation
    Product Name         Microsoft® Windows® Operating System
    Product Version      6.1.7100.0
    Original Filename    Kernelbase
    File Description     Windows NT BASE API Client DLL
    File Version         6.1.7100.0 (winmain_win7rc.090421-1700)
```

- Using Module Address to display information from a specific dll:

!dlls -c <moduleAddress>

```
0:801> !dlls -c 63390000

Dump dll containing 0x63390000:


0x00544998:
C:\Windows\WinSxS\x86_microsoft.vc90.debugcrt_1fc8b3b9a1e18e3b_9.0.30729.1_n
one_bb1f6aa1308c35eb\MSVCR90D.dll

      Base   0x63390000  EntryPoint  0x633cc6f0  Size        0x00123000

      Flags  0x90084004  LoadCount   0x0000ffff  TlsIndex    0x00000000

             LDRP_IMAGE_DLL

             LDRP_ENTRY_PROCESSED

             LDRP_PROCESS_ATTACH_CALLED

             LDRP_REDIRECTED
```

!dh

The **!dh** extension displays the PE header information from a specified module.

Example:

```
0:532> lm
start    end        module name
00400000 00427000   mtgdi      (deferred)
5a700000 5acaf000   mfc90d     (deferred)
692e0000 69403000   MSVCR90D   (deferred)
71270000 71283000   dwmapi     (deferred)
72cf0000 72d70000   UxTheme    (deferred)
73470000 73475000   MSIMG32    (deferred)
73b50000 73b5d000   MFC90ENU   (deferred)
74fd0000 75053000   COMCTL32   (deferred)
751d0000 751dc000   CRYPTBASE   (deferred)
751e0000 75240000   SspiCli    (deferred)
75240000 75259000   sechost    (deferred)
75260000 75ea6000   SHELL32    (deferred)
75ee0000 75f8c000   msvcrt     (deferred)
75fd0000 76060000   GDI32      (deferred)
76150000 76250000   kernel32   (deferred)
76250000 762ed000   USP10      (deferred)
763b0000 76410000   IMM32      (deferred)
76410000 7649f000   OLEAUT32   (deferred)
764a0000 764e4000   KERNELBASE   (deferred)
765c0000 766b0000   RPCRT4     (deferred)
766b0000 76733000   CLBCatQ    (deferred)
76a00000 76aa0000   ADVAPI32   (deferred)
76ce0000 76d37000   SHLWAPI    (deferred)
```

```
76f40000 77040000   USER32     (deferred)
77040000 7710c000   MSCTF      (deferred)
77110000 7726b000   ole32      (deferred)
77640000 7764a000   LPK        (deferred)
```

Now we use the start address as an argument:

```
0:532> !dh -a 5a700000

File Type: DLL
FILE HEADER VALUES
     14C machine (i386)
       4 number of sections
488F15C6 time date stamp Tue Jul 29 06:06:14 2008

       0 file pointer to symbol table
       0 number of symbols
      E0 size of optional header
    2102 characteristics
            Executable
            32 bit word machine
            DLL

OPTIONAL HEADER VALUES
     10B magic #
    9.00 linker version
  45B600 size of code
  151A00 size of initialized data
       0 size of uninitialized data
  3F66C0 address of entry point
    1000 base of code
         ----- new -----
5a700000 image base
```

(UL) .childdbg *Controls debugging of child processes* *0n33 0x21 0010 0001*

```
    1000 section alignment
     200 file alignment
       3 subsystem (Windows CUI)
    5.00 operating system version
    9.00 image version
    5.00 subsystem version
  5AF000 size of image
     400 size of headers
  5B030B checksum
00100000 size of stack reserve
00001000 size of stack commit
00100000 size of heap reserve
00001000 size of heap commit
     140  DLL characteristics
            Dynamic base
            NX compatible
  44D0A0 [    F4A5] address [size] of Export Directory
  448DB8 [      A0] address [size] of Import Directory
  46B000 [  106C18] address [size] of Resource Directory
       0 [       0] address [size] of Exception Directory
  5A7400 [    23F8] address [size] of Security Directory
  572000 [   38D08] address [size] of Base Relocation Directory
    21D0 [      1C] address [size] of Debug Directory
       0 [       0] address [size] of Description Directory
       0 [       0] address [size] of Special Directory
       0 [       0] address [size] of Thread Storage Directory
   59310 [      40] address [size] of Load Configuration Directory
       0 [       0] address [size] of Bound Import Directory
    1000 [     CEC] address [size] of Import Address Table Directory
  4471A4 [     200] address [size] of Delay Import Directory
       0 [       0] address [size] of COR20 Header Directory
       0 [       0] address [size] of Reserved Directory
SECTION HEADER #1
   .text name
```

```
  45B545 virtual size
    1000 virtual address
  45B600 size of raw data
     400 file pointer to raw data
       0 file pointer to relocation table
       0 file pointer to line numbers
       0 number of relocations
       0 number of line numbers
60000020 flags
         Code
         (no align specified)
         Execute Read


Debug Directories(1)
         Type       Size     Address  Pointer
         cv           28       59358    58758 Format: RSDS, guid, 17,
mfc90d.i386.pdb

SECTION HEADER #2
   .data name
    DC3C virtual size
  45D000 virtual address
    7E00 size of raw data
  45BA00 file pointer to raw data
       0 file pointer to relocation table
       0 file pointer to line numbers
       0 number of relocations
       0 number of line numbers
C0000040 flags
         Initialized Data
         (no align specified)
         Read Write
```

(UL) .closehandle *Closes handle(s) in a process* *0n35 0x23 0010 0011*

```
SECTION HEADER #3
   .rsrc name
  106C18 virtual size
  46B000 virtual address
  106E00 size of raw data
  463800 file pointer to raw data
       0 file pointer to relocation table
       0 file pointer to line numbers
       0 number of relocations
       0 number of line numbers
40000040 flags
         Initialized Data
         (no align specified)
         Read Only

SECTION HEADER #4
  .reloc name
   3CCD4 virtual size
  572000 virtual address
   3CE00 size of raw data
  56A600 file pointer to raw data
       0 file pointer to relocation table
       0 file pointer to line numbers
       0 number of relocations
       0 number of line numbers
42000040 flags
         Initialized Data
         Discardable
         (no align specified)
         Read Only
```

wt

According to WinDbg documentation this command runs through the whole function and then displays statistics when we execute it at the beginning of a function call. Thus, this command can be used only when doing live debugging, not a postmortem debugging (memory dump analysis). Its mnemonic is easy to remember: **w**atch and **t**race.

To demonstrate this command let's use this simple Visual C++ application that recursively calculates a Fibonacci number:

```
#include "stdafx.h"

using namespace std;

// Recursive function.
unsigned FiboRecursive(unsigned n, int nNum = 0)
{
    if(n <= 1)
    {
        return n;
    }

    return FiboRecursive(n - 1, 1) + FiboRecursive(n - 2, 2);
}

int _tmain(int argc, _TCHAR* argv[])
{
    cout << FiboRecursive(5) << endl;
    return 0;
}
```

Now we run the application from WinDbg and insert a breakpoint at the beginning of **_tmain**() function.

When the breakpoint is hit we disassemble the function:

```
0:000> uf Fibo!wmain

Fibo!wmain [c:\development\my tools\book\fibo\fibo\fibo.cpp @ 20]:

   20 001b1440 55              push    ebp

   20 001b1441 8bec            mov     ebp,esp

   20 001b1443 81ecc0000000    sub     esp,0C0h

   20 001b1449 53              push    ebx

   20 001b144a 56              push    esi

   20 001b144b 57              push    edi

   20 001b144c 8dbd40ffffff    lea     edi,[ebp-0C0h]

   20 001b1452 b930000000      mov     ecx,30h

   20 001b1457 b8cccccccc      mov     eax,0CCCCCCCCh

   20 001b145c f3ab            rep stos dword ptr es:[edi]

   21 001b145e 8bf4            mov     esi,esp

   21 001b1460 a198821b00      mov     eax,dword ptr
[Fibo!_imp_?endlstdYAAAV?$basic_ostreamDU?$char_traitsDstd (001b8298)]

   21 001b1465 50              push    eax

   21 001b1466 6a00            push    0

   21 001b1468 6a05            push    5

   21 001b146a e89bfbffff      call    Fibo!ILT+5(?FiboRecursiveYAIIHZ) (001b100a)

   21 001b146f 83c408          add     esp,8

   21 001b1472 8bfc            mov     edi,esp

   21 001b1474 50              push    eax

   21 001b1475 8b0d90821b00    mov     ecx,dword ptr [Fibo!_imp_?coutstd (001b8290)]

   21 001b147b ff1594821b00    call    dword ptr
[Fibo!_imp_??6?$basic_ostreamDU?$char_traitsDstdstdQAEAAV01IZ (001b8294)]

   21 001b1481 3bfc            cmp     edi,esp

   21 001b1483 e8d1fcffff      call    Fibo!ILT+340(__RTC_CheckEsp) (001b1159)

   21 001b1488 8bc8            mov     ecx,eax

   21 001b148a ff159c821b00    call    dword ptr
[Fibo!_imp_??6?$basic_ostreamDU?$char_traitsDstdstdQAEAAV01P6AAAV01AAV01ZZ (001b829c)]

   21 001b1490 3bf4            cmp     esi,esp

   21 001b1492 e8c2fcffff      call    Fibo!ILT+340(__RTC_CheckEsp) (001b1159)

   23 001b1497 33c0            xor     eax,eax

   24 001b1499 5f              pop     edi
```

```
24 001b149a 5e              pop     esi
24 001b149b 5b              pop     ebx
24 001b149c 81c4c0000000    add     esp,0C0h
24 001b14a2 3bec            cmp     ebp,esp
24 001b14a4 e8b0fcffff      call    Fibo!ILT+340(__RTC_CheckEsp) (001b1159)
24 001b14a9 8be5            mov     esp,ebp
24 001b14ab 5d              pop     ebp
24 001b14ac c3              ret
```

Let's use the address right before the recursive function call as the Start address and the address right after it as the End address of **wt** command. Note the "=" character right before the first address.

```
0:000> wt =001b1468  001b146f
   2     0 [  0] Fibo!wmain
   1     0 [  1]   Fibo!ILT+5(?FiboRecursiveYAIIHZ)
  64     0 [  1]   Fibo!FiboRecursive
   1     0 [  2]     Fibo!ILT+5(?FiboRecursiveYAIIHZ)
  64     0 [  2]     Fibo!FiboRecursive
   1     0 [  3]       Fibo!ILT+5(?FiboRecursiveYAIIHZ)
  64     0 [  3]       Fibo!FiboRecursive
   1     0 [  4]         Fibo!ILT+5(?FiboRecursiveYAIIHZ)
  64     0 [  4]         Fibo!FiboRecursive
   1     0 [  5]           Fibo!ILT+5(?FiboRecursiveYAIIHZ)
  67     0 [  5]           Fibo!FiboRecursive
   1     0 [  6]             Fibo!ILT+340(__RTC_CheckEsp)
   2     0 [  6]             Fibo!_RTC_CheckEsp
  70     3 [  5]           Fibo!FiboRecursive
  71    74 [  4]         Fibo!FiboRecursive
   1     0 [  5]           Fibo!ILT+5(?FiboRecursiveYAIIHZ)
  67     0 [  5]           Fibo!FiboRecursive
   1     0 [  6]             Fibo!ILT+340(__RTC_CheckEsp)
   2     0 [  6]             Fibo!_RTC_CheckEsp
  70     3 [  5]           Fibo!FiboRecursive
  79   148 [  4]         Fibo!FiboRecursive
   1     0 [  5]           Fibo!ILT+340(__RTC_CheckEsp)
```

```
    2      0 [  5]           Fibo!_RTC_CheckEsp
   82    151 [  4]         Fibo!FiboRecursive
   71    234 [  3]       Fibo!FiboRecursive
    1      0 [  4]         Fibo!ILT+5(?FiboRecursiveYAIIHZ)
   67      0 [  4]         Fibo!FiboRecursive
    1      0 [  5]           Fibo!ILT+340(__RTC_CheckEsp)
    2      0 [  5]           Fibo!_RTC_CheckEsp
   70      3 [  4]         Fibo!FiboRecursive
   79    308 [  3]       Fibo!FiboRecursive
    1      0 [  4]         Fibo!ILT+340(__RTC_CheckEsp)
    2      0 [  4]         Fibo!_RTC_CheckEsp
   82    311 [  3]       Fibo!FiboRecursive
   71    394 [  2]     Fibo!FiboRecursive
    1      0 [  3]       Fibo!ILT+5(?FiboRecursiveYAIIHZ)
   64      0 [  3]       Fibo!FiboRecursive
    1      0 [  4]         Fibo!ILT+5(?FiboRecursiveYAIIHZ)
   67      0 [  4]         Fibo!FiboRecursive
    1      0 [  5]           Fibo!ILT+340(__RTC_CheckEsp)
    2      0 [  5]           Fibo!_RTC_CheckEsp
   70      3 [  4]         Fibo!FiboRecursive
   71     74 [  3]       Fibo!FiboRecursive
    1      0 [  4]         Fibo!ILT+5(?FiboRecursiveYAIIHZ)
   67      0 [  4]         Fibo!FiboRecursive
    1      0 [  5]           Fibo!ILT+340(__RTC_CheckEsp)
    2      0 [  5]           Fibo!_RTC_CheckEsp
   70      3 [  4]         Fibo!FiboRecursive
   79    148 [  3]       Fibo!FiboRecursive
    1      0 [  4]         Fibo!ILT+340(__RTC_CheckEsp)
    2      0 [  4]         Fibo!_RTC_CheckEsp
   82    151 [  3]       Fibo!FiboRecursive
   79    628 [  2]     Fibo!FiboRecursive
    1      0 [  3]       Fibo!ILT+340(__RTC_CheckEsp)
    2      0 [  3]       Fibo!_RTC_CheckEsp
   82    631 [  2]     Fibo!FiboRecursive
   71    714 [  1]   Fibo!FiboRecursive
    1      0 [  2]     Fibo!ILT+5(?FiboRecursiveYAIIHZ)
   64      0 [  2]     Fibo!FiboRecursive
```

```
   1      0 [  3]        Fibo!ILT+5(?FiboRecursiveYAIIHZ)
  64      0 [  3]        Fibo!FiboRecursive
   1      0 [  4]          Fibo!ILT+5(?FiboRecursiveYAIIHZ)
  67      0 [  4]          Fibo!FiboRecursive
   1      0 [  5]            Fibo!ILT+340(__RTC_CheckEsp)
   2      0 [  5]            Fibo!_RTC_CheckEsp
  70      3 [  4]          Fibo!FiboRecursive
  71     74 [  3]        Fibo!FiboRecursive
   1      0 [  4]          Fibo!ILT+5(?FiboRecursiveYAIIHZ)
  67      0 [  4]          Fibo!FiboRecursive
   1      0 [  5]            Fibo!ILT+340(__RTC_CheckEsp)
   2      0 [  5]            Fibo!_RTC_CheckEsp
  70      3 [  4]          Fibo!FiboRecursive
  79    148 [  3]        Fibo!FiboRecursive
   1      0 [  4]          Fibo!ILT+340(__RTC_CheckEsp)
   2      0 [  4]          Fibo!_RTC_CheckEsp
  82    151 [  3]        Fibo!FiboRecursive
  71    234 [  2]      Fibo!FiboRecursive
   1      0 [  3]        Fibo!ILT+5(?FiboRecursiveYAIIHZ)
  67      0 [  3]        Fibo!FiboRecursive
   1      0 [  4]          Fibo!ILT+340(__RTC_CheckEsp)
   2      0 [  4]          Fibo!_RTC_CheckEsp
  70      3 [  3]        Fibo!FiboRecursive
  79    308 [  2]      Fibo!FiboRecursive
   1      0 [  3]        Fibo!ILT+340(__RTC_CheckEsp)
   2      0 [  3]        Fibo!_RTC_CheckEsp
  82    311 [  2]      Fibo!FiboRecursive
  79   1108 [  1]    Fibo!FiboRecursive
   1      0 [  2]      Fibo!ILT+340(__RTC_CheckEsp)
   2      0 [  2]      Fibo!_RTC_CheckEsp
  82   1111 [  1]    Fibo!FiboRecursive

1196 instructions were executed in 1195 events (0 from other threads)
```

```
Function Name                              Invocations MinInst MaxInst AvgInst

Fibo!FiboRecursive                                  15      70      82      75
Fibo!ILT+340(__RTC_CheckEsp)                        15       1       1       1
Fibo!ILT+5(?FiboRecursiveYAIIHZ)                    15       1       1       1
Fibo!_RTC_CheckEsp                                  15       2       2       2
Fibo!wmain                                           1       2       2       2

0 system calls were executed

eax=00000005 ebx=7efde000 ecx=00000000 edx=00000001 esi=00000000 edi=00000000
eip=001b146f esp=0045f914 ebp=0045f964 iopl=0         nv up ei pl zr na pe nc
cs=0023  ss=002b  ds=002b  es=002b  fs=0053  gs=002b             efl=00000246
Fibo!wmain+0x2f:
001b146f 83c408          add     esp,8
```

Notice that the first number right below the command specifies the number of instructions that were executed, the second number specifies the number of instructions executed by the function child calls, and the third number (in brackets) is the depth of the function on the stack.

MinInst, **MaxInst** and **AvgInst** mean the number of instructions by call.

u, ub, uf

When debugging sooner or later we need to do code disassembly to get better understanding of our problem. By unassembling or disassembling the code we get the mnemonics translated from the 0s and 1s that constitute the binary code. It is a low level view of the code, but the higher level than seeing just numbers.

To demonstrate this command let's use the simple Visual C++ application that recursively calculates the Fibonacci number from a specific number:

```
#include "stdafx.h"
using namespace std;

// Recursive function.
unsigned FiboRecursive(unsigned n, int nNum = 0)
{
    if(n <= 1)
    {
        return n;
    }

    return FiboRecursive(n - 1, 1) + FiboRecursive(n - 2, 2);
}

int _tmain(int argc, _TCHAR* argv[])
{
    cout << FiboRecursive(5) << endl;
    return 0;
}
```

Let's break the program execution at the first line of **main**() function using a breakpoint and then disassemble the **eip** register.

```
0:000> u @eip
Fibo!wmain+0x1e [c:\development\my tools\book\fibo\fibo\fibo.cpp @ 21]:
00a7145e 8bf4            mov     esi,esp
00a71460 a19882a700      mov     eax,dword ptr
[Fibo!_imp_?endlstdYAAAV?$basic_ostreamDU?$char_traitsDstd (00a78298)]
00a71465 50              push    eax
00a71466 6a00            push    0
00a71468 6a05            push    5
00a7146a e89bfbffff      call    Fibo!ILT+5(?FiboRecursiveYAIIHZ) (00a7100a)
00a7146f 83c408          add     esp,8
00a71472 8bfc            mov     edi,esp
```

Using this approach we see the disassembled code starting from **eip**. However, if we want to see the disassembled code that comes before **eip** we should use this approach (**b** is for backward):

```
0:000> ub @eip L8
Fibo!wmain+0x3 [c:\development\my tools\book\fibo\fibo\fibo.cpp @ 20]:
00a71443 81ecc0000000    sub     esp,0C0h
00a71449 53              push    ebx
00a7144a 56              push    esi
00a7144b 57              push    edi
00a7144c 8dbd40ffffff    lea     edi,[ebp-0C0h]
00a71452 b930000000      mov     ecx,30h
00a71457 b8cccccccc      mov     eax,0CCCCCCCCh
00a7145c f3ab            rep stos dword ptr es:[edi]
```

Let's suppose we want to disassemble the entire function without trying to find its beginning (start address). To accomplish that we use **uf** command and it automatically does that for us:

```
0:000> uf @eip
Fibo!wmain [c:\development\my tools\book\fibo\fibo\fibo.cpp @ 20]:
   20 00a71440 55              push    ebp
   20 00a71441 8bec            mov     ebp,esp
   20 00a71443 81ecc0000000    sub     esp,0C0h
   20 00a71449 53              push    ebx
   20 00a7144a 56              push    esi
   20 00a7144b 57              push    edi
   20 00a7144c 8dbd40ffffff    lea     edi,[ebp-0C0h]
   20 00a71452 b930000000      mov     ecx,30h
   20 00a71457 b8cccccccc      mov     eax,0CCCCCCCCh
   20 00a7145c f3ab            rep stos dword ptr es:[edi]
   21 00a7145e 8bf4            mov     esi,esp
   21 00a71460 a19882a700      mov     eax,dword ptr
[Fibo!_imp_?endlstdYAAAV?$basic_ostreamDU?$char_traitsDstd (00a78298)]
   21 00a71465 50              push    eax
   21 00a71466 6a00            push    0
   21 00a71468 6a05            push    5
   21 00a7146a e89bfbffff      call    Fibo!ILT+5(?FiboRecursiveYAIIHZ) (00a7100a)
   21 00a7146f 83c408          add     esp,8
   21 00a71472 8bfc            mov     edi,esp
   21 00a71474 50              push    eax
   21 00a71475 8b0d9082a700    mov     ecx,dword ptr [Fibo!_imp_?coutstd (00a78290)]
   21 00a7147b ff159482a700    call    dword ptr
[Fibo!_imp_??6?$basic_ostreamDU?$char_traitsDstdstdQAEAAV01IZ (00a78294)]
   21 00a71481 3bfc            cmp     edi,esp
   21 00a71483 e8d1fcffff      call    Fibo!ILT+340(__RTC_CheckEsp) (00a71159)
   21 00a71488 8bc8            mov     ecx,eax
   21 00a7148a ff159c82a700    call    dword ptr
[Fibo!_imp_??6?$basic_ostreamDU?$char_traitsDstdstdQAEAAV01P6AAAV01AAV01ZZ (00a7829c)]
   21 00a71490 3bf4            cmp     esi,esp
   21 00a71492 e8c2fcffff      call    Fibo!ILT+340(__RTC_CheckEsp) (00a71159)
   23 00a71497 33c0            xor     eax,eax
   24 00a71499 5f              pop     edi
   24 00a7149a 5e              pop     esi
   24 00a7149b 5b              pop     ebx
   24 00a7149c 81c4c0000000    add     esp,0C0h
   24 00a714a2 3bec            cmp     ebp,esp
   24 00a714a4 e8b0fcffff      call    Fibo!ILT+340(__RTC_CheckEsp) (00a71159)
```

```
24 00a714a9 8be5            mov     esp,ebp
24 00a714ab 5d              pop     ebp
24 00a714ac c3              ret
```

Let's see just the calls made by that function:

```
0:000> uf /c @eip
Fibo!wmain (00a71440) [c:\development\my tools\book\fibo\fibo\fibo.cpp @ 20]
  Fibo!wmain+0x2a (00a7146a) [c:\development\my tools\book\fibo\fibo\fibo.cpp @ 21]:
    call to Fibo!ILT+5(?FiboRecursiveYAIIHZ) (00a7100a)
  Fibo!wmain+0x3b (00a7147b) [c:\development\my tools\book\fibo\fibo\fibo.cpp @ 21]:
    call to MSVCP90D!std::basic_ostream<char,std::char_traits<char> >::operator<<
(690fa700)
  Fibo!wmain+0x43 (00a71483) [c:\development\my tools\book\fibo\fibo\fibo.cpp @ 21]:
    call to Fibo!ILT+340(__RTC_CheckEsp) (00a71159)
  Fibo!wmain+0x4a (00a7148a) [c:\development\my tools\book\fibo\fibo\fibo.cpp @ 21]:
    call to MSVCP90D!std::basic_ostream<char,std::char_traits<char> >::operator<<
(690f9f60)
  Fibo!wmain+0x52 (00a71492) [c:\development\my tools\book\fibo\fibo\fibo.cpp @ 21]:
    call to Fibo!ILT+340(__RTC_CheckEsp) (00a71159)
  Fibo!wmain+0x64 (00a714a4) [c:\development\my tools\book\fibo\fibo\fibo.cpp @ 24]:
    call to Fibo!ILT+340(__RTC_CheckEsp) (00a71159)
```

The following command creates linked callee names from the same function:

```
0:000> uf /D @eip
Fibo!wmain [c:\development\my tools\book\fibo\fibo\fibo.cpp @ 20]:
   20 00a71440 55              push    ebp
   20 00a71441 8bec            mov     ebp,esp
   20 00a71443 81ecc0000000    sub     esp,0C0h
   20 00a71449 53              push    ebx
   20 00a7144a 56              push    esi
   20 00a7144b 57              push    edi
   20 00a7144c 8dbd40ffffff    lea     edi,[ebp-0C0h]
   20 00a71452 b930000000      mov     ecx,30h
   20 00a71457 b8cccccccc      mov     eax,0CCCCCCCCh
```

```
   20 00a7145c f3ab            rep stos dword ptr es:[edi]

   21 00a7145e 8bf4            mov     esi,esp

   21 00a71460 a19882a700      mov     eax,dword ptr
[Fibo!_imp_?endlstdYAAAV?$basic_ostreamDU?$char_traitsDstd (00a78298)]

   21 00a71465 50              push    eax

   21 00a71466 6a00            push    0

   21 00a71468 6a05            push    5

   21 00a7146a e89bfbffff      call    Fibo!ILT+5(?FiboRecursiveYAIIHZ) (00a7100a)

   21 00a7146f 83c408          add     esp,8

   21 00a71472 8bfc            mov     edi,esp

   21 00a71474 50              push    eax

   21 00a71475 8b0d9082a700    mov     ecx,dword ptr [Fibo!_imp_?coutstd (00a78290)]

   21 00a7147b ff159482a700    call    dword ptr
[Fibo!_imp_??6?$basic_ostreamDU?$char_traitsDstdstdQAEAAV01IZ (00a78294)]

   21 00a71481 3bfc            cmp     edi,esp

   21 00a71483 e8d1fcffff      call    Fibo!ILT+340(__RTC_CheckEsp) (00a71159)

   21 00a71488 8bc8            mov     ecx,eax

   21 00a7148a ff159c82a700    call    dword ptr
[Fibo!_imp_??6?$basic_ostreamDU?$char_traitsDstdstdQAEAAV01P6AAAV01AAV01ZZ (00a7829c)]

   21 00a71490 3bf4            cmp     esi,esp

   21 00a71492 e8c2fcffff      call    Fibo!ILT+340(__RTC_CheckEsp) (00a71159)

   23 00a71497 33c0            xor     eax,eax

   24 00a71499 5f              pop     edi

   24 00a7149a 5e              pop     esi

   24 00a7149b 5b              pop     ebx

   24 00a7149c 81c4c0000000    add     esp,0C0h

   24 00a714a2 3bec            cmp     ebp,esp

   24 00a714a4 e8b0fcffff      call    Fibo!ILT+340(__RTC_CheckEsp) (00a71159)

   24 00a714a9 8be5            mov     esp,ebp

   24 00a714ab 5d              pop     ebp

   24 00a714ac c3              ret
```

This command sorts the output by address:

```
0:000> uf /o @eip

Fibo!wmain [c:\development\my tools\book\fibo\fibo\fibo.cpp @ 20]:

   20 00a71440 55              push    ebp

   20 00a71441 8bec            mov     ebp,esp

   20 00a71443 81ecc0000000    sub     esp,0C0h
```

```
20 00a71449 53              push    ebx
20 00a7144a 56              push    esi
20 00a7144b 57              push    edi
20 00a7144c 8dbd40ffffff    lea     edi,[ebp-0C0h]
20 00a71452 b930000000      mov     ecx,30h
20 00a71457 b8cccccccc      mov     eax,0CCCCCCCCh
20 00a7145c f3ab            rep stos dword ptr es:[edi]
21 00a7145e 8bf4            mov     esi,esp
21 00a71460 a19882a700      mov     eax,dword ptr
[Fibo!_imp_?endlstdYAAAV?$basic_ostreamDU?$char_traitsDstd (00a78298)]
21 00a71465 50              push    eax
21 00a71466 6a00            push    0
21 00a71468 6a05            push    5
21 00a7146a e89bfbffff      call    Fibo!ILT+5(?FiboRecursiveYAIIHZ) (00a7100a)
21 00a7146f 83c408          add     esp,8
21 00a71472 8bfc            mov     edi,esp
21 00a71474 50              push    eax
21 00a71475 8b0d9082a700    mov     ecx,dword ptr [Fibo!_imp_?coutstd (00a78290)]
21 00a7147b ff159482a700    call    dword ptr
[Fibo!_imp_??6?$basic_ostreamDU?$char_traitsDstdstdQAEAAV01IZ (00a78294)]
21 00a71481 3bfc            cmp     edi,esp
21 00a71483 e8d1fcffff      call    Fibo!ILT+340(__RTC_CheckEsp) (00a71159)
21 00a71488 8bc8            mov     ecx,eax
21 00a7148a ff159c82a700    call    dword ptr
[Fibo!_imp_??6?$basic_ostreamDU?$char_traitsDstdstdQAEAAV01P6AAAV01AAV01ZZ (00a7829c)]
21 00a71490 3bf4            cmp     esi,esp
21 00a71492 e8c2fcffff      call    Fibo!ILT+340(__RTC_CheckEsp) (00a71159)
23 00a71497 33c0            xor     eax,eax
24 00a71499 5f              pop     edi
24 00a7149a 5e              pop     esi
24 00a7149b 5b              pop     ebx
24 00a7149c 81c4c0000000    add     esp,0C0h
24 00a714a2 3bec            cmp     ebp,esp
24 00a714a4 e8b0fcffff      call    Fibo!ILT+340(__RTC_CheckEsp) (00a71159)
24 00a714a9 8be5            mov     esp,ebp
24 00a714ab 5d              pop     ebp
24 00a714ac c3              ret
```

The following command creates linked call lines to access call information and to create breakpoints:

```
0:000> uf /O @eip

Fibo!wmain [c:\development\my tools\book\fibo\fibo\fibo.cpp @ 20]:

   20 00a71440 55              push    ebp

   20 00a71441 8bec            mov     ebp,esp

   20 00a71443 81ecc0000000    sub     esp,0C0h

   20 00a71449 53              push    ebx

   20 00a7144a 56              push    esi

   20 00a7144b 57              push    edi

   20 00a7144c 8dbd40ffffff    lea     edi,[ebp-0C0h]

   20 00a71452 b930000000      mov     ecx,30h

   20 00a71457 b8cccccccc      mov     eax,0CCCCCCCCh

   20 00a7145c f3ab            rep stos dword ptr es:[edi]

   21 00a7145e 8bf4            mov     esi,esp

   21 00a71460 a19882a700      mov     eax,dword ptr
[Fibo!_imp_?endlstdYAAAV?$basic_ostreamDU?$char_traitsDstd (00a78298)]

   21 00a71465 50              push    eax

   21 00a71466 6a00            push    0

   21 00a71468 6a05            push    5

   21 00a7146a e89bfbffff      call    Fibo!ILT+5(?FiboRecursiveYAIIHZ) (00a7100a)

   21 00a7146f 83c408          add     esp,8

   21 00a71472 8bfc            mov     edi,esp

   21 00a71474 50              push    eax

   21 00a71475 8b0d9082a700    mov     ecx,dword ptr [Fibo!_imp_?coutstd (00a78290)]

   21 00a7147b ff159482a700    call    dword ptr
[Fibo!_imp_??6?$basic_ostreamDU?$char_traitsDstdstdQAEAAV01IZ (00a78294)]

   21 00a71481 3bfc            cmp     edi,esp

   21 00a71483 e8d1fcffff      call    Fibo!ILT+340(__RTC_CheckEsp) (00a71159)

   21 00a71488 8bc8            mov     ecx,eax

   21 00a7148a ff159c82a700    call    dword ptr
[Fibo!_imp_??6?$basic_ostreamDU?$char_traitsDstdstdQAEAAV01P6AAAV01AAV01ZZ (00a7829c)]

   21 00a71490 3bf4            cmp     esi,esp

   21 00a71492 e8c2fcffff      call    Fibo!ILT+340(__RTC_CheckEsp) (00a71159)

   23 00a71497 33c0            xor     eax,eax

   24 00a71499 5f              pop     edi

   24 00a7149a 5e              pop     esi

   24 00a7149b 5b              pop     ebx
```

(UL) .createdir *Controls the starting directory* *0n49 0x31 0011 0001*

```
   24 00a7149c 81c4c0000000     add     esp,0C0h
   24 00a714a2 3bec             cmp     ebp,esp
   24 00a714a4 e8b0fcffff       call    Fibo!ILT+340(__RTC_CheckEsp) (00a71159)
   24 00a714a9 8be5             mov     esp,ebp
   24 00a714ab 5d               pop     ebp
   24 00a714ac c3               ret
```

The last command variant shows the number of instructions in a function:

```
0:000> uf /i @eip
37 instructions scanned

Fibo!wmain [c:\development\my tools\book\fibo\fibo\fibo.cpp @ 20]:
   20 00a71440 55               push    ebp
   20 00a71441 8bec             mov     ebp,esp
   20 00a71443 81ecc0000000     sub     esp,0C0h
   20 00a71449 53               push    ebx
   20 00a7144a 56               push    esi
   20 00a7144b 57               push    edi
   20 00a7144c 8dbd40ffffff     lea     edi,[ebp-0C0h]
   20 00a71452 b930000000       mov     ecx,30h
   20 00a71457 b8cccccccc       mov     eax,0CCCCCCCCh
   20 00a7145c f3ab             rep stos dword ptr es:[edi]
   21 00a7145e 8bf4             mov     esi,esp
   21 00a71460 a19882a700       mov     eax,dword ptr
[Fibo!_imp_?endlstdYAAAV?$basic_ostreamDU?$char_traitsDstd (00a78298)]
   21 00a71465 50               push    eax
   21 00a71466 6a00             push    0
   21 00a71468 6a05             push    5
   21 00a7146a e89bfbffff       call    Fibo!ILT+5(?FiboRecursiveYAIIHZ) (00a7100a)
   21 00a7146f 83c408           add     esp,8
   21 00a71472 8bfc             mov     edi,esp
   21 00a71474 50               push    eax
   21 00a71475 8b0d9082a700     mov     ecx,dword ptr [Fibo!_imp_?coutstd (00a78290)]
   21 00a7147b ff159482a700     call    dword ptr
[Fibo!_imp_??6?$basic_ostreamDU?$char_traitsDstdstdQAEAAV01IZ (00a78294)]
```

```
   21 00a71481 3bfc            cmp     edi,esp

   21 00a71483 e8d1fcffff      call    Fibo!ILT+340(__RTC_CheckEsp) (00a71159)

   21 00a71488 8bc8            mov     ecx,eax

   21 00a7148a ff159c82a700    call    dword ptr
[Fibo!_imp_??6?$basic_ostreamDU?$char_traitsDstdstdQAEAAV01P6AAAV01AAV01ZZ (00a7829c)]

   21 00a71490 3bf4            cmp     esi,esp

   21 00a71492 e8c2fcffff      call    Fibo!ILT+340(__RTC_CheckEsp) (00a71159)

   23 00a71497 33c0            xor     eax,eax

   24 00a71499 5f              pop     edi

   24 00a7149a 5e              pop     esi

   24 00a7149b 5b              pop     ebx

   24 00a7149c 81c4c0000000    add     esp,0C0h

   24 00a714a2 3bec            cmp     ebp,esp

   24 00a714a4 e8b0fcffff      call    Fibo!ILT+340(__RTC_CheckEsp) (00a71159)

   24 00a714a9 8be5            mov     esp,ebp

   24 00a714ab 5d              pop     ebp

   24 00a714ac c3              ret
```

Editing memory (a, eb, ed, ew, eza, ezu)

When talking about editing memory we usually think about patching code. Patching code means changing the binary code in memory when we want to prove a hypothesis while debugging and we don't have access to the source code. This is a very exciting subject and WinDbg has the right tools to do the job.

To learn how to edit memory let's crack the application below. We will use the Debug version compiled as 32 bit project. This is just to make things easier because we can use alo 64 bit version or Release version. The techniques are the same.

```
// CrackMe.cpp : Defines the entry point for the console
application.

//

#include "stdafx.h"

#include <iostream>


using namespace std;  // Necessary for cout/cin.


// Declares prototypes.

void AskPassword(void);

bool IsRightPassword(int);

void GiveAccess(void);

void DenyAccess(void);


const int PASSWORD = 357;
```

```
void AskPassword()
{
   // User can try to input the password for three times.
   for(int i = 0; i < 3; i++)
   {
         cout << "Tentative " << i + 1 << "/3" << endl;
         cout << "Type the numeric secret password:" << endl;

         int nPassword = 0;

         cin >> nPassword;

         if(IsRightPassword(nPassword))
         {
             GiveAccess();
             break; // User got the right password. Don't need to
ask more.
         }
         else
         {
             DenyAccess();
         }
    }
}

void GiveAccess()
{
     cout << "You have access to the system." << endl;
}
```

```
void DenyAccess()
{
    cout << "Wrong password!" << endl;
}

inline bool IsRightPassword(int nPasswordToValidate)
{
    return PASSWORD == nPasswordToValidate;
}

int _tmain(int argc, _TCHAR* argv[])
{
    AskPassword();
    return 0;
}
```

From now on let's pretend we have never seen the source code and we don't have the right password. Let's use symbols to make things easier, but keep in mind that in real world scenarios we may not have application symbols.

Note: The answers from the tasks below are not meant to be the only right answers. There are many possible answers that can be used to show memory editing commands.

Task #1 – Finding out the right password.

We run the application from WinDbg and break into the debugger when prompted for the password. Then we disassemble **main()** function:

```
0:001> uf CrackMe!wmain
CrackMe!wmain [c:\development\my tools\book\crackme\crackme\crackme.cpp @ 59]:
   59 013f1c30 55              push    ebp
   59 013f1c31 8bec            mov     ebp,esp
   59 013f1c33 81ecc0000000    sub     esp,0C0h
   59 013f1c39 53              push    ebx
   59 013f1c3a 56              push    esi
   59 013f1c3b 57              push    edi
   59 013f1c3c 8dbd40ffffff    lea     edi,[ebp-0C0h]
   59 013f1c42 b930000000      mov     ecx,30h
   59 013f1c47 b8cccccccc      mov     eax,0CCCCCCCCh
   59 013f1c4c f3ab            rep stos dword ptr es:[edi]
   60 013f1c4e e8cbf3ffff      call    CrackMe!ILT+25(?AskPasswordYAXXZ) (013f101e)
   61 013f1c53 33c0            xor     eax,eax
   62 013f1c55 5f              pop     edi
   62 013f1c56 5e              pop     esi
   62 013f1c57 5b              pop     ebx
   62 013f1c58 81c4c0000000    add     esp,0C0h
   62 013f1c5e 3bec            cmp     ebp,esp
   62 013f1c60 e84ef5ffff      call    CrackMe!ILT+430(__RTC_CheckEsp) (013f11b3)
   62 013f1c65 8be5            mov     esp,ebp
   62 013f1c67 5d              pop     ebp
   62 013f1c68 c3              ret
```

AskPasswordYAXXZ looks interesting and we disassemble it:

```
0:001> uf 013f101e
CrackMe!AskPassword [c:\development\my tools\book\crackme\crackme\crackme.cpp @ 19]:
   19 013f4190 55              push    ebp
   19 013f4191 8bec            mov     ebp,esp
   19 013f4193 81ecd8000000    sub     esp,0D8h
   19 013f4199 53              push    ebx
   19 013f419a 56              push    esi
   19 013f419b 57              push    edi
   19 013f419c 8dbd28ffffff    lea     edi,[ebp-0D8h]
```

```
   19 013f41a2 b936000000      mov     ecx,36h

   19 013f41a7 b8cccccccc      mov     eax,0CCCCCCCCh

   19 013f41ac f3ab            rep stos dword ptr es:[edi]

   21 013f41ae c745f800000000  mov     dword ptr [ebp-8],0

   21 013f41b5 eb09            jmp     CrackMe!AskPassword+0x30 (013f41c0)


CrackMe!AskPassword+0x27 [c:\development\my tools\book\crackme\crackme\crackme.cpp @ 21]:

   21 013f41b7 8b45f8          mov     eax,dword ptr [ebp-8]

   21 013f41ba 83c001          add     eax,1

   21 013f41bd 8945f8          mov     dword ptr [ebp-8],eax


CrackMe!AskPassword+0x30 [c:\development\my tools\book\crackme\crackme\crackme.cpp @ 21]:

   21 013f41c0 837df803        cmp     dword ptr [ebp-8],3

   21 013f41c4 0f8dc2000000    jge     CrackMe!AskPassword+0xfc (013f428c)


CrackMe!AskPassword+0x3a [c:\development\my tools\book\crackme\crackme\crackme.cpp @ 23]:

   23 013f41ca 8bf4            mov     esi,esp

   23 013f41cc a110a33f01      mov     eax,dword ptr
[CrackMe!_imp_?endlstdYAAAV?$basic_ostreamDU?$char_traitsDstd (013fa310)]

   23 013f41d1 50              push    eax

   23 013f41d2 683c783f01      push    offset CrackMe!`string' (013f783c)

   23 013f41d7 8b4df8          mov     ecx,dword ptr [ebp-8]

   23 013f41da 83c101          add     ecx,1

   23 013f41dd 8bfc            mov     edi,esp

   23 013f41df 51              push    ecx

   23 013f41e0 6814783f01      push    offset CrackMe!`string' (013f7814)

   23 013f41e5 8b150ca33f01    mov     edx,dword ptr [CrackMe!_imp_?coutstd (013fa30c)]

   23 013f41eb 52              push    edx

   23 013f41ec e872cfffff      call
CrackMe!ILT+350(??$?6U?$char_traitsDstdstdYAAAV?$basic_ostreamDU?$char_traitsDstd
(013f1163)

   23 013f41f1 83c408          add     esp,8

   23 013f41f4 8bc8            mov     ecx,eax

   23 013f41f6 ff1554a33f01    call    dword ptr
[CrackMe!_imp_??6?$basic_ostreamDU?$char_traitsDstdstdQAEAAV01HZ (013fa354)]

   23 013f41fc 3bfc            cmp     edi,esp

   23 013f41fe e8b0cfffff      call    CrackMe!ILT+430(__RTC_CheckEsp) (013f11b3)
```

```
   23 013f4203 50              push    eax

   23 013f4204 e85acfffff      call
CrackMe!ILT+350(??$?6U?$char_traitsDstdstdYAAAV?$basic_ostreamDU?$char_traitsDstd
(013f1163)

   23 013f4209 83c408          add     esp,8

   23 013f420c 8bc8            mov     ecx,eax

   23 013f420e ff1508a33f01    call    dword ptr
[CrackMe!_imp_??6?$basic_ostreamDU?$char_traitsDstdstdQAEAAV01P6AAAV01AAV01ZZ
(013fa308)]

   23 013f4214 3bf4            cmp     esi,esp

   23 013f4216 e898cfffff      call    CrackMe!ILT+430(__RTC_CheckEsp) (013f11b3)

   24 013f421b 8bf4            mov     esi,esp

   24 013f421d a110a33f01      mov     eax,dword ptr
[CrackMe!_imp_?endlstdYAAAV?$basic_ostreamDU?$char_traitsDstd (013fa310)]

   24 013f4222 50              push    eax

   24 013f4223 68187b3f01      push    offset CrackMe!`string' (013f7b18)

   24 013f4228 8b0d0ca33f01    mov     ecx,dword ptr [CrackMe!_imp_?coutstd (013fa30c)]

   24 013f422e 51              push    ecx

   24 013f422f e82fcfffff      call
CrackMe!ILT+350(??$?6U?$char_traitsDstdstdYAAAV?$basic_ostreamDU?$char_traitsDstd
(013f1163)

   24 013f4234 83c408          add     esp,8

   24 013f4237 8bc8            mov     ecx,eax

   24 013f4239 ff1508a33f01    call    dword ptr
[CrackMe!_imp_??6?$basic_ostreamDU?$char_traitsDstdstdQAEAAV01P6AAAV01AAV01ZZ
(013fa308)]

   24 013f423f 3bf4            cmp     esi,esp

   24 013f4241 e86dcfffff      call    CrackMe!ILT+430(__RTC_CheckEsp) (013f11b3)

   26 013f4246 c745ec00000000  mov     dword ptr [ebp-14h],0

   28 013f424d 8bf4            mov     esi,esp

   28 013f424f 8d45ec          lea     eax,[ebp-14h]

   28 013f4252 50              push    eax

   28 013f4253 8b0d04a33f01    mov     ecx,dword ptr [CrackMe!_imp_?cinstd (013fa304)]

   28 013f4259 ff1500a33f01    call    dword ptr
[CrackMe!_imp_??5?$basic_istreamDU?$char_traitsDstdstdQAEAAV01AAHZ (013fa300)]

   28 013f425f 3bf4            cmp     esi,esp

   28 013f4261 e84dcfffff      call    CrackMe!ILT+430(__RTC_CheckEsp) (013f11b3)

   30 013f4266 8b45ec          mov     eax,dword ptr [ebp-14h]

   30 013f4269 50              push    eax

   30 013f426a e8eecfffff      call    CrackMe!ILT+600(?IsRightPasswordYA_NHZ)
(013f125d)

   30 013f426f 83c404          add     esp,4
```

```
   30 013f4272 0fb6c8          movzx   ecx,al
   30 013f4275 85c9            test    ecx,ecx
   30 013f4277 7409            je      CrackMe!AskPassword+0xf2 (013f4282)

CrackMe!AskPassword+0xe9 [c:\development\my tools\book\crackme\crackme\crackme.cpp @
32]:
   32 013f4279 e8e9cfffff      call    CrackMe!ILT+610(?GiveAccessYAXXZ) (013f1267)
   33 013f427e eb0c            jmp     CrackMe!AskPassword+0xfc (013f428c)

CrackMe!AskPassword+0xf2 [c:\development\my tools\book\crackme\crackme\crackme.cpp @
37]:
   37 013f4282 e8dbcfffff      call    CrackMe!ILT+605(?DenyAccessYAXXZ) (013f1262)
   38 013f4287 e92bffffff      jmp     CrackMe!AskPassword+0x27 (013f41b7)

CrackMe!AskPassword+0xfc [c:\development\my tools\book\crackme\crackme\crackme.cpp @
41]:
   41 013f428c 52              push    edx
   41 013f428d 8bcd            mov     ecx,ebp
   41 013f428f 50              push    eax
   41 013f4290 8d15b4423f01    lea     edx,[CrackMe!AskPassword+0x124 (013f42b4)]
   41 013f4296 e819ceffff      call    CrackMe!ILT+175(_RTC_CheckStackVars (013f10b4)
   41 013f429b 58              pop     eax
   41 013f429c 5a              pop     edx
   41 013f429d 5f              pop     edi
   41 013f429e 5e              pop     esi
   41 013f429f 5b              pop     ebx
   41 013f42a0 81c4d8000000    add     esp,0D8h
   41 013f42a6 3bec            cmp     ebp,esp
   41 013f42a8 e806cfffff      call    CrackMe!ILT+430(__RTC_CheckEsp) (013f11b3)
   41 013f42ad 8be5            mov     esp,ebp
   41 013f42af 5d              pop     ebp
   41 013f42b0 c3              ret

CrackMe!ILT+25(?AskPasswordYAXXZ):
013f101e e96d310000      jmp     CrackMe!AskPassword (013f4190)
```

After analyzing the code above we see two calls **coutstd** and **cinstd.** These names clearly suggests **cout** and **cin** from C++ Standard Template Library. We know that **cin** is used to receive information from a user.

Now we put a breakpoint just after the **cin** function call instruction.

```
0:001> bp 013f425f

0:001> bl
 0 e 013f425f     0001 (0001)  0:**** CrackMe!AskPassword+0xcf
```

We continue execution and type any number, like 543. We plan to track our number and see when it is compared against the right password. At this point the breakpoint is hit.

If we look at the disassembled code again we would see where our password was stored:

```
   28 013f424f 8d45ec          lea     eax,[ebp-14h]
   28 013f4252 50              push    eax
   28 013f4253 8b0d04a33f01    mov     ecx,dword ptr [CrackMe!_imp_?cinstd (013fa304)]
   28 013f4259 ff1500a33f01    call    dword ptr
[CrackMe!_imp_??5?$basic_istreamDU?$char_traitsDstdstdQAEAAV01AAHZ (013fa300)]
   28 013f425f 3bf4            cmp     esi,esp
   28 013f4261 e84dcfffff      call    CrackMe!ILT+430(__RTC_CheckEsp) (013f11b3)
   30 013f4266 8b45ec          mov     eax,dword ptr [ebp-14h]
   30 013f4269 50              push    eax
   30 013f426a e8eecfffff      call    CrackMe!ILT+600(?IsRightPasswordYA_NHZ)
(013f125d)
```

[ebp-14h] is a local variable used in **cin** and it is used again just before **IsRightPassword** is called. If this is true we should get the password we have typed:

```
0:000> dd [ebp-0x14]
001cf9dc  0000021f cccccccc cccccccc 00000000
001cf9ec  cccccccc 001cfac4 013f1c53 00000000
001cf9fc  00000000 7efde000 cccccccc cccccccc
001cfa0c  cccccccc cccccccc cccccccc cccccccc
001cfa1c  cccccccc cccccccc cccccccc cccccccc
001cfa2c  cccccccc cccccccc cccccccc cccccccc
001cfa3c  cccccccc cccccccc cccccccc cccccccc
001cfa4c  cccccccc cccccccc cccccccc cccccccc
```

```
0:000> ? 21f
Evaluate expression: 543 = 0000021f
```

This is the password we have just typed. We follow it through the code execution. It's being used as an argument here:

```
013f4266 8b45ec          mov     eax,dword ptr [ebp-14h] ss:002b:001cf9dc=0000021f
013f4269 50              push    eax
013f426a e8eecfffff      call    CrackMe!ILT+600(?IsRightPasswordYA_NHZ) (013f125d)
013f426f 83c404          add     esp,4
```

Note: Use **p** to step over and **t** to step into.

After stepping into **IsRightPassword**() and disassembling its code we have:

```
CrackMe!IsRightPassword:
013f16b0 55              push    ebp
013f16b1 8bec            mov     ebp,esp
013f16b3 81ecc0000000    sub     esp,0C0h
013f16b9 53              push    ebx
013f16ba 56              push    esi
013f16bb 57              push    edi
013f16bc 8dbd40ffffff    lea     edi,[ebp-0C0h]
013f16c2 b930000000      mov     ecx,30h
013f16c7 b8cccccccc      mov     eax,0CCCCCCCCh
013f16cc f3ab            rep stos dword ptr es:[edi]
013f16ce 33c0            xor     eax,eax
013f16d0 817d0865010000  cmp     dword ptr [ebp+8],165h
013f16d7 0f94c0          sete    al
013f16da 5f              pop     edi
013f16db 5e              pop     esi
013f16dc 5b              pop     ebx
013f16dd 8be5            mov     esp,ebp
013f16df 5d              pop     ebp
013f16e0 c3              ret
```

The line at the address **013f16d0** is the key because it compares the first function parameter with the specific number. The parameter happens to be our password, passed as an argument as we can see from the disassembly.

Now we put a breakpoint at the address **013f16d0** and continue execution.

```
0:000> g
Breakpoint 1 hit
eax=00000000 ebx=7efde000 ecx=00000000 edx=6952daa4 esi=001cf90c edi=001cf900
eip=013f16d0 esp=001cf834 ebp=001cf900 iopl=0         nv up ei pl zr na pe nc
cs=0023  ss=002b  ds=002b  es=002b  fs=0053  gs=002b             efl=00000246
CrackMe!IsRightPassword+0x20:
013f16d0 817d0865010000   cmp     dword ptr [ebp+8],165h ss:002b:001cf908=0000021f

0:000> dd [ebp+0x8] L1
001cf908  0000021f
```

The comparison value is our password:

```
0:000> ? 165
Evaluate expression: 357 = 00000165
```

So our password is being compared against 357. If we run the application again and use 357 we can prove that this is the right password.

Task #2 – Making the application to use 0 as a password.

Now we know the right password and we know where the user's password is tested against the application's password. So we just need to change the right password to 0. We also need to pay attention to the fact that the same password can be used from different parts of the program, so ideally all parts should be changed.

Let's restart the application and stop its execution when it asks for the password. After that let's disassemble **CrackMe!IsRightPassword** function and get the address just before the **cmp** instruction:

```
0:001> uf CrackMe!IsRightPassword
*** WARNING: Unable to verify checksum for CrackMe.exe
CrackMe!IsRightPassword [c:\development\my tools\book\crackme\crackme\crackme.cpp @ 54]:
   54 00d416b0 55              push    ebp
   54 00d416b1 8bec            mov     ebp,esp
   54 00d416b3 81ecc0000000    sub     esp,0C0h
   54 00d416b9 53              push    ebx
   54 00d416ba 56              push    esi
   54 00d416bb 57              push    edi
   54 00d416bc 8dbd40ffffff    lea     edi,[ebp-0C0h]
   54 00d416c2 b930000000      mov     ecx,30h
   54 00d416c7 b8cccccccc      mov     eax,0CCCCCCCCh
   54 00d416cc f3ab            rep stos dword ptr es:[edi]
   55 00d416ce 33c0            xor     eax,eax
   55 00d416d0 817d0865010000  cmp     dword ptr [ebp+8],165h
   55 00d416d7 0f94c0          sete    al
   56 00d416da 5f              pop     edi
   56 00d416db 5e              pop     esi
   56 00d416dc 5b              pop     ebx
   56 00d416dd 8be5            mov     esp,ebp
   56 00d416df 5d              pop     ebp
   56 00d416e0 c3              ret
```

After hitting the breakpoint at **00d416ce** we start the “surgery”.

```
0:000> a 00d416ce
00d416ce cmp dword ptr [ebp+8], 0
cmp dword ptr [ebp+8], 0
00d416d2
```

We get the new listing:

```
0:000>  uf CrackMe!IsRightPassword
CrackMe!IsRightPassword [c:\development\my
tools\book\crackme\crackme\crackme.cpp @ 54]:
   54 00d416b0 55              push    ebp
   54 00d416b1 8bec            mov     ebp,esp
   54 00d416b3 81ecc0000000    sub     esp,0C0h
   54 00d416b9 53              push    ebx
   54 00d416ba 56              push    esi
   54 00d416bb 57              push    edi
   54 00d416bc 8dbd40ffffff    lea     edi,[ebp-0C0h]
   54 00d416c2 b930000000      mov     ecx,30h
   54 00d416c7 b8cccccccc      mov     eax,0CCCCCCCCh
   54 00d416cc f3ab            rep stos dword ptr es:[edi]
   55 00d416ce 837d0800        cmp     dword ptr [ebp+8],0
   55 00d416d2 086501          or      byte ptr [ebp+1],ah
   55 00d416d5 0000            add     byte ptr [eax],al
   55 00d416d7 0f94c0          sete    al
   56 00d416da 5f              pop     edi
   56 00d416db 5e              pop     esi
   56 00d416dc 5b              pop     ebx
```

```
56 00d416dd 8be5            mov     esp,ebp
56 00d416df 5d              pop     ebp
56 00d416e0 c3              ret
```

Note that we messed up the function because the original code 817d0865010000 has more bytes than the new code has: 837d0800.

To correct that we need to insert NOP instructions just to fill the remaining bytes. We can calculate the number of instructions or see the disassembly after entering each NOP until we see the right code continuation according to the original listing. In our case we use:

```
a 00d416d2
```

and enter NOP instructions or we can try the approach below that uses the code corresponding to the mnemonic:

```
eb 00d416d2 90 90 90
```

If we use the Disassembly Window or if we use **uf** command again we will be able to see the modified version:

```
CrackMe!IsRightPassword:
003716b0 55              push    ebp
003716b1 8bec            mov     ebp,esp
003716b3 81ecc0000000    sub     esp,0C0h
003716b9 53              push    ebx
003716ba 56              push    esi
```

```
003716bb 57              push    edi
003716bc 8dbd40ffffff    lea     edi,[ebp-0C0h]
003716c2 b930000000      mov     ecx,30h
003716c7 b8cccccccc      mov     eax,0CCCCCCCCh
003716cc f3ab            rep stos dword ptr es:[edi]
003716ce 33c0            xor     eax,eax
003716d0 837d0800        cmp     dword ptr [ebp+8],0
003716d4 90              nop
003716d5 90              nop
003716d6 90              nop
003716d7 0f94c0          sete    al
003716da 5f              pop     edi
003716db 5e              pop     esi
003716dc 5b              pop     ebx
003716dd 8be5            mov     esp,ebp
003716df 5d              pop     ebp
003716e0 c3              ret
```

The original password is 0. Let's change the user's password to 0, too:

```
0:000> dd [ebp+8] L1
002bfaf0  00000003
```

In our case we used 3. Let's change our password to 0, too:

```
0:000> ed 002bfaf0  0
```

We can see that it was changed:

```
0:000> dd [ebp+8] L1
002bfaf0  00000000
```

At this point we should get the message: "You have access to the system." This happens because the application is comparing the user's password that is 0 (we changed it) against the original password that is also 0 (we changed it too).

By using debuggers like OllyDbg or hexadecimal editors we can go one step further and save another version of the binary, the patched version. That means the application will consider the number 0 as the right password whenever we run it.

Task #3 – Removing the test that validates the password.

After running the application again we break into the debugger when it asks for the password.

```
0:000> uf CrackMe!wmain
CrackMe!wmain [c:\development\my tools\book\crackme\crackme\crackme.cpp @ 59]:
   59 00ec1c30 55              push    ebp
   59 00ec1c31 8bec            mov     ebp,esp
   59 00ec1c33 81ecc0000000    sub     esp,0C0h
   59 00ec1c39 53              push    ebx
   59 00ec1c3a 56              push    esi
   59 00ec1c3b 57              push    edi
   59 00ec1c3c 8dbd40ffffff    lea     edi,[ebp-0C0h]
   59 00ec1c42 b930000000      mov     ecx,30h
   59 00ec1c47 b8cccccccc      mov     eax,0CCCCCCCCh
```

```
   59 00ec1c4c f3ab            rep stos dword ptr es:[edi]
   60 00ec1c4e e8cbf3ffff      call    CrackMe!ILT+25(?AskPasswordYAXXZ) (00ec101e)
   61 00ec1c53 33c0            xor     eax,eax
   62 00ec1c55 5f              pop     edi
   62 00ec1c56 5e              pop     esi
   62 00ec1c57 5b              pop     ebx
   62 00ec1c58 81c4c0000000    add     esp,0C0h
   62 00ec1c5e 3bec            cmp     ebp,esp
   62 00ec1c60 e84ef5ffff      call    CrackMe!ILT+430(__RTC_CheckEsp) (00ec11b3)
   62 00ec1c65 8be5            mov     esp,ebp
   62 00ec1c67 5d              pop     ebp
   62 00ec1c68 c3              ret
0:000> uf 00ec101e
CrackMe!AskPassword [c:\development\my tools\book\crackme\crackme\crackme.cpp @ 19]:
   19 00ec4190 55              push    ebp
   19 00ec4191 8bec            mov     ebp,esp
   19 00ec4193 81ecd8000000    sub     esp,0D8h
   19 00ec4199 53              push    ebx
   19 00ec419a 56              push    esi
   19 00ec419b 57              push    edi
   19 00ec419c 8dbd28ffffff    lea     edi,[ebp-0D8h]
   19 00ec41a2 b936000000      mov     ecx,36h
   19 00ec41a7 b8cccccccc      mov     eax,0CCCCCCCCh
   19 00ec41ac f3ab            rep stos dword ptr es:[edi]
   21 00ec41ae c745f800000000  mov     dword ptr [ebp-8],0
   21 00ec41b5 eb09            jmp     CrackMe!AskPassword+0x30 (00ec41c0)

CrackMe!AskPassword+0x27 [c:\development\my tools\book\crackme\crackme\crackme.cpp @
21]:
   21 00ec41b7 8b45f8          mov     eax,dword ptr [ebp-8]
   21 00ec41ba 83c001          add     eax,1
   21 00ec41bd 8945f8          mov     dword ptr [ebp-8],eax

CrackMe!AskPassword+0x30 [c:\development\my tools\book\crackme\crackme\crackme.cpp @
21]:
   21 00ec41c0 837df803        cmp     dword ptr [ebp-8],3
   21 00ec41c4 0f8dc2000000    jge     CrackMe!AskPassword+0xfc (00ec428c)
```

```
CrackMe!AskPassword+0x3a [c:\development\my tools\book\crackme\crackme\crackme.cpp @ 23]:

   23 00ec41ca 8bf4            mov     esi,esp

   23 00ec41cc a110a3ec00      mov     eax,dword ptr [CrackMe!_imp_?endlstdYAAAV?$basic_ostreamDU?$char_traitsDstd (00eca310)]

   23 00ec41d1 50              push    eax

   23 00ec41d2 683c78ec00      push    offset CrackMe!`string' (00ec783c)

   23 00ec41d7 8b4df8          mov     ecx,dword ptr [ebp-8]

   23 00ec41da 83c101          add     ecx,1

   23 00ec41dd 8bfc            mov     edi,esp

   23 00ec41df 51              push    ecx

   23 00ec41e0 681478ec00      push    offset CrackMe!`string' (00ec7814)

   23 00ec41e5 8b150ca3ec00    mov     edx,dword ptr [CrackMe!_imp_?coutstd (00eca30c)]

   23 00ec41eb 52              push    edx

   23 00ec41ec e872cfffff      call    CrackMe!ILT+350(??$?6U?$char_traitsDstdstdYAAAV?$basic_ostreamDU?$char_traitsDstd (00ec1163)

   23 00ec41f1 83c408          add     esp,8

   23 00ec41f4 8bc8            mov     ecx,eax

   23 00ec41f6 ff1554a3ec00    call    dword ptr [CrackMe!_imp_??6?$basic_ostreamDU?$char_traitsDstdstdQAEAAV01HZ (00eca354)]

   23 00ec41fc 3bfc            cmp     edi,esp

   23 00ec41fe e8b0cfffff      call    CrackMe!ILT+430(__RTC_CheckEsp) (00ec11b3)

   23 00ec4203 50              push    eax

   23 00ec4204 e85acfffff      call    CrackMe!ILT+350(??$?6U?$char_traitsDstdstdYAAAV?$basic_ostreamDU?$char_traitsDstd (00ec1163)

   23 00ec4209 83c408          add     esp,8

   23 00ec420c 8bc8            mov     ecx,eax

   23 00ec420e ff1508a3ec00    call    dword ptr [CrackMe!_imp_??6?$basic_ostreamDU?$char_traitsDstdstdQAEAAV01P6AAAV01AAV01ZZ (00eca308)]

   23 00ec4214 3bf4            cmp     esi,esp

   23 00ec4216 e898cfffff      call    CrackMe!ILT+430(__RTC_CheckEsp) (00ec11b3)

   24 00ec421b 8bf4            mov     esi,esp

   24 00ec421d a110a3ec00      mov     eax,dword ptr [CrackMe!_imp_?endlstdYAAAV?$basic_ostreamDU?$char_traitsDstd (00eca310)]

   24 00ec4222 50              push    eax

   24 00ec4223 68187bec00      push    offset CrackMe!`string' (00ec7b18)

   24 00ec4228 8b0d0ca3ec00    mov     ecx,dword ptr [CrackMe!_imp_?coutstd (00eca30c)]

   24 00ec422e 51              push    ecx
```

```
   24 00ec422f e82fcfffff      call
CrackMe!ILT+350(??$?6U?$char_traitsDstdstdYAAAV?$basic_ostreamDU?$char_traitsDstd
(00ec1163)

   24 00ec4234 83c408          add     esp,8

   24 00ec4237 8bc8            mov     ecx,eax

   24 00ec4239 ff1508a3ec00    call    dword ptr
[CrackMe!_imp_??6?$basic_ostreamDU?$char_traitsDstdstdQAEAAV01P6AAAV01AAV01ZZ
(00eca308)]

   24 00ec423f 3bf4            cmp     esi,esp

   24 00ec4241 e86dcfffff      call    CrackMe!ILT+430(__RTC_CheckEsp) (00ec11b3)

   26 00ec4246 c745ec00000000  mov     dword ptr [ebp-14h],0

   28 00ec424d 8bf4            mov     esi,esp

   28 00ec424f 8d45ec          lea     eax,[ebp-14h]

   28 00ec4252 50              push    eax

   28 00ec4253 8b0d04a3ec00    mov     ecx,dword ptr [CrackMe!_imp_?cinstd (00eca304)]

   28 00ec4259 ff1500a3ec00    call    dword ptr
[CrackMe!_imp_??5?$basic_istreamDU?$char_traitsDstdstdQAEAAV01AAHZ (00eca300)]

   28 00ec425f 3bf4            cmp     esi,esp

   28 00ec4261 e84dcfffff      call    CrackMe!ILT+430(__RTC_CheckEsp) (00ec11b3)

   30 00ec4266 8b45ec          mov     eax,dword ptr [ebp-14h]

   30 00ec4269 50              push    eax

   30 00ec426a e8eecfffff      call    CrackMe!ILT+600(?IsRightPasswordYA_NHZ)
(00ec125d)

   30 00ec426f 83c404          add     esp,4

   30 00ec4272 0fb6c8          movzx   ecx,al

   30 00ec4275 85c9            test    ecx,ecx

   30 00ec4277 7409            je      CrackMe!AskPassword+0xf2 (00ec4282)


CrackMe!AskPassword+0xe9 [c:\development\my tools\book\crackme\crackme\crackme.cpp @
32]:

   32 00ec4279 e8e9cfffff      call    CrackMe!ILT+610(?GiveAccessYAXXZ) (00ec1267)

   33 00ec427e eb0c            jmp     CrackMe!AskPassword+0xfc (00ec428c)


CrackMe!AskPassword+0xf2 [c:\development\my tools\book\crackme\crackme\crackme.cpp @
37]:

   37 00ec4282 e8dbcfffff      call    CrackMe!ILT+605(?DenyAccessYAXXZ) (00ec1262)

   38 00ec4287 e92bffffff      jmp     CrackMe!AskPassword+0x27 (00ec41b7)


CrackMe!AskPassword+0xfc [c:\development\my tools\book\crackme\crackme\crackme.cpp @
41]:

   41 00ec428c 52              push    edx
```

```
   41 00ec428d 8bcd            mov     ecx,ebp
   41 00ec428f 50              push    eax
   41 00ec4290 8d15b442ec00    lea     edx,[CrackMe!AskPassword+0x124 (00ec42b4)]
   41 00ec4296 e819ceffff      call    CrackMe!ILT+175(_RTC_CheckStackVars (00ec10b4)
   41 00ec429b 58              pop     eax
   41 00ec429c 5a              pop     edx
   41 00ec429d 5f              pop     edi
   41 00ec429e 5e              pop     esi
   41 00ec429f 5b              pop     ebx
   41 00ec42a0 81c4d8000000    add     esp,0D8h
   41 00ec42a6 3bec            cmp     ebp,esp
   41 00ec42a8 e806cfffff      call    CrackMe!ILT+430(__RTC_CheckEsp) (00ec11b3)
   41 00ec42ad 8be5            mov     esp,ebp
   41 00ec42af 5d              pop     ebp
   41 00ec42b0 c3              ret

CrackMe!ILT+25(?AskPasswordYAXXZ):
00ec101e e96d310000      jmp     CrackMe!AskPassword (00ec4190)
```

[ebp-14] holds the user password that is sent as the argument to **IsRightPassword**().

```
0:000> uf 00ec125d
CrackMe!IsRightPassword [c:\development\my
tools\book\crackme\crackme\crackme.cpp @ 54]:
   54 00ec16b0 55              push    ebp
   54 00ec16b1 8bec            mov     ebp,esp
   54 00ec16b3 81ecc0000000    sub     esp,0C0h
   54 00ec16b9 53              push    ebx
   54 00ec16ba 56              push    esi
   54 00ec16bb 57              push    edi
   54 00ec16bc 8dbd40ffffff    lea     edi,[ebp-0C0h]
   54 00ec16c2 b930000000      mov     ecx,30h
   54 00ec16c7 b8cccccccc      mov     eax,0CCCCCCCCh
```

```
54 00ec16cc f3ab            rep stos dword ptr es:[edi]
55 00ec16ce 33c0            xor     eax,eax
55 00ec16d0 817d0865010000  cmp     dword ptr [ebp+8],165h
55 00ec16d7 0f94c0          sete    al
56 00ec16da 5f              pop     edi
56 00ec16db 5e              pop     esi
56 00ec16dc 5b              pop     ebx
56 00ec16dd 8be5            mov     esp,ebp
56 00ec16df 5d              pop     ebp
56 00ec16e0 c3              ret

CrackMe!ILT+600(?IsRightPasswordYA_NHZ):
00ec125d e94e040000      jmp     CrackMe!IsRightPassword (00ec16b0)
```

Next step is to replace this code:

```
55 00ec16ce 33c0            xor     eax,eax
55 00ec16d0 817d0865010000  cmp     dword ptr [ebp+8],165h
```

with this new code:

```
55 00ec16ce        mov eax, 1
                   nop
                   nop
                   …
```

After the changes we have this code:

```
CrackMe!IsRightPassword:
00ec16b0 55              push    ebp
```

```
00ec16b1 8bec           mov     ebp,esp
00ec16b3 81ecc0000000   sub     esp,0C0h
00ec16b9 53             push    ebx
00ec16ba 56             push    esi
00ec16bb 57             push    edi
00ec16bc 8dbd40ffffff   lea     edi,[ebp-0C0h]
00ec16c2 b930000000     mov     ecx,30h
00ec16c7 b8cccccccc     mov     eax,0CCCCCCCCh
00ec16cc f3ab           rep stos dword ptr es:[edi]
00ec16ce b801000000     mov     eax,1
00ec16d3 650100         add     dword ptr gs:[eax],eax
00ec16d6 000f           add     byte ptr [edi],cl
00ec16d8 94             xchg    eax,esp
00ec16d9 c05f5e5b       rcr     byte ptr [edi+5Eh],5Bh
00ec16dd 8be5           mov     esp,ebp
00ec16df 5d             pop     ebp
00ec16e0 c3             ret
```

However, notice that we changed all other instructions because our instruction used more bytes than the original instruction. We fix that using NOP instructions.

```
0:000> eb 00ec16d3 90 90 90 90 90 90 90
```

Another approach is to use this command:

```
a 00ec16d3
```

and then type 7 NOP opcodes pressing Enter after each one.

The first approach has one key benefit: it can be used from scripts or breakpoints. And it is faster.

Our final code:

```
CrackMe!IsRightPassword:
00ec16b0 55              push    ebp
00ec16b1 8bec            mov     ebp,esp
00ec16b3 81ecc0000000    sub     esp,0C0h
00ec16b9 53              push    ebx
00ec16ba 56              push    esi
00ec16bb 57              push    edi
00ec16bc 8dbd40ffffff    lea     edi,[ebp-0C0h]
00ec16c2 b930000000      mov     ecx,30h
00ec16c7 b8cccccccc      mov     eax,0CCCCCCCCh
00ec16cc f3ab            rep stos dword ptr es:[edi]
00ec16ce b801000000      mov     eax,1
00ec16d3 90              nop
00ec16d4 90              nop
00ec16d5 90              nop
00ec16d6 90              nop
00ec16d7 90              nop
00ec16d8 90              nop
00ec16d9 90              nop
00ec16da 5f              pop     edi
00ec16db 5e              pop     esi
00ec16dc 5b              pop     ebx
00ec16dd 8be5            mov     esp,ebp
00ec16df 5d              pop     ebp
00ec16e0 c3              ret
```

Now **IsRightPassword()** function always returns **1** (TRUE). We use **g** to continue the execution and from the console window enter any number we want as a password.

Task #4 – Making the application to call the function that is called when typing the right password even when typing the wrong password.

After running the application and breaking into the debugger when asked for a password we start with what we call the "pre-surgery" phase.

```
0:000> kL 1000
ChildEBP RetAddr
0046f1ec 75f66f99 kernel32!ReadConsoleInternal+0x15
0046f274 75eeefc6 kernel32!ReadConsoleA+0x40
0046f2bc 67416c3c kernel32!ReadFileImplementation+0x75
0046f350 67416589 MSVCR90D!_read_nolock+0x62c
0046f3a0 673a4453 MSVCR90D!_read+0x219
0046f3c8 673a2748 MSVCR90D!_filbuf+0x113
0046f420 6ce5c8e0 MSVCR90D!fgetc+0x208
0046f430 6ce5c567 MSVCP90D!std::_Fgetc<char>+0x10
0046f518 6ce5c460 MSVCP90D!std::basic_filebuf<char,std::char_traits<char> >::uflow+0xb7
0046f530 6ce58c9a MSVCP90D!std::basic_filebuf<char,std::char_traits<char>
>::underflow+0x50
0046f540 6ce59104 MSVCP90D!std::basic_streambuf<char,std::char_traits<char>
>::sgetc+0x3a
0046f59c 6ce58c3a MSVCP90D!std::basic_istream<char,std::char_traits<char> >::_Ipfx+0x104
0046f5bc 6ce7eee6 MSVCP90D!std::basic_istream<char,std::char_traits<char>
>::sentry::sentry+0x4a
0046f634 0002425f MSVCP90D!std::basic_istream<char,std::char_traits<char>
>::operator>>+0x46
0046f724 00021c53 CrackMe!AskPassword+0xcf
0046f7f8 00022598 CrackMe!wmain+0x23
0046f848 000223df CrackMe!__tmainCRTStartup+0x1a8
0046f850 75ec3f39 CrackMe!wmainCRTStartup+0xf
0046f85c 77710409 kernel32!BaseThreadInitThunk+0xe
0046f89c 777103dc ntdll!__RtlUserThreadStart+0x70
0046f8b4 00000000 ntdll!_RtlUserThreadStart+0x1b
```

AskPassword() is called from **main**() and look suspicious. Let's investigate this further:

```
0:000> uf CrackMe!AskPassword
CrackMe!AskPassword [c:\development\my tools\book\crackme\crackme\crackme.cpp @ 19]:
   19 00024190 55              push    ebp
   19 00024191 8bec            mov     ebp,esp
   19 00024193 81ecd8000000    sub     esp,0D8h
   19 00024199 53              push    ebx
   19 0002419a 56              push    esi
   19 0002419b 57              push    edi
   19 0002419c 8dbd28ffffff    lea     edi,[ebp-0D8h]
   19 000241a2 b936000000      mov     ecx,36h
   19 000241a7 b8cccccccc      mov     eax,0CCCCCCCCh
   19 000241ac f3ab            rep stos dword ptr es:[edi]
   21 000241ae c745f800000000  mov     dword ptr [ebp-8],0
   21 000241b5 eb09            jmp     CrackMe!AskPassword+0x30 (000241c0)

CrackMe!AskPassword+0x27 [c:\development\my tools\book\crackme\crackme\crackme.cpp @
21]:
   21 000241b7 8b45f8          mov     eax,dword ptr [ebp-8]
   21 000241ba 83c001          add     eax,1
   21 000241bd 8945f8          mov     dword ptr [ebp-8],eax

CrackMe!AskPassword+0x30 [c:\development\my tools\book\crackme\crackme\crackme.cpp @
21]:
   21 000241c0 837df803        cmp     dword ptr [ebp-8],3
   21 000241c4 0f8dc2000000    jge     CrackMe!AskPassword+0xfc (0002428c)

CrackMe!AskPassword+0x3a [c:\development\my tools\book\crackme\crackme\crackme.cpp @
23]:
   23 000241ca 8bf4            mov     esi,esp
   23 000241cc a110a30200      mov     eax,dword ptr
[CrackMe!_imp_?endlstdYAAAV?$basic_ostreamDU?$char_traitsDstd (0002a310)]
   23 000241d1 50              push    eax
   23 000241d2 683c780200      push    offset CrackMe!`string' (0002783c)
   23 000241d7 8b4df8          mov     ecx,dword ptr [ebp-8]
   23 000241da 83c101          add     ecx,1
```

```
   23 000241dd 8bfc            mov     edi,esp

   23 000241df 51              push    ecx

   23 000241e0 6814780200      push    offset CrackMe!`string' (00027814)

   23 000241e5 8b150ca30200    mov     edx,dword ptr [CrackMe!_imp_?coutstd (0002a30c)]

   23 000241eb 52              push    edx

   23 000241ec e872cfffff      call
CrackMe!ILT+350(??$?6U?$char_traitsDstdstdYAAAV?$basic_ostreamDU?$char_traitsDstd
(00021163)

   23 000241f1 83c408          add     esp,8

   23 000241f4 8bc8            mov     ecx,eax

   23 000241f6 ff1554a30200    call    dword ptr
[CrackMe!_imp_??6?$basic_ostreamDU?$char_traitsDstdstdQAEAAV01HZ (0002a354)]

   23 000241fc 3bfc            cmp     edi,esp

   23 000241fe e8b0cfffff      call    CrackMe!ILT+430(__RTC_CheckEsp) (000211b3)

   23 00024203 50              push    eax

   23 00024204 e85acfffff      call
CrackMe!ILT+350(??$?6U?$char_traitsDstdstdYAAAV?$basic_ostreamDU?$char_traitsDstd
(00021163)

   23 00024209 83c408          add     esp,8

   23 0002420c 8bc8            mov     ecx,eax

   23 0002420e ff1508a30200    call    dword ptr
[CrackMe!_imp_??6?$basic_ostreamDU?$char_traitsDstdstdQAEAAV01P6AAAV01AAV01ZZ
(0002a308)]

   23 00024214 3bf4            cmp     esi,esp

   23 00024216 e898cfffff      call    CrackMe!ILT+430(__RTC_CheckEsp) (000211b3)

   24 0002421b 8bf4            mov     esi,esp

   24 0002421d a110a30200      mov     eax,dword ptr
[CrackMe!_imp_?endlstdYAAAV?$basic_ostreamDU?$char_traitsDstd (0002a310)]

   24 00024222 50              push    eax

   24 00024223 68187b0200      push    offset CrackMe!`string' (00027b18)

   24 00024228 8b0d0ca30200    mov     ecx,dword ptr [CrackMe!_imp_?coutstd (0002a30c)]

   24 0002422e 51              push    ecx

   24 0002422f e82fcfffff      call
CrackMe!ILT+350(??$?6U?$char_traitsDstdstdYAAAV?$basic_ostreamDU?$char_traitsDstd
(00021163)

   24 00024234 83c408          add     esp,8

   24 00024237 8bc8            mov     ecx,eax

   24 00024239 ff1508a30200    call    dword ptr
[CrackMe!_imp_??6?$basic_ostreamDU?$char_traitsDstdstdQAEAAV01P6AAAV01AAV01ZZ
(0002a308)]

   24 0002423f 3bf4            cmp     esi,esp

   24 00024241 e86dcfffff      call    CrackMe!ILT+430(__RTC_CheckEsp) (000211b3)
```

```
   26 00024246 c745ec00000000  mov     dword ptr [ebp-14h],0

   28 0002424d 8bf4            mov     esi,esp

   28 0002424f 8d45ec          lea     eax,[ebp-14h]

   28 00024252 50              push    eax

   28 00024253 8b0d04a30200    mov     ecx,dword ptr [CrackMe!_imp_?cinstd (0002a304)]

   28 00024259 ff1500a30200    call    dword ptr
[CrackMe!_imp_??5?$basic_istreamDU?$char_traitsDstdstdQAEAAV01AAHZ (0002a300)]

   28 0002425f 3bf4            cmp     esi,esp

   28 00024261 e84dcfffff      call    CrackMe!ILT+430(__RTC_CheckEsp) (000211b3)

   30 00024266 8b45ec          mov     eax,dword ptr [ebp-14h]

   30 00024269 50              push    eax

   30 0002426a e8eecfffff      call    CrackMe!ILT+600(?IsRightPasswordYA_NHZ)
(0002125d)

   30 0002426f 83c404          add     esp,4

   30 00024272 0fb6c8          movzx   ecx,al

   30 00024275 85c9            test    ecx,ecx

   30 00024277 7409            je      CrackMe!AskPassword+0xf2 (00024282)


CrackMe!AskPassword+0xe9 [c:\development\my tools\book\crackme\crackme\crackme.cpp @
32]:

   32 00024279 e8e9cfffff      call    CrackMe!ILT+610(?GiveAccessYAXXZ) (00021267)

   33 0002427e eb0c            jmp     CrackMe!AskPassword+0xfc (0002428c)


CrackMe!AskPassword+0xf2 [c:\development\my tools\book\crackme\crackme\crackme.cpp @
37]:

   37 00024282 e8dbcfffff      call    CrackMe!ILT+605(?DenyAccessYAXXZ) (00021262)

   38 00024287 e92bffffff      jmp     CrackMe!AskPassword+0x27 (000241b7)


CrackMe!AskPassword+0xfc [c:\development\my tools\book\crackme\crackme\crackme.cpp @
41]:

   41 0002428c 52              push    edx

   41 0002428d 8bcd            mov     ecx,ebp

   41 0002428f 50              push    eax

   41 00024290 8d15b4420200    lea     edx,[CrackMe!AskPassword+0x124 (000242b4)]

   41 00024296 e819ceffff      call    CrackMe!ILT+175(_RTC_CheckStackVars (000210b4)

   41 0002429b 58              pop     eax

   41 0002429c 5a              pop     edx

   41 0002429d 5f              pop     edi

   41 0002429e 5e              pop     esi
```

```
   41 0002429f 5b              pop     ebx
   41 000242a0 81c4d8000000    add     esp,0D8h
   41 000242a6 3bec            cmp     ebp,esp
   41 000242a8 e806cfffff      call    CrackMe!ILT+430(__RTC_CheckEsp) (000211b3)
   41 000242ad 8be5            mov     esp,ebp
   41 000242af 5d              pop     ebp
   41 000242b0 c3              ret
```

At this point it is necessary to analyze the dead listing in order to get a better understanding of the function and to make sure this is the right function.

We can see in bold above that what looks like the routine that checks the password displays the message when the wrong message is entered and probably shows another message when the right password is entered. Remember, we pretend that we don't know the source code, so to prove the point we should insert breakpoints, debug the application and see if **DenyAccessYAXXZ** above is called when we enter any invalid password.

Suppose that after running the application and using breakpoints we prove that point. However, we don't know what happens when we enter the right password but we suppose that **GiveAccessYAXXZ** is called. To prove that too let's analyze this function.

```
0:000> uf 00021267
CrackMe!GiveAccess [c:\development\my tools\book\crackme\crackme\crackme.cpp @ 44]:
   44 000215b0 55              push    ebp
   44 000215b1 8bec            mov     ebp,esp
   44 000215b3 81ecc0000000    sub     esp,0C0h
   44 000215b9 53              push    ebx
   44 000215ba 56              push    esi
   44 000215bb 57              push    edi
   44 000215bc 8dbd40ffffff    lea     edi,[ebp-0C0h]
   44 000215c2 b930000000      mov     ecx,30h
   44 000215c7 b8cccccccc      mov     eax,0CCCCCCCCh
```

```
   44 000215cc f3ab            rep stos dword ptr es:[edi]
   45 000215ce 8bf4            mov     esi,esp
   45 000215d0 a110a30200      mov     eax,dword ptr
[CrackMe!_imp_?endlstdYAAAV?$basic_ostreamDU?$char_traitsDstd (0002a310)]
   45 000215d5 50              push    eax
   45 000215d6 6840780200      push    offset CrackMe!`string' (00027840)
   45 000215db 8b0d0ca30200    mov     ecx,dword ptr [CrackMe!_imp_?coutstd (0002a30c)]
   45 000215e1 51              push    ecx
   45 000215e2 e87cfbffff      call
CrackMe!ILT+350(??$?6U?$char_traitsDstdstdYAAAV?$basic_ostreamDU?$char_traitsDstd
(00021163)
   45 000215e7 83c408          add     esp,8
   45 000215ea 8bc8            mov     ecx,eax
   45 000215ec ff1508a30200    call    dword ptr
[CrackMe!_imp_??6?$basic_ostreamDU?$char_traitsDstdstdQAEAAV01P6AAAV01AAV01ZZ
(0002a308)]
   45 000215f2 3bf4            cmp     esi,esp
   45 000215f4 e8bafbffff      call    CrackMe!ILT+430(__RTC_CheckEsp) (000211b3)
   46 000215f9 5f              pop     edi
   46 000215fa 5e              pop     esi
   46 000215fb 5b              pop     ebx
   46 000215fc 81c4c0000000    add     esp,0C0h
   46 00021602 3bec            cmp     ebp,esp
   46 00021604 e8aafbffff      call    CrackMe!ILT+430(__RTC_CheckEsp) (000211b3)
   46 00021609 8be5            mov     esp,ebp
   46 0002160b 5d              pop     ebp
   46 0002160c c3              ret

CrackMe!ILT+610(?GiveAccessYAXXZ):
00021267 e944030000      jmp     CrackMe!GiveAccess (000215b0)
```

After reviewing the code we located one string. Let's examine it:

```
0:000> db 00027840
00027840  59 6f 75 20 68 61 76 65-20 61 63 63 65 73 73 20  You have access
00027850  74 6f 20 74 68 65 20 73-79 73 74 65 6d 2e 00 00  to the system...
00027860  66 00 3a 00 5c 00 64 00-64 00 5c 00 76 00 63 00  f.:.\.d.d.\.v.c.
```

```
00027870  74 00 6f 00 6f 00 6c 00-73 00 5c 00 63 00 72 00  t.o.o.l.s.\.c.r.
00027880  74 00 5f 00 62 00 6c 00-64 00 5c 00 73 00 65 00  t._.b.l.d.\.s.e.
00027890  6c 00 66 00 5f 00 78 00-38 00 36 00 5c 00 63 00  l.f._.x.8.6.\.c.
000278a0  72 00 74 00 5c 00 73 00-72 00 63 00 5c 00 63 00  r.t.\.s.r.c.\.c.
000278b0  72 00 74 00 65 00 78 00-65 00 2e 00 63 00 00 00  r.t.e.x.e...c...
```

Excellent! This is the right function. The string is an ASCII string, not Unicode. A Unicode string should have two bytes for each character.

Here is another way to see that:

```
0:000> da 00027840
00027840  "You have access to the system."
```

Let's see two calls, for the right and wrong password:

```
0:000> uf /c CrackMe!AskPassword
CrackMe!AskPassword (00024190) [c:\development\my tools\book\crackme\crackme\crackme.cpp
@ 19]
  CrackMe!AskPassword+0x5c (000241ec) [c:\development\my
tools\book\crackme\crackme\crackme.cpp @ 23]:
    call to
CrackMe!ILT+350(??$?6U?$char_traitsDstdstdYAAAV?$basic_ostreamDU?$char_traitsDstd
(00021163)
  CrackMe!AskPassword+0x66 (000241f6) [c:\development\my
tools\book\crackme\crackme\crackme.cpp @ 23]:
    call to MSVCP90D!std::basic_ostream<char,std::char_traits<char> >::operator<<
(6ce7a520)
  CrackMe!AskPassword+0x6e (000241fe) [c:\development\my
tools\book\crackme\crackme\crackme.cpp @ 23]:
    call to CrackMe!ILT+430(__RTC_CheckEsp) (000211b3)
  CrackMe!AskPassword+0x74 (00024204) [c:\development\my
tools\book\crackme\crackme\crackme.cpp @ 23]:
    call to
CrackMe!ILT+350(??$?6U?$char_traitsDstdstdYAAAV?$basic_ostreamDU?$char_traitsDstd
(00021163)
```

```
  CrackMe!AskPassword+0x7e (0002420e) [c:\development\my
tools\book\crackme\crackme\crackme.cpp @ 23]:

    call to MSVCP90D!std::basic_ostream<char,std::char_traits<char> >::operator<<
(6ce79f60)

  CrackMe!AskPassword+0x86 (00024216) [c:\development\my
tools\book\crackme\crackme\crackme.cpp @ 23]:

    call to CrackMe!ILT+430(__RTC_CheckEsp) (000211b3)

  CrackMe!AskPassword+0x9f (0002422f) [c:\development\my
tools\book\crackme\crackme\crackme.cpp @ 24]:

    call to
CrackMe!ILT+350(??$?6U?$char_traitsDstdstdYAAAV?$basic_ostreamDU?$char_traitsDstd
(00021163)

  CrackMe!AskPassword+0xa9 (00024239) [c:\development\my
tools\book\crackme\crackme\crackme.cpp @ 24]:

    call to MSVCP90D!std::basic_ostream<char,std::char_traits<char> >::operator<<
(6ce79f60)

  CrackMe!AskPassword+0xb1 (00024241) [c:\development\my
tools\book\crackme\crackme\crackme.cpp @ 24]:

    call to CrackMe!ILT+430(__RTC_CheckEsp) (000211b3)

  CrackMe!AskPassword+0xc9 (00024259) [c:\development\my
tools\book\crackme\crackme\crackme.cpp @ 28]:

    call to MSVCP90D!std::basic_istream<char,std::char_traits<char> >::operator>>
(6ce7eea0)

  CrackMe!AskPassword+0xd1 (00024261) [c:\development\my
tools\book\crackme\crackme\crackme.cpp @ 28]:

    call to CrackMe!ILT+430(__RTC_CheckEsp) (000211b3)

  CrackMe!AskPassword+0xda (0002426a) [c:\development\my
tools\book\crackme\crackme\crackme.cpp @ 30]:

    call to CrackMe!ILT+600(?IsRightPasswordYA_NHZ) (0002125d)

  CrackMe!AskPassword+0xe9 (00024279) [c:\development\my
tools\book\crackme\crackme\crackme.cpp @ 32]:

    call to CrackMe!ILT+610(?GiveAccessYAXXZ) (00021267)

  CrackMe!AskPassword+0xf2 (00024282) [c:\development\my
tools\book\crackme\crackme\crackme.cpp @ 37]:

    call to CrackMe!ILT+605(?DenyAccessYAXXZ) (00021262)

  CrackMe!AskPassword+0x106 (00024296) [c:\development\my
tools\book\crackme\crackme\crackme.cpp @ 41]:

    call to CrackMe!ILT+175(_RTC_CheckStackVars (000210b4)

  CrackMe!AskPassword+0x118 (000242a8) [c:\development\my
tools\book\crackme\crackme\crackme.cpp @ 41]:

    call to CrackMe!ILT+430(__RTC_CheckEsp) (000211b3)
```

Hopefully the number of bytes is the same:

```
CrackMe!AskPassword+0xe9 [c:\development\my tools\book\crackme\crackme\crackme.cpp @
32]:
   32 00024279 e8e9cfffff      call    CrackMe!ILT+610(?GiveAccessYAXXZ) (00021267)
   33 0002427e eb0c            jmp     CrackMe!AskPassword+0xfc (0002428c)

CrackMe!AskPassword+0xf2 [c:\development\my tools\book\crackme\crackme\crackme.cpp @
37]:
   37 00024282 e8dbcfffff      call    CrackMe!ILT+605(?DenyAccessYAXXZ) (00021262)
```

We are ready to start the "surgery":

```
0:000> u 00021267
CrackMe!ILT+610(?GiveAccessYAXXZ):
00021267 e944030000      jmp     CrackMe!GiveAccess (000215b0)
```

We see the indirection to **000215b0** address:

```
0:000> u 000215b0
CrackMe!GiveAccess [c:\development\my tools\book\crackme\crackme\crackme.cpp @ 44]:
000215b0 55              push    ebp
000215b1 8bec            mov     ebp,esp
000215b3 81ecc0000000    sub     esp,0C0h
000215b9 53              push    ebx
000215ba 56              push    esi
000215bb 57              push    edi
000215bc 8dbd40ffffff    lea     edi,[ebp-0C0h]
000215c2 b930000000      mov     ecx,30h

0:000> a 00024282
00024282 call CrackMe!GiveAccess
call CrackMe!GiveAccess
00024287
```

The new listing:

```
00024277 7409          je      CrackMe!AskPassword+0xf2 (00024282)
00024279 e8e9cfffff    call    CrackMe!ILT+610(?GiveAccessYAXXZ)
(00021267)
0002427e eb0c          jmp     CrackMe!AskPassword+0xfc (0002428c)
00024280 eb05          jmp     CrackMe!AskPassword+0xf7 (00024287)
00024282 e829d3ffff    call    CrackMe!GiveAccess (000215b0)
00024287 e92bffffff    jmp     CrackMe!AskPassword+0x27 (000241b7)
0002428c 52            push    edx
0002428d 8bcd          mov     ecx,ebp
0002428f 50            push    eax
```

Now, if we type "g" and continue the execution entering any invalid password the application shows the message that says we have access to the system. However, the application is going to ask us the password again because we typed the wrong password. In other words, after changing the application according to the instructions above, it calls the function that is supposed to be called only if we type the right password! We can create a WinDbg script that patches the application on the fly, avoiding the manual work of retyping commands all over again.

Here is a fun demonstration for Windows XP on 32 bits:
http://blogs.msdn.com/debuggingtoolbox/archive/2007/03/28/windbg-script-playing-with-minesweeper.aspx

In Windows 7, Vista and Windows Server 2008 the addresses change whenever the application is loaded so it means more work but it is still possible anyway to crack this application.

k*

The **k*** command is used to display a call stack. It has several variations, for example, kL, kpn or kPn. Some of them are used most of the time and in subsequent sections we show when to use them.

The **k*** command is also useful for reconstructing a corrupt call stack. To do that we need to use the following format:

kbn = BasePointer StackPointer InstructionPointer

Example with a regular call stack:

```
0:024> r
eax=0397fd28 ebx=00000000 ecx=5d6a999c edx=00010001 esi=00422600 edi=00000000
eip=76ef9a94 esp=0397fcd0 ebp=0397fd34 iopl=0         nv up ei pl nz ac pe cy
cs=001b  ss=0023  ds=0023  es=0023  fs=003b  gs=0000             efl=00000217
ntdll!KiFastSystemCallRet:
76ef9a94 c3              ret

0:024> kbn = 0397fd34 0397fcd0 76ef9a94
 # ChildEBP RetAddr  Args to Child
00 0397fccc 76ef9254 76ee33b4 000000f4 00000000 ntdll!KiFastSystemCallRet
01 0397fcd0 76ee33b4 000000f4 00000000 00000000 ntdll!ZwWaitForSingleObject+0xc
02 0397fd34 76ee323c 00000000 00000000 03183ae8 ntdll!RtlpWaitOnCriticalSection+0x155
03 0397fd5c 00414ee7 00422600 00000000 00000000 ntdll!RtlEnterCriticalSection+0x152
04 0397fdc8 00414834 00000000 00000000 03183ae8 mtgdi!CBallThread::SingleStep+0x147
[c:\downloads\mtgdi\threads.cpp @ 180]
05 0397fe20 00414d8c 00000000 00000000 03183ae8 mtgdi!CGDIThread::InitInstance+0x44
[c:\downloads\mtgdi\threads.cpp @ 65]
06 0397fe78 5d57d973 d323d041 00000000 00000000 mtgdi!CBallThread::InitInstance+0x2c
[c:\downloads\mtgdi\threads.cpp @ 156]
07 0397ff40 5f1edfd3 0012f7dc d323d82c 00000000 mfc90d!_AfxThreadEntry+0x303
08 0397ff7c 5f1edf69 03183d38 0397ff94 75934911 MSVCR90D!_beginthreadex+0x243
09 0397ff88 75934911 03183d38 0397ffd4 76ede4b6 MSVCR90D!_beginthreadex+0x1d9
0a 0397ff94 76ede4b6 03183ae8 75fef35c 00000000 kernel32!BaseThreadInitThunk+0xe
0b 0397ffd4 76ede489 5f1edee0 03183ae8 00000000 ntdll!__RtlUserThreadStart+0x23
0c 0397ffec 00000000 5f1edee0 03183ae8 00000000 ntdll!_RtlUserThreadStart+0x1b
```

kL 1000

kL command displays a stack trace without any additional information. We can use **kL** whenever we need to send a call stack to external customers without information from private symbols like arguments and source code line numbers.

Tip: using 1000 after the command forces it to display the entire call stack in most scenarios. 1000 is sufficient 99% of the time. Another approach is to use **.kframes** to specify the number of frames to be displayed.

Example:

```
  24  Id: a9c.15d4 Suspend: 1 Teb: 7ffa3000 Unfrozen
ChildEBP RetAddr
0397fccc 76ef9254 ntdll!KiFastSystemCallRet
0397fcd0 76ee33b4 ntdll!ZwWaitForSingleObject+0xc
0397fd34 76ee323c ntdll!RtlpWaitOnCriticalSection+0x155
0397fd5c 00414ee7 ntdll!RtlEnterCriticalSection+0x152
0397fdc8 00414834 mtgdi!CBallThread::SingleStep+0x147
0397fe20 00414d8c mtgdi!CGDIThread::InitInstance+0x44
0397fe78 5d57d973 mtgdi!CBallThread::InitInstance+0x2c
0397ff40 5f1edfd3 mfc90d!_AfxThreadEntry+0x303
0397ff7c 5f1edf69 MSVCR90D!_beginthreadex+0x243
0397ff88 75934911 MSVCR90D!_beginthreadex+0x1d9
0397ff94 76ede4b6 kernel32!BaseThreadInitThunk+0xe
0397ffd4 76ede489 ntdll!__RtlUserThreadStart+0x23
0397ffec 00000000 ntdll!_RtlUserThreadStart+0x1b
```

kpn 1000

This variation of **k** command shows all parameters for each method/function on a call stack.

Tip: this command is useful when we have private symbols that give us information like parameters and source code line numbers.

Using **n** with **kb**, **kP** or **kp** commands shows frame numbers.

If we have only public symbols, we might want to use **kbn** command variant instead.

Example:

```
   0  Id: a9c.10d0 Suspend: 1 Teb: 7ffdf000 Unfrozen
 # ChildEBP RetAddr
00 0012fe08 76d9f837 ntdll!KiFastSystemCallRet
01 0012fe0c 76d959e5 USER32!NtUserGetMessage+0xc
02 0012fe30 5d57daa3 USER32!GetMessageA+0x8a
03 0012fe5c 5d57f13e mfc90d!AfxInternalPumpMessage+0x23
04 0012fe68 5d57e90d mfc90d!CWinThread::PumpMessage+0xe
05 0012fe84 5d581179 mfc90d!CWinThread::Run+0x8d
06 0012fe98 5d50648f mfc90d!CWinApp::Run+0x59
07 0012febc 0041903a mfc90d!AfxWinMain+0xef
08 0012fed4 00416a18 mtgdi!WinMain+0x1a
09 0012ff80 0041677f mtgdi!__tmainCRTStartup(void)+0x288
0a 0012ff88 75934911 mtgdi!WinMainCRTStartup(void)+0xf
0b 0012ff94 76ede4b6 kernel32!BaseThreadInitThunk+0xe
0c 0012ffd4 76ede489 ntdll!__RtlUserThreadStart+0x23
0d 0012ffec 00000000 ntdll!_RtlUserThreadStart+0x1b
```

kbn 1000

This variation shows the first three parameters passed to each function/method in a stack trace.

Tip: this command is useful when we have public symbols. It should help us to figure out the first three parameters.

Example:

```
 # ChildEBP RetAddr  Args to Child
00 0012fe08 76d9f837 76d959e5 00178370 00000000 ntdll!KiFastSystemCallRet
01 0012fe0c 76d959e5 00178370 00000000 00000000 USER32!NtUserGetMessage+0xc
02 0012fe30 5d57daa3 00178370 00000000 00000000 USER32!GetMessageA+0x8a
03 0012fe5c 5d57f13e 00422528 0012fe84 5d57e90d mfc90d!AfxInternalPumpMessage+0x23
04 0012fe68 5d57e90d 00000001 00422528 00178340 mfc90d!CWinThread::PumpMessage+0xe
05 0012fe84 5d581179 00422528 00419c7a ffffffff mfc90d!CWinThread::Run+0x8d
06 0012fe98 5d50648f 00000000 00000000 00000000 mfc90d!CWinApp::Run+0x59
07 0012febc 0041903a 00400000 00000000 001728c4 mfc90d!AfxWinMain+0xef
08 0012fed4 00416a18 00400000 00000000 001728c4 mtgdi!WinMain+0x1a
09 0012ff80 0041677f 0012ff94 75934911 7ffd7000 mtgdi!__tmainCRTStartup+0x288
0a 0012ff88 75934911 7ffd7000 0012ffd4 76ede4b6 mtgdi!WinMainCRTStartup+0xf
0b 0012ff94 76ede4b6 7ffd7000 767bf35c 00000000 kernel32!BaseThreadInitThunk+0xe
0c 0012ffd4 76ede489 00411929 7ffd7000 00000000 ntdll!__RtlUserThreadStart+0x23
0d 0012ffec 00000000 00411929 7ffd7000 00000000 ntdll!_RtlUserThreadStart+0x1b
```

Task: compare the output above against the **kpn** command.

kvn 1000

If our functions on a stack trace uses Frame Pointer Omission (FPO), which is some kind of register use optimization, we may want to use **kvn** command to see the number of parameters.

WinDbg **k** command documentation shows meanings for various FPO text combinations

Tip: usually we see FPO only when debugging optimized 32-bit C/C++ code. The command also shows function calling convention, for example *stdcall*.

Example:

```
 # ChildEBP RetAddr  Args to Child
00 0012fe08 76d9f837 76d959e5 00178370 00000000 ntdll!KiFastSystemCallRet (FPO: [0,0,0])
01 0012fe0c 76d959e5 00178370 00000000 00000000 USER32!NtUserGetMessage+0xc (FPO:
[4,0,0])
02 0012fe30 5d57daa3 00178370 00000000 00000000 USER32!GetMessageA+0x8a (FPO: [4,0,4])
03 0012fe5c 5d57f13e 00422528 0012fe84 5d57e90d mfc90d!AfxInternalPumpMessage+0x23 (FPO:
[0,5,0])
04 0012fe68 5d57e90d 00000001 00422528 00178340 mfc90d!CWinThread::PumpMessage+0xe (FPO:
[0,1,0])
05 0012fe84 5d581179 00422528 00419c7a ffffffff mfc90d!CWinThread::Run+0x8d (FPO:
[0,5,0])
06 0012fe98 5d50648f 00000000 00000000 00000000 mfc90d!CWinApp::Run+0x59 (FPO: [0,3,0])
07 0012febc 0041903a 00400000 00000000 001728c4 mfc90d!AfxWinMain+0xef (FPO: [4,7,0])
08 0012fed4 00416a18 00400000 00000000 001728c4 mtgdi!WinMain+0x1a (CONV: stdcall)
09 0012ff80 0041677f 0012ff94 75934911 7ffd7000 mtgdi!__tmainCRTStartup+0x288 (CONV:
cdecl)
0a 0012ff88 75934911 7ffd7000 0012ffd4 76ede4b6 mtgdi!WinMainCRTStartup+0xf (CONV:
cdecl)
0b 0012ff94 76ede4b6 7ffd7000 767bf35c 00000000 kernel32!BaseThreadInitThunk+0xe (FPO:
[1,0,0])
0c 0012ffd4 76ede489 00411929 7ffd7000 00000000 ntdll!__RtlUserThreadStart+0x23 (FPO:
[SEH])
0d 0012ffec 00000000 00411929 7ffd7000 00000000 ntdll!_RtlUserThreadStart+0x1b (FPO:
[2,2,0])
```

kPn 1000

When using this **k** command variation we see only one function parameter on each line of output and not side-by-side like in the case of **kpn** command.

Tip: use it when we have stack frames with many parameters. It should be easier to read them.

Example:

```
 # ChildEBP RetAddr
00 0012fe08 76d9f837 ntdll!KiFastSystemCallRet
01 0012fe0c 76d959e5 USER32!NtUserGetMessage+0xc
02 0012fe30 5d57daa3 USER32!GetMessageA+0x8a
03 0012fe5c 5d57f13e mfc90d!AfxInternalPumpMessage+0x23
04 0012fe68 5d57e90d mfc90d!CWinThread::PumpMessage+0xe
05 0012fe84 5d581179 mfc90d!CWinThread::Run+0x8d
06 0012fe98 5d50648f mfc90d!CWinApp::Run+0x59
07 0012febc 0041903a mfc90d!AfxWinMain+0xef
08 0012fed4 00416a18 mtgdi!WinMain(
                        struct HINSTANCE__ * hInstance = 0x00400000,
                        struct HINSTANCE__ * hPrevInstance = 0x00000000,
                        char * lpCmdLine = 0x001728c4 "",
                        int nCmdShow = 10)+0x1a
09 0012ff80 0041677f mtgdi!__tmainCRTStartup(void)+0x288
0a 0012ff88 75934911 mtgdi!WinMainCRTStartup(void)+0xf
0b 0012ff94 76ede4b6 kernel32!BaseThreadInitThunk+0xe
0c 0012ffd4 76ede489 ntdll!__RtlUserThreadStart+0x23
0d 0012ffec 00000000 ntdll!_RtlUserThreadStart+0x1b
```

kf 1000

This **k** command variation additionally shows the distance between adjacent frames in a separate column. This distance is the number of bytes that separate the frames on the actual stack.

Example:

```
  Memory       ChildEBP RetAddr
               0397fccc 76ef9254 ntdll!KiFastSystemCallRet
        4      0397fcd0 76ee33b4 ntdll!ZwWaitForSingleObject+0xc
       64      0397fd34 76ee323c ntdll!RtlpWaitOnCriticalSection+0x155
       28      0397fd5c 00414ee7 ntdll!RtlEnterCriticalSection+0x152
       6c      0397fdc8 00414834 mtgdi!CBallThread::SingleStep+0x147
[c:\downloads\mtgdi\threads.cpp @ 180]
       58      0397fe20 00414d8c mtgdi!CGDIThread::InitInstance+0x44
[c:\downloads\mtgdi\threads.cpp @ 65]
       58      0397fe78 5d57d973 mtgdi!CBallThread::InitInstance+0x2c
[c:\downloads\mtgdi\threads.cpp @ 156]
       c8      0397ff40 5f1edfd3 mfc90d!_AfxThreadEntry+0x303
       3c      0397ff7c 5f1edf69 MSVCR90D!_beginthreadex+0x243
        c      0397ff88 75934911 MSVCR90D!_beginthreadex+0x1d9
        c      0397ff94 76ede4b6 kernel32!BaseThreadInitThunk+0xe
       40      0397ffd4 76ede489 ntdll!__RtlUserThreadStart+0x23
       18      0397ffec 00000000 ntdll!_RtlUserThreadStart+0x1b
```

kpM

This command uses DML (Debugger Markup Language) to display a call stack. Besides that, it gives us hyperlinks for each frame. When we click on a specific hyperlink, it shows us local variables for this particular frame.

Example:

```
# ChildEBP RetAddr
00 0397fccc 76ef9254 ntdll!KiFastSystemCallRet
01 0397fcd0 76ee33b4 ntdll!ZwWaitForSingleObject+0xc
02 0397fd34 76ee323c ntdll!RtlpWaitOnCriticalSection+0x155
03 0397fd5c 00414ee7 ntdll!RtlEnterCriticalSection+0x152
04 0397fdc8 00414834 mtgdi!CBallThread::SingleStep(void)+0x147
05 0397fe20 00414d8c mtgdi!CGDIThread::InitInstance(void)+0x44
06 0397fe78 5d57d973 mtgdi!CBallThread::InitInstance(void)+0x2c
07 0397ff40 5f1edfd3 mfc90d!_AfxThreadEntry+0x303
08 0397ff7c 5f1edf69 MSVCR90D!_beginthreadex+0x243
09 0397ff88 75934911 MSVCR90D!_beginthreadex+0x1d9
0a 0397ff94 76ede4b6 kernel32!BaseThreadInitThunk+0xe
0b 0397ffd4 76ede489 ntdll!__RtlUserThreadStart+0x23
0c 0397ffec 00000000 ntdll!_RtlUserThreadStart+0x1b
```

d*

The **d*** command and its variations are among the most commonly used commands. It is used to display information from memory, including heap and stack. The information can be presented in different formats.

dd

WinDbg **dd** command is useful to see the memory contents using double word (4 bytes or 32 bits) format.

The default count is 32 DWORDs (128 bytes).

Example:

```
0:024> dd 0397fdc8
0397fdc8  0397fe20 00414834 00000000 00000000
0397fdd8  03183ae8 fffffffe 0397fdf0 5d4d1107
0397fde8  00000001 00000000 0397fe04 5d506062
0397fdf8  00000001 03183bb8 00000001 0397fe1c
0397fe08  5d54ffd2 60101c2a 0318344c 0318344c
0397fe18  03183bb8 031833c0 0397fe78 00414d8c
0397fe28  00000000 00000000 03183ae8 0397fe4c
0397fe38  5d4cac88 00000000 00000000 0397fe00
```

If we want to limit the output for clarity in case we are only interested in a few double words we can use the count parameter:

```
0:024> dd 0397fdc8 l1
0397fdc8  0397fe20
```

db

WinDbg **db** command is useful to see the data in byte format.

Tip: when we don't know the data format, use **db**. In **db** command output we can see numbers, ASCII and Unicode characters. This is the variation of **d*** command the author uses most of the time.

Example:

```
0:000> db 0x001728c4
001728c4  61 00 62 00 63 00 64 00-00 00 ee fe 00 00 00 00  a.b.c.d.........
001728d4  00 00 00 00 16 a8 d5 4c-cd 35 00 1c 43 00 3a 00  .......L.5..C.:.
001728e4  5c 00 57 00 69 00 6e 00-64 00 6f 00 77 00 73 00  \.W.i.n.d.o.w.s.
001728f4  5c 00 73 00 79 00 73 00-74 00 65 00 6d 00 33 00  \.s.y.s.t.e.m.3.
00172904  32 00 3b 00 43 00 3a 00-5c 00 57 00 69 00 6e 00  2.;.C.:.\.W.i.n.
00172914  64 00 6f 00 77 00 73 00-5c 00 73 00 79 00 73 00  d.o.w.s.\.s.y.s.
00172924  74 00 65 00 6d 00 3b 00-43 00 3a 00 5c 00 57 00  t.e.m.;.C.:.\.W.
00172934  69 00 6e 00 64 00 6f 00-77 00 73 00 3b 00 00 00  i.n.d.o.w.s.;...
```

Tip: when we want to see more byte output we can specify the larger count parameter, for example:

```
0:000> db 0x001728c4 l1000
[output skipped]
```

du

This variation is used to display Unicode strings.

Example:

```
0:000> du 001728e4
001728e4  "This is a test to show the Unico"
00172924  "de strings and how we can see th"
00172964  "em using WinDbg."
```

Notice that we can display more characters in the same column using **/c**. By using the **/c** option we can specify the number of columns to be displayed in the same row.

Example:

```
0:000> du /c 0n100 001728e4
001728e4  "This is a test to show the Unicode strings and how we
can see them using WinDbg."
```

da

This variation is used to display ASCII strings. The **/c** option is also valid when using **da**.

Tip: if **da** command shows characters followed by ".", like:

```
T.e.s.t
```

and **du** shows the same string, but without ".", it is a Unicode string, not an ASCII string. For the former we may want to use **du** command.

Example:

```
0:000> da /c 0n100 001728ff
001728ff  "This is another string test. This string is not
Unicode!"
```

dc

This command displays double word values (4 bytes) and ASCII characters.

Example:

```
0:000> dc 001728ff
001728ff  73696854 20736920 746f6e61 20726568  This is another
0017290f  69727473 7420676e 2e747365 69685420  string test. Thi
0017291f  74732073 676e6972 20736920 20746f6e  s string is not
0017292f  63696e55 2165646f 61002000 64006e00  Unicode!. .a.n.d
0017293f  68002000 77006f00 79002000 75006f00  . .h.o.w. .y.o.u
0017294f  63002000 6e006100 73002000 65006500  . .c.a.n. .s.e.e
0017295f  74002000 65006800 20006d00 73007500  . .t.h.e.m. .u.s
0017296f  6e006900 20006700 69005700 44006e00  .i.n.g. .W.i.n.D
```

Sometimes we need to dereference a pointer and see what it is pointing to. This is the way to do that:

```
0:000> dd 0012fee4  L1
0012fee4  001728c4


0:000> dc poi(0012fee4)
001728c4  00620061 00640063 feee0000 00000000  a.b.c.d.........
001728d4  00000000 4cd5a816 1c0035cd 003a0043  .......L.5..C.:.
001728e4  73696854 20736920 65742061 74207473  This is a test t
001728f4  6873206f 7420776f 54206568 20736968  o show the This
00172904  61207369 68746f6e 73207265 6e697274  is another strin
00172914  65742067 202e7473 73696854 72747320  g test. This str
00172924  20676e69 6e207369 5520746f 6f63696e  ing is not Unico
00172934  00216564 00610020 0064006e 00680020  de!. .a.n.d. .h.


0:000> dc poi(0012fee4 ) L4
001728c4  00620061 00640063 feee0000 00000000  a.b.c.d.........
```

dyb

This command displays binary and byte values.

Tip: it offers an easy way to see each byte for a double word value and its corresponding bits.

Example:

```
0:000> dyb 001728ff
          76543210 76543210 76543210 76543210
          -------- -------- -------- --------
001728ff  01010100 01101000 01101001 01110011  54 68 69 73
00172903  00100000 01101001 01110011 00100000  20 69 73 20
00172907  01100001 01101110 01101111 01110100  61 6e 6f 74
0017290b  01101000 01100101 01110010 00100000  68 65 72 20
0017290f  01110011 01110100 01110010 01101001  73 74 72 69
00172913  01101110 01100111 00100000 01110100  6e 67 20 74
00172917  01100101 01110011 01110100 00101110  65 73 74 2e
0017291b  00100000 01010100 01101000 01101001  20 54 68 69
```

.formats

A command similar to **dyb** is **.formats**. The most frequent variations are: **.formats <value>** and **.formats poi(<address>).**

Examples:

```
0:000> .formats 54
Evaluate expression:
  Hex:     00000054
  Decimal: 84
  Octal:   00000000124
  Binary:  00000000 00000000 00000000 01010100
  Chars:   ...T
  Time:    Wed Dec 31 16:01:24 1969
  Float:   low 1.17709e-043 high 0
  Double:  4.15015e-322
```

```
0:000> .formats poi(7c9118f1)
Evaluate expression:
  Hex:     3359066a
  Decimal: 861472362
  Octal:   06326203152
  Binary:  00110011 01011001 00000110 01101010
  Chars:   3Y.j
  Time:    Sat Apr 19 18:52:42 1997
  Float:   low 5.05301e-008 high 0
  Double:  4.25624e-315
```

0n100 0x64 0110 0100 ***!finddata*** *Shows cached data at a file offset*

dp*

The **dp*** command and its variations are among the most commonly used commands. It is used to display information from memory, including heap and the raw call stack. The information can be presented in different formats.

dpa

dpa <address> L<range>

dpa <startAddr> <endAddr>

This command allows us to see a range of ASCII strings, for example, strings from the call stack.

Example (shown in smaller font for visual clarity):

```
0:543> dpa @esp L300
2473fcd0  76ef9254 ".."
2473fcd4  76ee33b4 "=.."
2473fcd8  000000f0
2473fcdc  00000000
2473fce0  00000000
2473fce4  00422600 "..."
2473fce8  00422604 "....."
2473fcec  24141638 "...................................................."
2473fcf0  0000007c
2473fcf4  00000001
2473fcf8  647d37c0 "example.cpp"
2473fcfc  0000001d
2473fd00  24141db0 ""
2473fd04  24141e30 ""
2473fd08  ffffffff
2473fd0c  2473fd24 ""
2473fd10  6481156a "...]...................U...E.P.M.Q.U.R.E.P........]..."
2473fd14  0000007c
2473fd18  00000001
2473fd1c  647d37c0 "example.cpp"
2473fd20  00000000
2473fd24  00000000
2473fd28  7fd9c000 "4.s
```

dpu

dpu <address> L<range>

dpu <startAddress> <endAddress>

When using this command we can see a range of Unicode strings, for example, strings from a call stack.

Tip: poi(@$teb+0x8) is the beginning of a call stack.

poi(@$teb+0x4) is the end of a call stack.

Example:

```
0:000> dpu poi(@$teb+0x8) poi(@$teb+0x4)
0012759c  00000000
001275a0  0000006e
001275a4  001c4af8 "."
001275a8  0012bb60 "C:\Windows\winsxs\x86_microsoft.vc90.debugcrt_1fc8b3b9a"
…
001275b4  00127ac8 "C:\Windows\WinSxS\x86_microsoft.vc90.debugcrt_1fc8b3b9a"
001275b8  00000000
001275bc  001275f4 "msvcr90d.dll"
001275c0  0012bc3a ""
001275c4  0000006d
001275c8  00000020
001275cc  15be8624
00127720  00000000
00127724  00000002
00127728  00180018 " "
0012772c  001409fc "msvcr90d.dll"
00127840  0012bb84 "x86_microsoft.vc90.debugcrt_1fc8b3b9a1e18e3b_9.0.21022."
0012fd74  001c8370 "This is an Unicode string"
```

dps

dps <address> L<range>

dps <startAddr> <endAddr>

This command is very useful because we can see the raw call stack.

Tip: we can see the stack even if it's corrupt. We can also use **dps** command to see data from the heap memory.

Example:

```
0:043> dps poi(@$teb+0x8) poi(@$teb+0x4)
04c7f000  00000000
04c7f004  00000000
04c7f008  00000000
…
04c7f0dc  00000000
04c7f0e0  00000000
04c7f0e4  76ee429e ntdll!RtlImageNtHeaderEx+0xf1
04c7f0e8  4108a9c0
04c7f0ec  00000000
04c7f0f0  7ffdf000
04c7f0f4  00000000
04c7f0f8  004000e8 mtgdi!_enc$textbss$begin <PERF> (mtgdi+0xe8)
04c7f0fc  00000000
04c7f100  04c7f0e8
04c7f104  00000000
04c7f108  04c7fc88
04c7f10c  76ea9834 ntdll!_except_handler4
04c7f110  333f1190
04c7f114  fffffffe
04c7f118  76ee429e ntdll!RtlImageNtHeaderEx+0xf1
04c7f11c  76ee0e36 ntdll!RtlImageNtHeader+0x1b
04c7f120  00000001
```

Why do we see 00000000 values above? This is because the stack grows from the higher addresses to the lower addresses. Therefore, the beginning of the stack is still empty, which means the stack wasn't totally used.

dpp

```
dpp <address> L<range>
```

```
dpp <startAddress> <endAddress>
```

This is a very useful command. It displays pointers! By using it we can see pointers that are being referenced from a call stack.

When using this command we can find virtual pointer tables that appear in a specific memory range. It is a great approach to identify classes for virtual pointer tables.

Example:

```
0:043> dpp @esp L200
04c7fce8  00422604 fffff788
04c7fcec  02d91940 00000000
04c7fcf0  02d91940 00000000
04c7fcf4  04c7fd04 02d91e50
04c7fcf8  64828a09 33fc4589
04c7fcfc  00000001
04c7fd00  001fed58 647d3a2c mfc90d!AFX_MODULE_THREAD_STATE::`vftable'
04c7fd04  02d91e50 00000008
04c7fd08  6488fe2c 8bf04589
04c7fd0c  8d66a0fd
04c7fd10  02d92d90 01900010
04c7fd14  75b37d9f 900014c2
04c7fd18  75b37d87 5d5b5e5f
04c7fd1c  02d918fc 647deb2c mfc90d!CBrush::`vftable'
04c7fd20  00000000
```

dv

The **dv** command stands for **d**isplay **v**ariables. It's easy to memorize. The reality, though, is this: in the trenches we won't use the standard format of **dv** command because it doesn't give us enough information.

Here is the most common usage of this command:

`dv /i /t /V`

/i option shows the variable kind like parameter or function.

/t option includes the data type for each variable.

/V (uppercase) option shows the virtual memory address or register location of each variable and also the address of a variable relative to the referencing base register.

Below we use the regular variation so we can compare with the advanced variation.

```
0:000> dv
lock_free           = 0x00000000
fiberid             = 0x00130000
nested              = 0
inDoubleQuote       = 0
lpszCommandLine     = 0x002528c4 ""
StartupInfo         = struct _STARTUPINFOA
```

Now compare it against the advanced variation:

```
dv /i /t /V

prv local  0012ff0c @ebp-0x74 void * lock_free = 0x00000000

prv local  0012ff10 @ebp-0x70 void * fiberid = 0x00130000

prv local  0012ff14 @ebp-0x6c int nested = 0

prv local  0012ff18 @ebp-0x68 int inDoubleQuote = 0

prv local  0012ff1c @ebp-0x64 unsigned char * lpszCommandLine =
0x002528c4 ""

prv local  0012ff20 @ebp-0x60 struct _STARTUPINFOA StartupInfo =
struct _STARTUPINFOA
```

!for_each_frame

Most of the time we want to see local variables for each frame of a specific call stack. To accomplish that we can use this extension command that executes another debugger command one time for each frame in the stack of the current thread. Combining it with **dv** command gives us all variables for each frame.

Example:

```
0:025> !for_each_frame dv /i /t /V

- - - - - - - - - - - - - - - - -

00 0532fcd0 776f8edc ntdll!NtWaitForSingleObject+0x15

Unable to enumerate locals, HRESULT 0x80004005

Private symbols (symbols.pri) are required for locals.

Type ".hh dbgerr005" for details.

- - - - - - - - - - - - - - - - -

01 0532fd34 776f8dc0 ntdll!RtlpWaitOnCriticalSection+0x13e

Unable to enumerate locals, HRESULT 0x80004005

Private symbols (symbols.pri) are required for locals.

Type ".hh dbgerr005" for details.

- - - - - - - - - - - - - - - - -

02 0532fd5c 00414ee7 ntdll!RtlEnterCriticalSection+0x150

Unable to enumerate locals, HRESULT 0x80004005

Private symbols (symbols.pri) are required for locals.

Type ".hh dbgerr005" for details.

- - - - - - - - - - - - - - - - -

03 0532fdc8 00414834 mtgdi!CBallThread::SingleStep+0x147
[c:\downloads\mtgdi\threads.cpp @ 180]

prv local  0532fdc4 @ebp-0x04 class CBallThread * this = 0x043349f0

- - - - - - - - - - - - - - - - -

04 0532fe20 00414d8c mtgdi!CGDIThread::InitInstance+0x44
[c:\downloads\mtgdi\threads.cpp @ 65]

prv local  0532fe1c @ebp-0x04 class CGDIThread * this = 0x043349f0

- - - - - - - - - - - - - - - - -

05 0532fe78 5a67d3e3 mtgdi!CBallThread::InitInstance+0x2c
[c:\downloads\mtgdi\threads.cpp @ 156]

prv local  0532fe74 @ebp-0x04 class CBallThread * this = 0x043349f0
```

```
- - - - - - - - - - - - - - - - -
06 0532ff40 6d97dfd3 mfc90d!_AfxThreadEntry+0x303
Unable to enumerate locals, HRESULT 0x80004005
Private symbols (symbols.pri) are required for locals.
Type ".hh dbgerr005" for details.
- - - - - - - - - - - - - - - - -
07 0532ff7c 6d97df69 MSVCR90D!_callthreadstartex+0x53
Unable to enumerate locals, HRESULT 0x80004005
Private symbols (symbols.pri) are required for locals.
Type ".hh dbgerr005" for details.
- - - - - - - - - - - - - - - - -
08 0532ff88 75ec3f39 MSVCR90D!_threadstartex+0x89
Unable to enumerate locals, HRESULT 0x80004005
Private symbols (symbols.pri) are required for locals.
Type ".hh dbgerr005" for details.
- - - - - - - - - - - - - - - - -
09 0532ff94 77710409 kernel32!BaseThreadInitThunk+0xe
Unable to enumerate locals, HRESULT 0x80004005
Private symbols (symbols.pri) are required for locals.
Type ".hh dbgerr005" for details.
- - - - - - - - - - - - - - - - -
0a 0532ffd4 777103dc ntdll!__RtlUserThreadStart+0x70
Unable to enumerate locals, HRESULT 0x80004005
Private symbols (symbols.pri) are required for locals.
Type ".hh dbgerr005" for details.
- - - - - - - - - - - - - - - - -
0b 0532ffec 00000000 ntdll!_RtlUserThreadStart+0x1b
Unable to enumerate locals, HRESULT 0x80004005
Private symbols (symbols.pri) are required for locals.
Type ".hh dbgerr005" for details.
```

We need to keep in mind that to see variables we need private symbols. Public symbols don't have information about parameters and local variables.

~*

When debugging, most of the time, if not all the time, we have to see all stacks for all threads or set the context for a specific thread in order to analyze it. To do that we use the **~** command and according to the WinDbg documentation we have these variants:

Thread identifier	Description
~.	Identifies the current thread
~#	Identifies the thread that caused the current debug event or exception
~*	Identifies all threads in the process
~*Number*	Identifies the *Number* thread
~~[*TID*]	Identifies the thread with *TID* (Thread *ID*)

This command is very easy to use, but it has some nuances. Note that the **s** after the thread number, in examples below, forces the debugger to change the thread context. In other words, all **k*** commands are going to operate on the new thread.

Examples:

```
0:005> ~.
.  5  Id: 1ff0.14b0 Suspend: 1 Teb: 7ffd9000 Unfrozen
      Start: ntdll!RtlUserThreadStart (77b89a78)
      Priority: -15  Priority class: 32  Affinity: 3

0:005> ~#
#385  Id: 1ff0.1518 Suspend: 1 Teb: 7fe3a000 Unfrozen
      Start: ntdll!RtlUserThreadStart (77b89a78)
      Priority: 0  Priority class: 32  Affinity: 3
```

```
0:005> ~*
   0  Id: 1ff0.1904 Suspend: 1 Teb: 7ffdf000 Unfrozen
      Start: mtgdi!ILT+2340(_WinMainCRTStartup) (00411929)
      Priority: 0  Priority class: 32  Affinity: 3
   1  Id: 1ff0.1ab8 Suspend: 1 Teb: 7ffde000 Unfrozen
      Start: ntdll!RtlUserThreadStart (77b89a78)
      Priority: -15  Priority class: 32  Affinity: 3
   2  Id: 1ff0.1608 Suspend: 1 Teb: 7ffdd000 Unfrozen
      Start: ntdll!RtlUserThreadStart (77b89a78)
      Priority: -15  Priority class: 32  Affinity: 3
   3  Id: 1ff0.1384 Suspend: 1 Teb: 7ffdc000 Unfrozen
      Start: ntdll!RtlUserThreadStart (77b89a78)
      Priority: -15  Priority class: 32  Affinity: 3
   4  Id: 1ff0.1270 Suspend: 1 Teb: 7ffdb000 Unfrozen
      Start: ntdll!RtlUserThreadStart (77b89a78)
      Priority: -15  Priority class: 32  Affinity: 3
.  5  Id: 1ff0.14b0 Suspend: 1 Teb: 7ffd9000 Unfrozen
      Start: MSVCR90D!_beginthreadex+0x150 (6313dee0)
      Priority: -15  Priority class: 32  Affinity: 3
   6  Id: 1ff0.176c Suspend: 1 Teb: 7ffd8000 Unfrozen
      Start: ntdll!RtlUserThreadStart (77b89a78)
      Priority: -15  Priority class: 32  Affinity: 3

0:005> ~10s
eax=00000000 ebx=00000000 ecx=02a4fcd0 edx=77b89a94 esi=00422600 edi=00000000
eip=77b89a94 esp=02a4fcd0 ebp=02a4fd34 iopl=0         nv up ei pl nz ac pe cy
cs=001b  ss=0023  ds=0023  es=0023  fs=003b  gs=0000             efl=00000217
ntdll!KiFastSystemCallRet:
77b89a94 c3              ret

0:010> ~5s
eax=00000010 ebx=00000000 ecx=00290000 edx=0028aaf0 esi=00422600 edi=00000000
eip=77b89a94 esp=0254fcd0 ebp=0254fd34 iopl=0         nv up ei pl nz ac pe cy
cs=001b  ss=0023  ds=0023  es=0023  fs=003b  gs=0000             efl=00000217
ntdll!KiFastSystemCallRet:
77b89a94 c3              ret
```

```
0:005> ~~[960]s

eax=17233000 ebx=02efca38 ecx=17232fe8 edx=00001000 esi=00000000 edi=00000000
eip=77b89a94 esp=1a60fdec ebp=1a60fe5c iopl=0         nv up ei pl zr na pe nc
cs=001b  ss=0023  ds=0023  es=0023  fs=003b  gs=0000             efl=00000246
ntdll!KiFastSystemCallRet:
77b89a94 c3              ret
```

Now, things are going to be more interesting. We're going to execute commands for each thread (some output is shown in the smaller font for visual clarity).

```
0:384> ~* kvn 1000
   0  Id: 1ff0.1904 Suspend: 1 Teb: 7ffdf000 Unfrozen
 # ChildEBP RetAddr  Args to Child
00 0012f7a8 77b88f74 77cc030d 000018ec 00000003 ntdll!KiFastSystemCallRet (FPO: [0,0,0])
01 0012f7ac 77cc030d 000018ec 00000003 0012f7f8 ntdll!NtSetInformationThread+0xc (FPO:
[4,0,0])
02 0012f7ec 62cd26d7 000018ec fffffff0 02efc310 kernel32!SetThreadPriority+0x153 (FPO:
[2,8,0])
03 0012f800 00413af4 fffffff1 24e6b85a 0012fcb0
mfc90d!CWinThread::SetThreadPriority+0x37 (FPO: [1,1,0])
04 0012f8c4 00413ee1 00000002 0012fcb0 006082b0 mtgdi!CThreadView::StartThread+0x4c4
(FPO: [Non-Fpo]) (CONV: thiscall) [c:\downloads\mtgdi\mtgdivw.cpp @ 147]
05 0012f924 62bc75a2 00000000 00000176 00000004
mtgdi!CThreadView::On25newrectangles+0x31 (FPO: [Non-Fpo]) (CONV: thiscall)
[c:\downloads\mtgdi\mtgdivw.cpp @ 223]
06 0012f968 62bc7cea 00286070 0000800a 00000000 mfc90d!_AfxDispatchCmdMsg+0xb2 (FPO:
[7,15,0])
07 0012f9cc 62bd0a42 0000800a 00000000 00000000 mfc90d!CCmdTarget::OnCmdMsg+0x2ea (FPO:
[4,16,0])
08 0012fa08 62b6b36b 0000800a 00000000 00000000 mfc90d!CView::OnCmdMsg+0x42 (FPO:
[4,8,4])
09 0012fa58 62b608b4 0000800a 00000000 00000000 mfc90d!CFrameWnd::OnCmdMsg+0x6b (FPO:
[4,13,4])
0a 0012fabc 62b69e8e 0000800a 00000000 00285c08 mfc90d!CWnd::OnCommand+0x174 (FPO:
[2,19,0])
0b 0012fadc 62b5f529 0000800a 00000000 27422836 mfc90d!CFrameWnd::OnCommand+0xbe (FPO:
[2,4,0])
0c 0012fc2c 62b5f462 00000111 0000800a 00000000 mfc90d!CWnd::OnWndMsg+0x79 (FPO:
[4,79,4])
0d 0012fc4c 62b5c8e0 00000111 0000800a 00000000 mfc90d!CWnd::WindowProc+0x32 (FPO:
[3,2,0])
0e 0012fcc8 62b5cea6 00285c08 0005046e 00000111 mfc90d!AfxCallWndProc+0xf0 (FPO:
```

```
[5,22,0])

0f 0012fce8 62b5885b 0005046e 00000111 0000800a mfc90d!AfxWndProc+0xa6 (FPO: [4,1,0])

10 0012fd24 763cf8d2 0005046e 00000111 0000800a mfc90d!AfxWndProcBase+0x5b (FPO:
[4,8,4])

11 0012fd50 763cf794 62b58800 0005046e 00000111 USER32!InternalCallWinProc+0x23

12 0012fdc8 763d0008 00609cd4 62b58800 0005046e USER32!UserCallWinProcCheckWow+0x14b
(FPO: [SEH])

13 0012fe2c 763c5a2c 62b58800 00000001 0012fe5c USER32!DispatchMessageWorker+0x322 (FPO:
[SEH])

14 0012fe3c 62bedb82 00608268 00000000 00000000 USER32!DispatchMessageA+0xf (FPO:
[1,0,0])

15 0012fe5c 62bef13e 00422528 0012fe84 62bee90d mfc90d!AfxInternalPumpMessage+0x102
(FPO: [0,5,0])

16 0012fe68 62bee90d 00000001 00422528 00608238 mfc90d!CWinThread::PumpMessage+0xe (FPO:
[0,1,0])

17 0012fe84 62bf1179 00422528 00419c7a ffffffff mfc90d!CWinThread::Run+0x8d (FPO:
[0,5,0])

18 0012fe98 62b7648f 00000000 00000000 00000000 mfc90d!CWinApp::Run+0x59 (FPO: [0,3,0])

19 0012febc 0041903a 00400000 00000000 00602774 mfc90d!AfxWinMain+0xef (FPO: [4,7,0])

1a 0012fed4 00416a18 00400000 00000000 00602774 mtgdi!WinMain+0x1a (CONV: stdcall)

1b 0012ff80 0041677f 0012ff94 77ce4911 7ffda000 mtgdi!__tmainCRTStartup+0x288 (CONV:
cdecl)

1c 0012ff88 77ce4911 7ffda000 0012ffd4 77b6e4b6 mtgdi!WinMainCRTStartup+0xf (CONV:
cdecl)

1d 0012ff94 77b6e4b6 7ffda000 7643b3ab 00000000 kernel32!BaseThreadInitThunk+0xe (FPO:
[1,0,0])

1e 0012ffd4 77b6e489 00411929 7ffda000 00000000 ntdll!__RtlUserThreadStart+0x23 (FPO:
[SEH])

1f 0012ffec 00000000 00411929 7ffda000 00000000 ntdll!_RtlUserThreadStart+0x1b (FPO:
[2,2,0])


   1  Id: 1ff0.1ab8 Suspend: 1 Teb: 7ffde000 Unfrozen

 # ChildEBP RetAddr  Args to Child

00 0211fccc 77b89254 77b733b4 000000f4 00000000 ntdll!KiFastSystemCallRet (FPO: [0,0,0])

01 0211fcd0 77b733b4 000000f4 00000000 00000000 ntdll!ZwWaitForSingleObject+0xc (FPO:
[3,0,0])

02 0211fd34 77b7323c 00000000 00000000 002880f8 ntdll!RtlpWaitOnCriticalSection+0x155
(FPO: [2,17,4])

03 0211fd5c 00414ee7 00422600 00000000 00000000 ntdll!RtlEnterCriticalSection+0x152
(FPO: [1,3,4])

04 0211fdc8 00414834 00000000 00000000 002880f8 mtgdi!CBallThread::SingleStep+0x147
(CONV: thiscall) [c:\downloads\mtgdi\threads.cpp @ 180]

05 0211fe20 00414d8c 00000000 00000000 002880f8 mtgdi!CGDIThread::InitInstance+0x44
(CONV: thiscall) [c:\downloads\mtgdi\threads.cpp @ 65]

06 0211fe78 62bed973 25412b5a 00000000 00000000 mtgdi!CBallThread::InitInstance+0x2c
(CONV: thiscall) [c:\downloads\mtgdi\threads.cpp @ 156]

07 0211ff40 6313dfd3 0012f7e0 25412489 00000000 mfc90d!_AfxThreadEntry+0x303 (FPO:
[1,44,0])
```

```
08 0211ff7c 6313df69 00288348 0211ff94 77ce4911 MSVCR90D!_beginthreadex+0x243 (FPO:
[SEH])

09 0211ff88 77ce4911 00288348 0211ffd4 77b6e4b6 MSVCR90D!_beginthreadex+0x1d9 (FPO:
[1,1,0])

0a 0211ff94 77b6e4b6 002880f8 7440b3ab 00000000 kernel32!BaseThreadInitThunk+0xe (FPO:
[1,0,0])

0b 0211ffd4 77b6e489 6313dee0 002880f8 00000000 ntdll!__RtlUserThreadStart+0x23 (FPO:
[SEH])

0c 0211ffec 00000000 6313dee0 002880f8 00000000 ntdll!_RtlUserThreadStart+0x1b (FPO:
[2,2,0])


   2  Id: 1ff0.1608 Suspend: 1 Teb: 7ffdd000 Unfrozen

 # ChildEBP RetAddr  Args to Child

00 0224fccc 77b89254 77b733b4 000000f4 00000000 ntdll!KiFastSystemCallRet (FPO: [0,0,0])

01 0224fcd0 77b733b4 000000f4 00000000 00000000 ntdll!ZwWaitForSingleObject+0xc (FPO:
[3,0,0])

02 0224fd34 77b7323c 00000000 00000000 00289280 ntdll!RtlpWaitOnCriticalSection+0x155
(FPO: [2,17,4])

03 0224fd5c 004153e7 00422600 00000000 00000000 ntdll!RtlEnterCriticalSection+0x152
(FPO: [1,3,4])

04 0224fdc8 00414834 00000000 00000000 00289280 mtgdi!CRectThread::SingleStep+0x147
(CONV: thiscall) [c:\downloads\mtgdi\threads.cpp @ 249]

05 0224fe20 0041528c 00000000 00000000 00289280 mtgdi!CGDIThread::InitInstance+0x44
(CONV: thiscall) [c:\downloads\mtgdi\threads.cpp @ 65]

06 0224fe78 62bed973 25742b5a 00000000 00000000 mtgdi!CRectThread::InitInstance+0x2c
(CONV: thiscall) [c:\downloads\mtgdi\threads.cpp @ 225]

07 0224ff40 6313dfd3 0012f7dc 25742489 00000000 mfc90d!_AfxThreadEntry+0x303 (FPO:
[1,44,0])

08 0224ff7c 6313df69 002894d0 0224ff94 77ce4911 MSVCR90D!_beginthreadex+0x243 (FPO:
[SEH])

09 0224ff88 77ce4911 002894d0 0224ffd4 77b6e4b6 MSVCR90D!_beginthreadex+0x1d9 (FPO:
[1,1,0])

0a 0224ff94 77b6e4b6 00289280 7475b3ab 00000000 kernel32!BaseThreadInitThunk+0xe (FPO:
[1,0,0])

0b 0224ffd4 77b6e489 6313dee0 00289280 00000000 ntdll!__RtlUserThreadStart+0x23 (FPO:
[SEH])

0c 0224ffec 00000000 6313dee0 00289280 00000000 ntdll!_RtlUserThreadStart+0x1b (FPO:
[2,2,0])


0:384> ~* e !gle

LastErrorValue: (Win32) 0 (0) - The operation completed successfully.

LastStatusValue: (NTSTATUS) 0xc0000034 - Object Name not found.

LastErrorValue: (Win32) 0 (0) - The operation completed successfully.

LastStatusValue: (NTSTATUS) 0xc000000d - An invalid parameter was passed to a service or
function.

LastErrorValue: (Win32) 0 (0) - The operation completed successfully.

LastStatusValue: (NTSTATUS) 0xc000000d - An invalid parameter was passed to a service or
function.
```

(AA) .fnent *Shows function data (extends **ln**)* *0n115 0x73 0111 0011*

```
LastErrorValue: (Win32) 0 (0) - The operation completed successfully.

LastStatusValue: (NTSTATUS) 0xc000000d - An invalid parameter was passed to a service or
function.

LastErrorValue: (Win32) 0 (0) - The operation completed successfully.

LastStatusValue: (NTSTATUS) 0xc000000d - An invalid parameter was passed to a service or
function.

LastErrorValue: (Win32) 0 (0) - The operation completed successfully.

LastStatusValue: (NTSTATUS) 0xc000000d - An invalid parameter was passed to a service or
function.

LastErrorValue: (Win32) 0 (0) - The operation completed successfully.

LastStatusValue: (NTSTATUS) 0xc000000d - An invalid parameter was passed to a service or
function.

LastErrorValue: (Win32) 0 (0) - The operation completed successfully.

LastStatusValue: (NTSTATUS) 0xc000000d - An invalid parameter was passed to a service or
function.

LastErrorValue: (Win32) 0 (0) - The operation completed successfully.

LastStatusValue: (NTSTATUS) 0xc000000d - An invalid parameter was passed to a service or
function.

LastErrorValue: (Win32) 0 (0) - The operation completed successfully.

LastStatusValue: (NTSTATUS) 0xc000000d - An invalid parameter was passed to a service or
function.

LastErrorValue: (Win32) 0 (0) - The operation completed successfully.

LastStatusValue: (NTSTATUS) 0xc000000d - An invalid parameter was passed to a service or
function.

LastErrorValue: (Win32) 0 (0) - The operation completed successfully.

LastStatusValue: (NTSTATUS) 0xc000000d - An invalid parameter was passed to a service or
function.

LastErrorValue: (Win32) 0 (0) - The operation completed successfully.

LastStatusValue: (NTSTATUS) 0xc000000d - An invalid parameter was passed to a service or
function.

LastErrorValue: (Win32) 0 (0) - The operation completed successfully.

LastStatusValue: (NTSTATUS) 0xc000000d - An invalid parameter was passed to a service or
function.

LastErrorValue: (Win32) 0 (0) - The operation completed successfully.

LastStatusValue: (NTSTATUS) 0xc000000d - An invalid parameter was passed to a service or
function.

LastErrorValue: (Win32) 0 (0) - The operation completed successfully.

LastStatusValue: (NTSTATUS) 0xc000000d - An invalid parameter was passed to a service or
function.

LastErrorValue: (Win32) 0 (0) - The operation completed successfully.

LastStatusValue: (NTSTATUS) 0xc000000d - An invalid parameter was passed to a service or
```

```
function.

LastErrorValue: (Win32) 0 (0) - The operation completed successfully.

LastStatusValue: (NTSTATUS) 0xc000000d - An invalid parameter was passed to a service or function.

LastErrorValue: (Win32) 0 (0) - The operation completed successfully.

LastStatusValue: (NTSTATUS) 0xc000000d - An invalid parameter was passed to a service or function.

LastErrorValue: (Win32) 0 (0) - The operation completed successfully.

LastStatusValue: (NTSTATUS) 0xc000000d - An invalid parameter was passed to a service or function.

LastErrorValue: (Win32) 0 (0) - The operation completed successfully.
```

Have you noticed the **e**? The **e** is necessary when we need to execute a debugger extension or commands that start with a dot (**.**) or a bang (**!**).

Tip: The last command above is just to demonstrate the usage of **e**. It's better and simpler to use this approach:

```
0:384> !gle -all


Last error for thread 0:

LastErrorValue: (Win32) 0 (0) - The operation completed successfully.

LastStatusValue: (NTSTATUS) 0xc0000034 - Object Name not found.


Last error for thread 1:

LastErrorValue: (Win32) 0 (0) - The operation completed successfully.

LastStatusValue: (NTSTATUS) 0xc000000d - An invalid parameter was passed to a service or function.


Last error for thread 2:

LastErrorValue: (Win32) 0 (0) - The operation completed successfully.

LastStatusValue: (NTSTATUS) 0xc000000d - An invalid parameter was passed to a service or function.


Last error for thread 3:

LastErrorValue: (Win32) 0 (0) - The operation completed successfully.

LastStatusValue: (NTSTATUS) 0xc000000d - An invalid parameter was passed to a service or function.


Last error for thread 4:
```

```
LastErrorValue: (Win32) 0 (0) - The operation completed successfully.
LastStatusValue: (NTSTATUS) 0xc000000d - An invalid parameter was passed to a service or
function.

Last error for thread 5:
LastErrorValue: (Win32) 0 (0) - The operation completed successfully.
LastStatusValue: (NTSTATUS) 0xc000000d - An invalid parameter was passed to a service or
function.

Last error for thread 6:
LastErrorValue: (Win32) 0 (0) - The operation completed successfully.
LastStatusValue: (NTSTATUS) 0xc000000d - An invalid parameter was passed to a service or
function.

Last error for thread 7:
LastErrorValue: (Win32) 0 (0) - The operation completed successfully.
LastStatusValue: (NTSTATUS) 0xc000000d - An invalid parameter was passed to a service or
function.

Last error for thread 8:
LastErrorValue: (Win32) 0 (0) - The operation completed successfully.
LastStatusValue: (NTSTATUS) 0xc000000d - An invalid parameter was passed to a service or
function.

Last error for thread 9:
LastErrorValue: (Win32) 0 (0) - The operation completed successfully.
LastStatusValue: (NTSTATUS) 0xc000000d - An invalid parameter was passed to a service or
function.
```

Please look what happens if we don't use **e** when we need to:

```
0:384> ~* .echo Displaying a message.
         ^ Syntax error in '~* .echo Displaying a message.'
```

This works fine:

```
0:384> ~* e .echo Displaying a message.
Displaying a message.
Displaying a message.
Displaying a message.
Displaying a message.
Displaying a message.
Displaying a message.
Displaying a message.
Displaying a message.
Displaying a message.
Displaying a message.
Displaying a message.
Displaying a message.
Displaying a message.
Displaying a message.
Displaying a message.
Displaying a message.
Displaying a message.
Displaying a message.
Displaying a message.
Displaying a message.
Displaying a message.
Displaying a message.
Displaying a message.
Displaying a message.
Displaying a message.
Displaying a message.
Displaying a message.
```

Semicolon (**;**) is used to aggregate commands, so we can do this:

```
0:384> ~* e .echo Thread ID:; r @$tid; .echo =================
Thread ID:
$tid=00001904
=================
Thread ID:
$tid=00001ab8
=================
Thread ID:
$tid=00001608
=================
Thread ID:
$tid=00001384
=================
Thread ID:
$tid=00001270
=================
Thread ID:
$tid=000014b0
=================
Thread ID:
$tid=0000176c
=================
Thread ID:
$tid=000013d8
=================
Thread ID:
$tid=000004ac
=================
Thread ID:
$tid=00001e98
```

```
=================
Thread ID:
$tid=00001ee4
=================
Thread ID:
$tid=000012b4
=================
Thread ID:
$tid=00001924
=================
Thread ID:
$tid=00000330
=================
Thread ID:
$tid=0000129c
=================
Thread ID:
$tid=0000122c
=================
Thread ID:
$tid=00001784
=================
```

Pseudo-register **$tid** gives us the thread ID.

(AA) .force_radix_output *Decimal/default radix 0n121 0x79 0111 1001*

x*

The **x*** command has powerful capabilities. It's very flexible, too. We can use different parameter combinations; though, we recommend looking at and checking WinDbg documentation to explore other variations.

Notice that some parameters may not display information if we use public symbols and others work with public and private symbols.

Some useful options:

`/t`	Shows the data type of every symbol (if known).
`/v`	Shows the symbol type like global, parameter or function and its size.
`/s` ***`size`***	Shows only symbols that have a nonzero ***size***, in bytes.
`/a /n /z`	Sorts the output by addresses, name or size.

Example of displaying all symbols for the specified module:

```
0:002> x mtgdi!*
0041f580 mtgdi!ATL::CVarTypeInfo<unsigned __int64>::pmField = 0x00000008
004225f4 mtgdi!ATL::CFixedStringMgr::s_pLog = 0x00000000
004223d8 mtgdi!__security_cookie_complement = 0xdb0bbf61
0041fbe0 mtgdi!IID_IAxWinAmbientDispatchEx = struct _GUID {b2d0778b-ac99-4c58-a5c8-e7724e5316b5}
0041fed8 mtgdi!multiszStringVal = 0x0041fb38 "M"
0041fbf8 mtgdi!multiszStringVal = 0x0041fb38 "M"
0041fc7c mtgdi!multiszStringVal = 0x0041fb38 "M"
00422664 mtgdi!envp = 0x00281cc0
0041f5a0 mtgdi!ATL::CVarTypeInfo<double>::pmField = 0x00000008
0042266c mtgdi!managedapp = 0
00422654 mtgdi!ATL::CComApartment::ATL_CREATE_OBJECT = 0
0041fedc mtgdi!szDwordVal = 0x0041fb34 "D"
```

```
0041fbfc mtgdi!szDwordVal = 0x0041fb34 "D"

0041fc80 mtgdi!szDwordVal = 0x0041fb34 "D"

00422a5c mtgdi!_afxInitAppState = 1 ''

00422a4c mtgdi!_commode = 0

0041f548 mtgdi!ATL::CVarTypeInfo<unsigned int *>::pmField = 0x00000008

0041f550 mtgdi!ATL::CVarTypeInfo<long>::pmField = 0x00000008

00420d5c mtgdi!__rtc_taa = <function> *[1]

00421658 mtgdi!__pobjMapEntryLast = 0x00000000

0041f500 mtgdi!ATL::CVarTypeInfo<char *>::pmField = 0x00000008

00422a50 mtgdi!_fmode = 0

0041f540 mtgdi!ATL::CVarTypeInfo<unsigned int>::pmField = 0x00000008

0041f558 mtgdi!ATL::CVarTypeInfo<long *>::pmField = 0x00000008

00420b54 mtgdi!__rtc_iaa = <function> *[1]

0041e000 mtgdi!__xc_a = <function> *[]

0041e000 mtgdi!__xc_a = <function> *[1]

0041f4f0 mtgdi!ATL::CVarTypeInfo<char>::pmField = 0x00000008 "--- memory
read error at address 0x00000008 ---"

0041fb7c mtgdi!IID_IAxWinHostWindow = struct _GUID {b6ea2050-048a-11d1-82b9-
00c04fb9942e}

00422634 mtgdi!ATL::_AtlRegisterPerUser = false

0041fee8 mtgdi!szForceRemove = 0x0041fb1c "ForceRemove"

0041fc08 mtgdi!szForceRemove = 0x0041fb1c "ForceRemove"

0041fc8c mtgdi!szForceRemove = 0x0041fb1c "ForceRemove"

0041f588 mtgdi!ATL::CVarTypeInfo<unsigned __int64 *>::pmField = 0x00000008

00422a80 mtgdi!__dyn_tls_init_callback = 0x00000000

0041e830 mtgdi!__xi_z = <function> *[]

0041e830 mtgdi!__xi_z = <function> *[1]

0041f5a8 mtgdi!ATL::CVarTypeInfo<double *>::pmField = 0x00000008

0041f518 mtgdi!ATL::CVarTypeInfo<short *>::pmField = 0x00000008

00422404 mtgdi!__native_vcclrit_reason = 0xffffffff

0041f5e4 mtgdi!ATL::CVarTypeInfo<tagCY>::pmField = 0x00000008

0041f054 mtgdi!CThreadView::classCThreadView = struct CRuntimeClass

004226e0 mtgdi!GS_ContextRecord = struct _CONTEXT

0041e628 mtgdi!pcinit = 0x00416630

0041f520 mtgdi!ATL::CVarTypeInfo<unsigned short>::pmField = 0x00000008

004226d8 mtgdi!DebuggerWasPresent = 0

00422638 mtgdi!ATL::_pAtlModule = 0x00000000

00422324 mtgdi!THIS_FILE = char [31] "c:\downloads\mtgdi\threads.cpp"
```

(AA) .force_tb *Allow branch tracing earlier* *0n123 0x7B 0111 1011*

```
004221d4 mtgdi!THIS_FILE = char [31] "c:\downloads\mtgdi\mtgdivw.cpp"

00422170 mtgdi!THIS_FILE = char [32] "c:\downloads\mtgdi\mtgdidoc.cpp"

004220b8 mtgdi!THIS_FILE = char [29] "c:\downloads\mtgdi\mtgdi.cpp"

00422000 mtgdi!THIS_FILE = char [31] "c:\downloads\mtgdi\mainfrm.cpp"

0041e208 mtgdi!_afxInitAppState$initializer$ = 0x0041b1a0

00422a70 mtgdi!__native_startup_lock = 0x00000000

00422624 mtgdi!ATL::_pAtlAutoThreadModule = 0x00000000

0041fc60 mtgdi!ATL::CRegParser::cbNeverDelete = 12

0041f560 mtgdi!ATL::CVarTypeInfo<unsigned long>::pmField = 0x00000008

0041f5bc mtgdi!ATL::CVarTypeInfo<wchar_t * *>::pmField = 0x00000008

0041fb90 mtgdi!IID_IAxWinAmbientDispatch = struct _GUID {b6ea2051-048a-11d1-
82b9-00c04fb9942e}

00422528 mtgdi!theApp = class CThreadApp

0041f794 mtgdi!CRectThread::classCRectThread = struct CRuntimeClass

0041fba4 mtgdi!IID_IInternalConnection = struct _GUID {72ad0770-6a9f-11d1-
bcec-0060088f444e}

00422400 mtgdi!__native_dllmain_reason = 0xffffffff

00422628 mtgdi!_afxForceEXCLUDE = 0

0041f598 mtgdi!ATL::CVarTypeInfo<float *>::pmField = 0x00000008

0041f5d4 mtgdi!ATL::CVarTypeInfo<IDispatch *>::pmField = 0x00000008

0041f7b8 mtgdi!CLineThread::classCLineThread = struct CRuntimeClass

0041f770 mtgdi!CBallThread::classCBallThread = struct CRuntimeClass

0041f538 mtgdi!ATL::CVarTypeInfo<int *>::pmField = 0x00000008

0041fed4 mtgdi!szStringVal = 0x0041fb3c "S"

0041fbf4 mtgdi!szStringVal = 0x0041fb3c "S"

0041fc78 mtgdi!szStringVal = 0x0041fb3c "S"

0042267c mtgdi!has_cctor = 0

0041f4f8 mtgdi!ATL::CVarTypeInfo<unsigned char>::pmField = 0x00000008 "---
memory read error at address 0x00000008 ---"

0041f528 mtgdi!ATL::CVarTypeInfo<unsigned short *>::pmField = 0x00000008

0042263c mtgdi!ATL::CAtlModule::m_libid = struct _GUID {00000000-0000-0000-
0000-000000000000}

00422678 mtgdi!mainret = 0

00422a58 mtgdi!_newmode = 0

00423980 mtgdi!_imp___adjust_fdiv = 0x632166cc

0041f578 mtgdi!ATL::CVarTypeInfo<__int64 *>::pmField = 0x00000008

0042262c mtgdi!ATL::_pPerfRegFunc = 0x00000000

00422a84 mtgdi!__onexitend = 0x59366304
```

```
0041e318 mtgdi!CGDIThread::m_hAnotherDead$initializer$ = 0x0041b0f0

0042265c mtgdi!_afxForceSTDAFX = 0

0042395c mtgdi!_imp___onexit = 0x631cf660

0041fb40 mtgdi!LIBID_ATLLib = struct _GUID {44ec0535-400f-11d0-9dcd-
00a0c90391d3}

0041e524 mtgdi!__xi_a = <function> *[]

0041e524 mtgdi!__xi_a = <function> *[1]

004239ac mtgdi!_imp___acmdln = 0x63215aa4 "@'`"

00422670 mtgdi!argret = 0

0041fd88 mtgdi!GS_ExceptionPointers = struct _EXCEPTION_POINTERS

. . .

. . .

. . .

. . .
```

Example of displaying all symbols for the specified module, plus the data type, symbol type, and sorted by name in ascending order:

```
0:002> x /t /v /n  mtgdi!*

pub global 0041fd98    0 <NoType>
mtgdi!<CrtImplementationDetails>::NativeDll::ProcessAttach = <no type
information>

pub global 0041fd94    0 <NoType>
mtgdi!<CrtImplementationDetails>::NativeDll::ProcessDetach = <no type
information>

pub global 0041fda4    0 <NoType>
mtgdi!<CrtImplementationDetails>::NativeDll::ProcessVerifier = <no type
information>

pub global 0041fd9c    0 <NoType>
mtgdi!<CrtImplementationDetails>::NativeDll::ThreadAttach = <no type
information>

pub global 0041fda0    0 <NoType>
mtgdi!<CrtImplementationDetails>::NativeDll::ThreadDetach = <no type
information>

pub global 0041f4c0    0 <NoType> mtgdi!ATL::AtlLimits<__int64>::_Max = <no
type information>

pub global 0041f4b0    0 <NoType> mtgdi!ATL::AtlLimits<__int64>::_Min = <no
type information>
```

```
pub global 0041f490    0 <NoType> mtgdi!ATL::AtlLimits<int>::_Max = <no type
information>

pub global 0041f48c    0 <NoType> mtgdi!ATL::AtlLimits<int>::_Min = <no type
information>

pub global 0041f4a0    0 <NoType> mtgdi!ATL::AtlLimits<long>::_Max = <no
type information>

pub global 0041f49c    0 <NoType> mtgdi!ATL::AtlLimits<long>::_Min = <no
type information>

pub global 0041f4e0    0 <NoType> mtgdi!ATL::AtlLimits<unsigned
__int64>::_Max = <no type information>

pub global 0041f4d0    0 <NoType> mtgdi!ATL::AtlLimits<unsigned
__int64>::_Min = <no type information>

pub global 0041f498    0 <NoType> mtgdi!ATL::AtlLimits<unsigned int>::_Max =
<no type information>

pub global 0041f494    0 <NoType> mtgdi!ATL::AtlLimits<unsigned int>::_Min =
<no type information>

pub global 0041f4a8    0 <NoType> mtgdi!ATL::AtlLimits<unsigned long>::_Max
= <no type information>

pub global 0041f4a4    0 <NoType> mtgdi!ATL::AtlLimits<unsigned long>::_Min
= <no type information>

prv global 004225f0    1 bool mtgdi!ATL::CAtlBaseModule::m_bInitFailed =
false

prv global 0042263c   10 struct _GUID mtgdi!ATL::CAtlModule::m_libid =
struct _GUID {00000000-0000-0000-0000-000000000000}

prv global 00422654    4 unsigned int
mtgdi!ATL::CComApartment::ATL_CREATE_OBJECT = 0

prv func   00416380   19 <function> mtgdi!ATL::CComBSTR::~CComBSTR ()

prv func   004162d0   6c <function>
mtgdi!ATL::CComTypeInfoHolder::stringdispid::`vector deleting destructor' ()

prv func   00416360   15 <function>
mtgdi!ATL::CComTypeInfoHolder::stringdispid::~stringdispid ()

pub global 0041f640    0 <NoType> mtgdi!ATL::CFileTime::Day = <no type
information>

pub global 0041f630    0 <NoType> mtgdi!ATL::CFileTime::Hour = <no type
information>

pub global 0041f600    0 <NoType> mtgdi!ATL::CFileTime::Millisecond = <no
type information>

pub global 0041f620    0 <NoType> mtgdi!ATL::CFileTime::Minute = <no type
information>

pub global 0041f610    0 <NoType> mtgdi!ATL::CFileTime::Second = <no type
information>

pub global 0041f650    0 <NoType> mtgdi!ATL::CFileTime::Week = <no type
information>

prv global 004225f4    4 class ATL::IFixedStringLog *
mtgdi!ATL::CFixedStringMgr::s_pLog = 0x00000000
```

```
prv global 004225ec    4 <function> *
mtgdi!ATL::CNoUIAssertHook::s_pfnPrevHook = 0x00000000

pub global 0041fc20    0 <NoType> mtgdi!ATL::CRegParser::MAX_TYPE = <no type
information>

pub global 0041fc1c    0 <NoType> mtgdi!ATL::CRegParser::MAX_VALUE = <no
type information>

prv global 0041fc60    4 int mtgdi!ATL::CRegParser::cbNeverDelete = 12

prv global 0041fc24   30 char *[12] mtgdi!ATL::CRegParser::rgszNeverDelete =
char *[12]

pub global 0041616c    0 <NoType>
mtgdi!ATL::CSimpleStringT<char,1>::operator char const * = <no type
information>

pub global 00416178    0 <NoType>
mtgdi!ATL::CStringT<char,StrTraitMFC_DLL<char,ATL::ChTraitsCRT<char> >
>::CStringT<char,StrTraitMFC_DLL<char,ATL::ChTraitsCRT<char> > > = <no type
information>

pub global 00416166    0 <NoType>
mtgdi!ATL::CStringT<char,StrTraitMFC_DLL<char,ATL::ChTraitsCRT<char> >
>::Format = <no type information>

pub global 00416172    0 <NoType>
mtgdi!ATL::CStringT<char,StrTraitMFC_DLL<char,ATL::ChTraitsCRT<char> >
>::LoadStringA = <no type information>

pub global 00416160    0 <NoType>
mtgdi!ATL::CStringT<char,StrTraitMFC_DLL<char,ATL::ChTraitsCRT<char> >
>::~CStringT<char,StrTraitMFC_DLL<char,ATL::ChTraitsCRT<char> > > = <no type
information>

pub global 0041f5d8    0 <NoType> mtgdi!ATL::CVarTypeInfo<IDispatch * *>::VT
= <no type information>

prv global 0041f5dc    4 struct IDispatch ***
mtgdi!ATL::CVarTypeInfo<IDispatch * *>::pmField = 0x00000008

pub global 0041f5d0    0 <NoType> mtgdi!ATL::CVarTypeInfo<IDispatch *>::VT =
<no type information>

prv global 0041f5d4    4 struct IDispatch **
mtgdi!ATL::CVarTypeInfo<IDispatch *>::pmField = 0x00000008

pub global 0041f5c8    0 <NoType> mtgdi!ATL::CVarTypeInfo<IUnknown * *>::VT
= <no type information>

prv global 0041f5cc    4 struct IUnknown ***
mtgdi!ATL::CVarTypeInfo<IUnknown * *>::pmField = 0x00000008

pub global 0041f5c0    0 <NoType> mtgdi!ATL::CVarTypeInfo<IUnknown *>::VT =
<no type information>

prv global 0041f5c4    4 struct IUnknown ** mtgdi!ATL::CVarTypeInfo<IUnknown
*>::pmField = 0x00000008

pub global 0041f574    0 <NoType> mtgdi!ATL::CVarTypeInfo<__int64 *>::VT =
<no type information>

prv global 0041f578    4 int64 ** mtgdi!ATL::CVarTypeInfo<__int64
*>::pmField = 0x00000008
```

```
pub global 0041f56c    0 <NoType> mtgdi!ATL::CVarTypeInfo<__int64>::VT = <no type information>

prv global 0041f570    4 int64 * mtgdi!ATL::CVarTypeInfo<__int64>::pmField = 0x00000008

pub global 0041f4fc    0 <NoType> mtgdi!ATL::CVarTypeInfo<char *>::VT = <no type information>

prv global 0041f500    4 char ** mtgdi!ATL::CVarTypeInfo<char *>::pmField = 0x00000008

pub global 0041f4ec    0 <NoType> mtgdi!ATL::CVarTypeInfo<char>::VT = <no type information>

prv global 0041f4f0    4 char * mtgdi!ATL::CVarTypeInfo<char>::pmField = 0x00000008 "--- memory read error at address 0x00000008 ---"

pub global 0041f5a4    0 <NoType> mtgdi!ATL::CVarTypeInfo<double *>::VT = <no type information>

prv global 0041f5a8    4 double ** mtgdi!ATL::CVarTypeInfo<double *>::pmField = 0x00000008

pub global 0041f59c    0 <NoType> mtgdi!ATL::CVarTypeInfo<double>::VT = <no type information>

prv global 0041f5a0    4 double * mtgdi!ATL::CVarTypeInfo<double>::pmField = 0x00000008

pub global 0041f594    0 <NoType> mtgdi!ATL::CVarTypeInfo<float *>::VT = <no type information>

prv global 0041f598    4 float ** mtgdi!ATL::CVarTypeInfo<float *>::pmField = 0x00000008

pub global 0041f58c    0 <NoType> mtgdi!ATL::CVarTypeInfo<float>::VT = <no type information>

prv global 0041f590    4 float * mtgdi!ATL::CVarTypeInfo<float>::pmField = 0x00000008

pub global 0041f534    0 <NoType> mtgdi!ATL::CVarTypeInfo<int *>::VT = <no type information>

prv global 0041f538    4 int ** mtgdi!ATL::CVarTypeInfo<int *>::pmField = 0x00000008

pub global 0041f52c    0 <NoType> mtgdi!ATL::CVarTypeInfo<int>::VT = <no type information>

prv global 0041f530    4 int * mtgdi!ATL::CVarTypeInfo<int>::pmField = 0x00000008

pub global 0041f554    0 <NoType> mtgdi!ATL::CVarTypeInfo<long *>::VT = <no type information>

prv global 0041f558    4 long ** mtgdi!ATL::CVarTypeInfo<long *>::pmField = 0x00000008

pub global 0041f54c    0 <NoType> mtgdi!ATL::CVarTypeInfo<long>::VT = <no type information>

prv global 0041f550    4 long * mtgdi!ATL::CVarTypeInfo<long>::pmField = 0x00000008

pub global 0041f514    0 <NoType> mtgdi!ATL::CVarTypeInfo<short *>::VT = <no type information>
```

```
prv global 0041f518    4 short ** mtgdi!ATL::CVarTypeInfo<short *>::pmField
= 0x00000008

pub global 0041f50c    0 <NoType> mtgdi!ATL::CVarTypeInfo<short>::VT = <no
type information>

prv global 0041f510    4 short * mtgdi!ATL::CVarTypeInfo<short>::pmField =
0x00000008

pub global 0041f5e8    0 <NoType> mtgdi!ATL::CVarTypeInfo<tagCY *>::VT = <no
type information>

prv global 0041f5ec    4 union tagCY ** mtgdi!ATL::CVarTypeInfo<tagCY
*>::pmField = 0x00000008

pub global 0041f5e0    0 <NoType> mtgdi!ATL::CVarTypeInfo<tagCY>::VT = <no
type information>

prv global 0041f5e4    4 union tagCY *
mtgdi!ATL::CVarTypeInfo<tagCY>::pmField = 0x00000008

pub global 0041f5ac    0 <NoType> mtgdi!ATL::CVarTypeInfo<tagVARIANT>::VT =
<no type information>

pub global 0041f584    0 <NoType> mtgdi!ATL::CVarTypeInfo<unsigned __int64
*>::VT = <no type information>

prv global 0041f588    4 unsigned int64 ** mtgdi!ATL::CVarTypeInfo<unsigned
__int64 *>::pmField = 0x00000008

pub global 0041f57c    0 <NoType> mtgdi!ATL::CVarTypeInfo<unsigned
__int64>::VT = <no type information>

prv global 0041f580    4 unsigned int64 * mtgdi!ATL::CVarTypeInfo<unsigned
__int64>::pmField = 0x00000008

pub global 0041f504    0 <NoType> mtgdi!ATL::CVarTypeInfo<unsigned char
*>::VT = <no type information>

prv global 0041f508    4 unsigned char ** mtgdi!ATL::CVarTypeInfo<unsigned
char *>::pmField = 0x00000008

pub global 0041f4f4    0 <NoType> mtgdi!ATL::CVarTypeInfo<unsigned char>::VT
= <no type information>

prv global 0041f4f8    4 unsigned char * mtgdi!ATL::CVarTypeInfo<unsigned
char>::pmField = 0x00000008 "--- memory read error at address 0x00000008 ---
"

pub global 0041f544    0 <NoType> mtgdi!ATL::CVarTypeInfo<unsigned int
*>::VT = <no type information>

prv global 0041f548    4 unsigned int ** mtgdi!ATL::CVarTypeInfo<unsigned
int *>::pmField = 0x00000008

pub global 0041f53c    0 <NoType> mtgdi!ATL::CVarTypeInfo<unsigned int>::VT
= <no type information>

prv global 0041f540    4 unsigned int * mtgdi!ATL::CVarTypeInfo<unsigned
int>::pmField = 0x00000008

pub global 0041f564    0 <NoType> mtgdi!ATL::CVarTypeInfo<unsigned long
*>::VT = <no type information>

prv global 0041f568    4 unsigned long ** mtgdi!ATL::CVarTypeInfo<unsigned
long *>::pmField = 0x00000008
```

```
pub global 0041f55c     0 <NoType> mtgdi!ATL::CVarTypeInfo<unsigned long>::VT
= <no type information>

prv global 0041f560     4 unsigned long * mtgdi!ATL::CVarTypeInfo<unsigned
long>::pmField = 0x00000008

pub global 0041f524     0 <NoType> mtgdi!ATL::CVarTypeInfo<unsigned short
*>::VT = <no type information>

prv global 0041f528     4 unsigned short ** mtgdi!ATL::CVarTypeInfo<unsigned
short *>::pmField = 0x00000008

pub global 0041f51c     0 <NoType> mtgdi!ATL::CVarTypeInfo<unsigned
short>::VT = <no type information>

prv global 0041f520     4 unsigned short * mtgdi!ATL::CVarTypeInfo<unsigned
short>::pmField = 0x00000008

pub global 0041f5b8     0 <NoType> mtgdi!ATL::CVarTypeInfo<wchar_t * *>::VT =
<no type information>

prv global 0041f5bc     4 wchar_t *** mtgdi!ATL::CVarTypeInfo<wchar_t *
*>::pmField = 0x00000008

pub global 0041f5b0     0 <NoType> mtgdi!ATL::CVarTypeInfo<wchar_t *>::VT =
<no type information>

prv global 0041f5b4     4 wchar_t ** mtgdi!ATL::CVarTypeInfo<wchar_t
*>::pmField = 0x00000008

prv global 00422634     1 bool mtgdi!ATL::_AtlRegisterPerUser = false

pub global 0041f5f0     0 <NoType>
mtgdi!ATL::_CSTRING_IMPL_::_MFCDLLTraitsCheck<char,StrTraitMFC_DLL<char,ATL:
:ChTraitsCRT<char> > >::c_bIsMFCDLLTraits = <no type information>

pub global 0041f5f1     0 <NoType>
mtgdi!ATL::_CSTRING_IMPL_::_MFCDLLTraitsCheck<wchar_t,StrTraitMFC_DLL<wchar_
t,ATL::ChTraitsCRT<wchar_t> > >::c_bIsMFCDLLTraits = <no type information>

prv global 00422624     4 struct ATL::IAtlAutoThreadModule *
mtgdi!ATL::_pAtlAutoThreadModule = 0x00000000

prv global 00422638     4 class ATL::CAtlModule * mtgdi!ATL::_pAtlModule =
0x00000000

prv global 00422650     4 class ATL::CComModule * mtgdi!ATL::_pModule =
0x00000000

prv global 0042262c     4 <function> * mtgdi!ATL::_pPerfRegFunc = 0x00000000

prv global 00422630     4 <function> * mtgdi!ATL::_pPerfUnRegFunc =
0x00000000

prv global 0041f65c     4 char * mtgdi!ATL::szInvalidDateTime = 0x0041f478
"Invalid DateTime"

prv global 0041f660     4 char * mtgdi!ATL::szInvalidDateTimeSpan =
0x0041f45c "Invalid DateTimeSpan"

pub global 0041618a     0 <NoType> mtgdi!AfxAssertFailedLine = <no type
information>

pub global 0041619c     0 <NoType> mtgdi!AfxAssertValidObject = <no type
information>

pub global 00419110     0 <NoType> mtgdi!AfxGetModuleState = <no type
information>
```

```
prv func   00419050   56 <function> mtgdi!AfxInitialize ()

pub global 004161b4    0 <NoType> mtgdi!AfxStaticDownCast = <no type
information>

pub global 0041910a    0 <NoType> mtgdi!AfxWinMain = <no type information>

prv func   00416e00   2e <function> mtgdi!ArrayUnwindFilter ()

pub global 00422138    0 <NoType> mtgdi!CAboutDlg `RTTI Type Descriptor' =
<no type information>

. . .

. . .

. . .

. . .
```

??, @@c++() and poi()

We really like using C/C++ expressions from WinDbg. It's a natural way to extract information from C and C++ applications if an engineer knows these programming languages; therefore, it's important to master the related commands.

First, let's talk about **poi().** It is used to get pointer-sized data. Think about the ***** pointer dereferencing operation in C and C++.

For example:

```
0:000> dc poi(0012fee4) L4
00602774  73696854 20736920 65742061 002e7473  This is a test..
```

Therefore, **poi()** is the best operator to use if we want pointer-sized data. The double question mark (**??**) command evaluates and displays the value of an expression according to C++ expression rules. This is how we get a pointer value using **poi()** and **??**. The single question mark (**?**) is used to evaluate expressions.

Tip: By using **?** we can easily convert a number from hexadecimal to decimal or vice versa. The prefix **0x** should be used for hexadecimal and **0n** for decimal numbers.

Examples:

```
0:000>  ? 0n15
Evaluate expression: 15 = 0000000f

0:000> ? 0xF
Evaluate expression: 15 = 0000000f
```

Finally, we have the C++ expression parser - **@@c++()** - that supports all forms of C++ expression syntax, such as:

- Numbers in C++ expressions
- Characters and strings in C++ expressions
- Symbols in C++ expressions (see WinDbg documentation for details)
- Operators in C++ expressions
- Registers and pseudo-registers in C++ expressions
- Macros in C++ expressions

Examples:

```
0:005> ?? @@c++(this->m_bAutoDelete)
int 0

0:005> ?? (int) this->m_bAutoDelete
int 0

0:005> ?? this->m_bAutoDelete
int 0

0:005> ?? @@c++(sizeof(this->m_rectPosition))
unsigned int 0x10

0:005> ?? @@c++(sizeof(&this->m_rectPosition))
unsigned int 4

0:005> ?? @@c++(&this->m_rectPosition)
class CRect * 0x0028ab08
   +0x000 left             : 171
   +0x004 top              : 84
   +0x008 right            : 193
   +0x00c bottom           : 144
```

z

When doing live debugging, it is not uncommon to repeat a set of commands until a condition becomes true or false. There are several ways to do that, and one of them is by using the *z* command. We can create automated commands using this instruction: just think about the possibilities!

Here is an example that shows call stacks and executes the next instruction while EIP is different from 66FCA607:

```
0:809> tr; .echo CALL STACK; kL 1000; z(@eip != 66FCA607 )
CALL STACK
ChildEBP RetAddr
3510ff2c 77b88aa4 ntdll!KiFastSystemCall+0x2
3510ff30 77b6ec1d ntdll!ZwQueryInformationThread+0xc
3510ff54 77bbd0f1 ntdll!RtlExitUserThread+0x1c
3510ff88 77ce4911 ntdll!DbgUiRemoteBreakin+0x53
3510ff94 77b6e4b6 kernel32!BaseThreadInitThunk+0xe
3510ffd4 77b6e489 ntdll!__RtlUserThreadStart+0x23
3510ffec 00000000 ntdll!_RtlUserThreadStart+0x1b
redo [1] tr; .echo CALL STACK; kL 1000; z(@eip != 66FCA607 )
CALL STACK
ChildEBP RetAddr
3510ff30 77b6ec1d ntdll!ZwQueryInformationThread+0xc
3510ff54 77bbd0f1 ntdll!RtlExitUserThread+0x1c
3510ff88 77ce4911 ntdll!DbgUiRemoteBreakin+0x53
3510ff94 77b6e4b6 kernel32!BaseThreadInitThunk+0xe
3510ffd4 77b6e489 ntdll!__RtlUserThreadStart+0x23
3510ffec 00000000 ntdll!_RtlUserThreadStart+0x1b
redo [1] tr; .echo CALL STACK; kL 1000; z(@eip != 66FCA607 )
CALL STACK
ChildEBP RetAddr
3510ff54 77bbd0f1 ntdll!RtlExitUserThread+0x1c
3510ff88 77ce4911 ntdll!DbgUiRemoteBreakin+0x53
```

```
3510ff94 77b6e4b6 kernel32!BaseThreadInitThunk+0xe
3510ffd4 77b6e489 ntdll!__RtlUserThreadStart+0x23
3510ffec 00000000 ntdll!_RtlUserThreadStart+0x1b
redo [1] tr; .echo CALL STACK; kL 1000; z(@eip != 66FCA607 )
CALL STACK
ChildEBP RetAddr
3520ff40 77b6ec31 ntdll!TpCheckTerminateWorker+0x50
3520ff54 77bbd0f1 ntdll!RtlExitUserThread+0x30
3520ff88 77ce4911 ntdll!DbgUiRemoteBreakin+0x53
3520ff94 77b6e4b6 kernel32!BaseThreadInitThunk+0xe
3520ffd4 77b6e489 ntdll!__RtlUserThreadStart+0x23
3520ffec 00000000 ntdll!_RtlUserThreadStart+0x1b
redo [1] tr; .echo CALL STACK; kL 1000; z(@eip != 66FCA607 )
CALL STACK
ChildEBP RetAddr
3520ff54 77bbd0f1 ntdll!TpCheckTerminateWorker+0x51
3520ff88 77ce4911 ntdll!DbgUiRemoteBreakin+0x53
3520ff94 77b6e4b6 kernel32!BaseThreadInitThunk+0xe
3520ffd4 77b6e489 ntdll!__RtlUserThreadStart+0x23
3520ffec 00000000 ntdll!_RtlUserThreadStart+0x1b
. . .
. . .
. . .
```

At some point, when the next instruction address is 66FCA607, it stops the execution.

!address

Let's say that we get a memory address and we want to know if it is from a heap, a stack, or something else. Or yet, let's say we have a .NET application consuming a lot of memory, and we want to get a better understanding of this memory consumption.

The **!address** command is helpful in both situations mentioned above and probably in others not mentioned here.

Usage:

`!address <address>` ← gives us information about the address type.

`!address -summary` ← displays all addresses and a summary at the end.

Interpretation of address usage results like **RegionUsageIsVAD**, **RegionUsageImage**, and many others is available from WinDbg entry describing this command.

Examples:

!address <address>

```
0:017> !address 79360acf
    790c0000 : 79340000 - 0033f000
                    Type     01000000 MEM_IMAGE
                    Protect  00000020 PAGE_EXECUTE_READ
                    State    00001000 MEM_COMMIT
                    Usage    RegionUsageImage
                    FullPath
C:\WINDOWS\assembly\NativeImages_v2.0.50727_32\mscorlib\5b1ea64ba1
04acf854cc21ed4cf9d18e\mscorlib.ni.dll
```

```
0:017> !address 00250000

    00250000 : 00250000 - 0000a000
                    Type     00020000 MEM_PRIVATE
                    Protect  00000004 PAGE_READWRITE
                    State    00001000 MEM_COMMIT
                    Usage    RegionUsageHeap
                    Handle   00250000

0:017> !address 0a7bef7c
    0a6c0000 : 0a7be000 - 00002000
                    Type     00020000 MEM_PRIVATE
                    Protect  00000004 PAGE_READWRITE
                    State    00001000 MEM_COMMIT
                    Usage    RegionUsageStack
                    Pid.Tid  15c4.320

0:017> !address -summary
 ProcessParameters 003e1860 in range 003e0000 004b0000
 Environment 003e0808 in range 003e0000 004b0000

-------------------- Usage SUMMARY --------------------------
    TotSize (      KB)   Pct(Tots) Pct(Busy)   Usage
    3b09000 (   60452) : 02.88%    41.28%    : RegionUsageIsVAD ←
Location where .NET allocates heaps.
   770f1000 ( 1950660) : 93.02%    00.00%    : RegionUsageFree ← Not
committed memory or not reserved memory.
    46ff000 (   72700) : 03.47%    49.65%    : RegionUsageImage
     6ff000 (    7164) : 00.34%    04.89%    : RegionUsageStack ← Used
for stacks.
       7000 (      28) : 00.00%    00.02%    : RegionUsageTeb ← Used
for Thread Environment Block.
     5f0000 (    6080) : 00.29%    04.15%    : RegionUsageHeap ← Heaps
from unmanaged code allocations.
          0 (       0) : 00.00%    00.00%    : RegionUsagePageHeap
       1000 (       4) : 00.00%    00.00%    : RegionUsagePeb
```

(AA) .holdmem *Saves or compares memory range* *0n137 0x89 1000 1001*

```
         0 (        0) : 00.00%    00.00%    :
RegionUsageProcessParametrs
         0 (        0) : 00.00%    00.00%    :
RegionUsageEnvironmentBlock
       Tot: 7fff0000 (2097088 KB) Busy: 08eff000 (146428 KB)

-------------------- Type SUMMARY --------------------------
    TotSize (      KB)   Pct(Tots)  Usage
   770f1000 ( 1950660) : 93.02%   : <free>
    46ff000 (   72700) : 03.47%   : MEM_IMAGE
    181f000 (   24700) : 01.18%   : MEM_MAPPED
    2fe1000 (   49028) : 02.34%   : MEM_PRIVATE

-------------------- State SUMMARY --------------------------
    TotSize (      KB)   Pct(Tots)  Usage
    5d48000 (   95520) : 04.55%   : MEM_COMMIT
   770f1000 ( 1950660) : 93.02%   : MEM_FREE
    31b7000 (   50908) : 02.43%   : MEM_RESERVE

Largest free region: Base 04950000 - Size 5ee50000 (1554752 KB)
```

.foreach

This is by far one of the most powerful WinDbg commands. Even if we don't create scripts we will benefit from this command. It is powerful because it is flexible. We can use it for a huge variety of operations. It parses the output of debugger commands (InCmds, String or FileName) and uses each output value as the input to other commands (OutCmds).

Syntax

```
.foreach [Options] ( Var  { InCmds } ) { OutCmds }
.foreach [Options] /s ( Var  "String" ) { OutCmds }
.foreach [Options] /f ( Var  "FileName" ) { OutCmds }
```

Options can be:

`/pS InitSkipNum`

to skip the number of initial tokens and

`/ps SkipNum`

to skip the number of tokens repeatedly.

It may look complicated. To help in understanding the variations, below are several different examples ranging from the simplest to the most complex. We start from dumping virtual memory addresses that have the "nt" string:

```
0:000> .foreach(obj {s -[1]a 0 0FFFFFFF "nt"}){da /c 0n100 ${obj}}

0014086a  "nt.dll"

001532f1  "nts and Settings\All Users\Start Menu\AABS\Process and
Analytics\EY Global Analytics.lnk"

0015377f  "ntec Corporation1.0...U....Symantec Root
CA0...010501000000Z..110430235959Z0:1.0...U....Symantec Cor"
```

```
001537e3  "poration1.0...U....Symantec Root CA0.."0...*.H......."

0015379e  "ntec Root
CA0...010501000000Z..110430235959Z0:1.0...U....Symantec
Corporation1.0...U....Symantec Roo"

00153802  "t CA0.."0...*.H......."

001537db  "ntec Corporation1.0...U....Symantec Root
CA0.."0...*.H......."

001537fa  "ntec Root CA0.."0...*.H......."

00153978
"ntec.com/sympki/cps0...U........0...U..............#g.....5_.un0.
..*.H......."

001542e7  "nt.w..mr..'K.H."

00156741  "ntation."

00156791  "ntTrend."

001567e5  "nta."

00157cfc  "ntat."

00157ea3  "ntryS."

00157fbc  "ntat"

0015957e  "nt."

00163c57  "nternet1.0...U....VeriSign, Inc.1301..U...*VeriSign
Commercial Software Publishers CA0...96040900000"

00163cbb
"0Z..040107235959Z0a1.0...U....Internet1.0...U....VeriSign,
Inc.1301..U...*VeriSign Commercial Softwa"

00163d1f  "re Publishers CA0..0...*.H......."

00163cda  "nternet1.0...U....VeriSign, Inc.1301..U...*VeriSign
Commercial Software Publishers CA0..0...*.H....."

00163d3e  ".."

00172610  "ntimeLibrary"

00172648  "ntimelibrary"

00179f50  "nternet1.0...U....VeriSign, Inc.1301..U...*VeriSign
Commercial Software Publishers CA..010324000000Z"

00179fb4
"..040107235959Z0i0!...Q..7$9..T.BF7.j..010130000124Z0!..u.@...G..
V..N.....010131000049Z0!..w.ZCY.]_z"
```

```
0017a018  "u.....".000831000056Z..0.0...U....0"
00183845  "nt"
00184c0f  "ntrast Black (large)"
0018d5fe  "nt."
0018fa27  "ntermediate CA1.0...U....Microsoft
Corporation110/..U...(Microsoft Windows Hardware Compatibility0.."
0018fa8b  "0...*.H......."
00197dbc  "nt"
0019bd38  "ntVersion\Internet Settings\ZoneMap\"
0019bd43  "nternet Settings\ZoneMap\"
001a272c  "nt"
001a42c5  "nterpriseLibrary.Security.Cryptography"
001a789c  "nt.dll"
001afb17  "ntrolEvidence."
001bc0bc  "nt"
001bc73d  "nterpriseLibrary.Data"
001bf29c  "nt.dll"
001bfa4d  "nt.Interfaces"
001bfa51  "nterfaces"
001bfe59  "ntoolbars.v8.2.dll"
001c07cd  "nterpriseLibrary.Security.Cryptography.dll"
001c494d  "nterpriselibrary.security.cryptography.dll"
001c58ad  "nt"
001c58e5  "nt"
001cb3c5  "nterpriseLibrary.Common"
001cc25d  "nt.dll"
001d60cd  "nt"
```

Now we use **!DumpObj** command for each object address from the output of **!DumpStackObjects** command (both commands are from the extension **sos.dll**):

```
0:000> .foreach /pS 1 /ps 2 (obj {.shell -i - -ci "!dso" FIND
"System."}){!do ${obj}}
```

In bold below is the part skipped using **/pS 1** (skips 1 token) and in italic are the parts skipped using **/ps 2** (causes 2 tokens to be skipped repeatedly). The output is from !DumpStackObjects command:

```
OS Thread Id: 0x1d3c (0)
ESP/REG  Object   Name
ebx      01d9eb80 System.Windows.Forms.Application+ThreadContext
esi      01e56a84 System.Collections.Hashtable+HashtableEnumerator
002df0a4 01e434e4 System.Windows.Forms.NativeMethods+MSG[]
002df0a8 01d9eb80 System.Windows.Forms.Application+ThreadContext
002df0b0 01d9ee10 System.Windows.Forms.Application+ComponentManager
002df0fc 01f63884 System.Windows.Forms.ApplicationContext
002df104 01f63884 System.Windows.Forms.ApplicationContext
002df128 01d9eb80 System.Windows.Forms.Application+ThreadContext
002df178 01f63884 System.Windows.Forms.ApplicationContext
002df17c 01e62b28 System.Windows.Forms.Application+ThreadContext
002df18c 01df1130 System.Windows.Forms.ApplicationContext
002df194 01f505a0 System.ComponentModel.EventHandlerList
002df198 01f63898 System.EventHandler
002df1a0 01f63898 System.EventHandler
002df1a4 01f63898 System.EventHandler
002df1a8 01e9e33c NetWiz.frmNetWiz
002df1ac 01f63884 System.Windows.Forms.ApplicationContext
002df1b0 01e62b28 System.Windows.Forms.Application+ThreadContext
002df1bc 01f63884 System.Windows.Forms.ApplicationContext
002df1c4 01e9e33c NetWiz.frmNetWiz
002df1d0 01d9ef48 System.IO.FileStream
002df1d4 01d9e960 System.Object[]    (System.Diagnostics.Process[])
002df1d8 01d85a10 System.Diagnostics.Process
```

The following command runs commands stored in a string:

```
0:017> $$ Create an alias with several different commands

0:017> as ${/v:CommandString} kb r !clrstack

0:017> $$ Extract commands from the string and execute them

0:017> .foreach /s (obj "CommandString") {${obj}}
ChildEBP RetAddr  Args to Child
0a7bee54 7c90e9ab 7c8094e2 00000002 0a7bee80 ntdll!KiFastSystemCallRet
0a7bee58 7c8094e2 00000002 0a7bee80 00000001
ntdll!ZwWaitForMultipleObjects+0xc
0a7beef4 79f46ef1 00000002 0a7bf080 00000000
kernel32!WaitForMultipleObjectsEx+0x12c
0a7bef5c 79f46e7d 00000002 0a7bf080 00000000
mscorwks!WaitForMultipleObjectsEx_SO_TOLERANT+0x6f
0a7bef7c 79f46ddb 00000002 0a7bf080 00000000
mscorwks!Thread::DoAppropriateAptStateWait+0x3c
0a7bf000 79f46c7b 00000002 0a7bf080 00000000
mscorwks!Thread::DoAppropriateWaitWorker+0x144
0a7bf050 7a076262 00000002 0a7bf080 00000000
mscorwks!Thread::DoAppropriateWait+0x40
0a7bf198 793d3ac9 00000000 00000000 000073f7
mscorwks!WaitHandleNative::CorWaitMultipleNative+0x1ee
*** WARNING: Unable to verify checksum for System.ni.dll
0178f95c 7a5d551c 00000000 00000000 00000000
mscorlib_ni!System.Threading.WaitHandle.WaitAny(System.Threading.WaitHa
ndle[], Int32, Boolean)+0x7d
0a7bf208 793d70fb 00000000 00000000 00000000
System_ni!System.Net.TimerThread.ThreadProc()+0x2b8
0a7bf220 79360acf 00000000 00000000 00000000
mscorlib_ni!System.Threading.ThreadHelper.ThreadStart_Context(System.Ob
ject)+0x3b
```

```
0a7bf220 79e7be1b 00000000 00000000 00000000
mscorlib_ni!System.Threading.ExecutionContext.runTryCode(System.Object)
+0x43

0a7bf230 79e7bd9b 0a7bf300 00000000 0a7bf2d0
mscorwks!CallDescrWorker+0x33

0a7bf2b0 79e7bce8 0a7bf300 00000000 0a7bf2d0
mscorwks!CallDescrWorkerWithHandler+0xa3

0a7bf3f0 79e7bbd0 796802ac 0a7bf534 0a7bf43c
mscorwks!MethodDesc::CallDescr+0x19c

0a7bf408 79e802f4 796802ac 0a7bf534 0a7bf43c
mscorwks!MethodDesc::CallTargetWorker+0x20

0a7bf41c 79e92d42 0a7bf43c cf190c5b 073c1240
mscorwks!MethodDescCallSite::CallWithValueTypes_RetArgSlot+0x18

0a7bf5e8 79e92c4d 0a7bf67c cf190eb7 025e101c
mscorwks!ExecuteCodeWithGuaranteedCleanupHelper+0xb2

0a7bf698 79360a1b 0a7bf63c 0170b5c8 0163d8e8
mscorwks!ReflectionInvocation::ExecuteCodeWithGuaranteedCleanup+0xf9

0170b5fc 7936090e 00000000 00000000 00000000
mscorlib_ni!System.Threading.ExecutionContext.RunInternal(System.Thread
ing.ExecutionContext, System.Threading.ContextCallback,
System.Object)+0xa7

eax=2ab6df5b ebx=0a7bee80 ecx=ffffffff edx=00000000 esi=00000000
edi=7ffde000

eip=7c90eb94 esp=0a7bee58 ebp=0a7beef4 iopl=0         nv up ei pl zr na
pe nc

cs=001b  ss=0023  ds=0023  es=0023  fs=003b  gs=0000
efl=00000246

ntdll!KiFastSystemCallRet:

7c90eb94 c3              ret

OS Thread Id: 0x320 (17)

ESP       EIP

0a7bf0dc 7c90eb94 [HelperMethodFrame_1OBJ: 0a7bf0dc]
System.Threading.WaitHandle.WaitMultiple(System.Threading.WaitHandle[],
Int32, Boolean, Boolean)

0a7bf1a8 793d3ac9
System.Threading.WaitHandle.WaitAny(System.Threading.WaitHandle[],
Int32, Boolean)

0a7bf1c4 7a5d551c System.Net.TimerThread.ThreadProc()
```

```
0a7bf210 793d70fb
System.Threading.ThreadHelper.ThreadStart_Context(System.Object)

0a7bf218 79360acf
System.Threading.ExecutionContext.runTryCode(System.Object)

0a7bf63c 79e7be1b [HelperMethodFrame_PROTECTOBJ: 0a7bf63c]
System.Runtime.CompilerServices.RuntimeHelpers.ExecuteCodeWithGuarantee
dCleanup(TryCode, CleanupCode, System.Object)

0a7bf6a4 79360a1b
System.Threading.ExecutionContext.RunInternal(System.Threading.Executio
nContext, System.Threading.ContextCallback, System.Object)

0a7bf6bc 7936090e
System.Threading.ExecutionContext.Run(System.Threading.ExecutionContext
, System.Threading.ContextCallback, System.Object)

0a7bf6d4 793d71dc System.Threading.ThreadHelper.ThreadStart()

0a7bf8f8 79e7be1b [GCFrame: 0a7bf8f8]
```

Same thing, but gets the commands from a text file:

```
0:017> .foreach /f (obj "C:\downloads\test.txt") {${obj}}
```

where the text file has this content:

```
kpn !clrstack !dso r
```

(KL) .kdfiles *Reads driver replacement map file* *0n145 0x91 1001 0001*

.shell

This is a very powerful command! It launches a shell process and redirects its output either to a WinDbg window or to a file.

Usage:

```
.shell [Options] [ShellCmd]
.shell -i InFile [-o OutFile [-e ErrFile]] [Options] ShellCmd
```

According to the WinDbg help, options can be:

-ci "*Cmd1; Cmd2; …*"

> Processes any number of debugger commands and then passes their output as an input to the process being launched.

-x

> Causes any process being launched to be completely detached from WinDbg and thus to continue running after WinDbg session ends.

The way we can use it is:

```
.shell -i - -ci "command" FIND "string" /i
```

Why do we use **FIND**? The **FIND** command is not a part of **.shell**. It's a DOS command. .shell gives us access to the OS command shell. We use FIND to extract specific information from the "command" output. It searches for a text string in a file or from the piped input. The /i option ignores character case.

The combination of **.shell** and **FIND** is very powerful and it's the most common way to use this command. Let's see a few examples.

Example #1 – Searching for a specific managed object:

```
0:000> .shell -i - -ci "~* e !dso" FIND "System.Threading" /i
0012e570 016d9d68 System.Threading.ExecutionContext
0012e57c 015e64e0 System.Threading.Thread
0012ef9c 01659134 System.Threading.ContextCallback
0012efb4 01659134 System.Threading.ContextCallback
0012f020 01702ddc System.Threading.ExecutionContext+ExecutionContextRunData
0012f044 01659134 System.Threading.ContextCallback
0012f04c 01603e9c System.Threading.ExecutionContext
0012f458 015e183c System.Threading.Mutex
07b4fb50 0163d024 System.Threading.ParameterizedThreadStart
0a65f490 01762700 System.Threading._ThreadPoolWaitCallback
0a65f4a0 01763a6c System.Threading.ExecutionContext+ExecutionContextRunData
0a65f560 01763a6c System.Threading.ExecutionContext+ExecutionContextRunData
0a65f6d0 01763a6c System.Threading.ExecutionContext+ExecutionContextRunData
0a65f888 01763a6c System.Threading.ExecutionContext+ExecutionContextRunData
0a65f88c 0166ede8 System.Threading.ContextCallback
0a65f898 01762714 System.Threading.ExecutionContext
0a65f89c 01763a6c System.Threading.ExecutionContext+ExecutionContextRunData
0a65f8ac 01762714 System.Threading.ExecutionContext
0a65f910 01763a6c System.Threading.ExecutionContext+ExecutionContextRunData
0a65f924 01762714 System.Threading.ExecutionContext
0a65f930 01762700 System.Threading._ThreadPoolWaitCallback
0a65f934 0166ede8 System.Threading.ContextCallback
0a65f938 01762714 System.Threading.ExecutionContext
0a65f944 01762700 System.Threading._ThreadPoolWaitCallback
0a65f950 01762700 System.Threading._ThreadPoolWaitCallback
0a65f954 01762714 System.Threading.ExecutionContext
0a65f95c 01762700 System.Threading._ThreadPoolWaitCallback
0a65fb0c 01762700 System.Threading._ThreadPoolWaitCallback
0a65fb10 01762700 System.Threading._ThreadPoolWaitCallback
0a7bf098 01691498 System.Threading.AutoResetEvent
0a7bf0a0 016915b8 System.Object[]    (System.Threading.WaitHandle[])
```

```
0a7bf0b8 016915b8 System.Object[]    (System.Threading.WaitHandle[])
0a7bf100 016915b8 System.Object[]    (System.Threading.WaitHandle[])
0a7bf17c 0178f95c System.Object[]    (System.Threading.WaitHandle[])
0a7bf184 016915b8 System.Object[]    (System.Threading.WaitHandle[])
0a7bf198 0178f95c System.Object[]    (System.Threading.WaitHandle[])
0a7bf684 016996dc System.Threading.ExecutionContext+ExecutionContextRunData
0a7bf6b8 01698730 System.Threading.ThreadHelper
0a7bf950 01698744 System.Threading.ThreadStart
0a7bf958 016986fc System.Threading.Thread
.shell: Process exited
```

The better variant:

```
0:000> .shell -ci "~* e !dso" FIND "System.Threading" /i
0012e570 016d9d68 System.Threading.ExecutionContext
0012e57c 015e64e0 System.Threading.Thread
0012ef9c 01659134 System.Threading.ContextCallback
0012efb4 01659134 System.Threading.ContextCallback
0012f020 01702ddc System.Threading.ExecutionContext+ExecutionContextRunData
0012f044 01659134 System.Threading.ContextCallback
0012f04c 01603e9c System.Threading.ExecutionContext
0012f458 015e183c System.Threading.Mutex
07b4fb50 0163d024 System.Threading.ParameterizedThreadStart
0a65f490 01762700 System.Threading._ThreadPoolWaitCallback
0a65f4a0 01763a6c System.Threading.ExecutionContext+ExecutionContextRunData
0a65f560 01763a6c System.Threading.ExecutionContext+ExecutionContextRunData
0a65f6d0 01763a6c System.Threading.ExecutionContext+ExecutionContextRunData
0a65f888 01763a6c System.Threading.ExecutionContext+ExecutionContextRunData
0a65f88c 0166ede8 System.Threading.ContextCallback
0a65f898 01762714 System.Threading.ExecutionContext
0a65f89c 01763a6c System.Threading.ExecutionContext+ExecutionContextRunData
0a65f8ac 01762714 System.Threading.ExecutionContext
0a65f910 01763a6c System.Threading.ExecutionContext+ExecutionContextRunData
0a65f924 01762714 System.Threading.ExecutionContext
0a65f930 01762700 System.Threading._ThreadPoolWaitCallback
```

```
0a65f934 0166ede8 System.Threading.ContextCallback
0a65f938 01762714 System.Threading.ExecutionContext
0a65f944 01762700 System.Threading._ThreadPoolWaitCallback
0a65f950 01762700 System.Threading._ThreadPoolWaitCallback
0a65f954 01762714 System.Threading.ExecutionContext
0a65f95c 01762700 System.Threading._ThreadPoolWaitCallback
0a65fb0c 01762700 System.Threading._ThreadPoolWaitCallback
0a65fb10 01762700 System.Threading._ThreadPoolWaitCallback
0a7bf098 01691498 System.Threading.AutoResetEvent
0a7bf0b8 016915b8 System.Object[]    (System.Threading.WaitHandle[])
0a7bf198 0178f95c System.Object[]    (System.Threading.WaitHandle[])
0a7bf684 016996dc System.Threading.ExecutionContext+ExecutionContextRunData
0a7bf6b8 01698730 System.Threading.ThreadHelper
0a7bf950 01698744 System.Threading.ThreadStart
0a7bf958 016986fc System.Threading.Thread
.shell: Process exited
```

Example #2 – Searching for a specific mnemonic from the disassembled code:

```
0:000> .shell -ci "uf USER32!InternalCallWinProc" FIND "cmp" /i
7e418742 817c2404cdabbadc cmp     dword ptr [esp+4],0DCBAABCDh
7e440378 813c24cdabbadc   cmp     dword ptr [esp],0DCBAABCDh
.shell: Process exited
```

Example #3 – Dumping the part of a raw call stack and searching for USER32 calls:

```
0:000> .shell -ci "dps @$csp L300" FIND "MSCORWKS" /i
0012db58  79e7bf32 mscorwks!Binder::RawGetClass+0x23
0012db6c  79e80a2d mscorwks!Binder::IsClass+0x21
0012db78  79f55dff mscorwks!Binder::IsException+0x13
0012db88  79f55b05 mscorwks!RaiseTheExceptionInternalOnly+0x226
0012dbd8  79f55eb6 mscorwks!_except_handler4
0012dbe8  7a0905dc mscorwks!JIT_Rethrow+0xbf
0012dc38  7a090531 mscorwks!JIT_Rethrow+0x14
0012dc40  79e719e0 mscorwks!HelperMethodFrame::`vftable'
0012dc80  7a31e1f0 mscorwks!GetManagedNameForTypeInfo+0x1b401
0012dc94  79fc84c6 mscorwks!COMPlusNestedExceptionHandler
0012dd74  79e93728 mscorwks!MarshalNative::GCHandleInternalAlloc+0x13b
0012df34  79e7be1b mscorwks!CallDescrWorker+0x33
0012df64  79e7bd9b mscorwks!CallDescrWorkerWithHandler+0xa3
0012df80  79f54466 mscorwks!COMPlusFrameHandler
0012dfd4  79f55eb6 mscorwks!_except_handler4
0012dfe4  79e7bce8 mscorwks!MethodDesc::CallDescr+0x19c
0012e014  79e7b6e8 mscorwks!MetaSig::MetaSig+0x38
0012e020  79e7bc6a mscorwks!MethodDesc::CallDescr+0xaf
0012e02c  79e7bc7a mscorwks!MethodDesc::CallDescr+0xbb
0012e090  79f1554a mscorwks!CanAccess+0x235
0012e0a4  79e725a0 mscorwks!GCFrame::`vftable'
0012e0ac  79e74e5c mscorwks!HelperMethodFrame::LazyInit+0x17
0012e0b4  79e70000 mscorwks!_imp__GetKernelObjectSecurity <PERF>
(mscorwks+0x0)
0012e0b8  7a11e152 mscorwks!RuntimeMethodHandle::InvokeMethodFast
0012e0c4  79e7cb94
mscorwks!HelperMethodFrame_1OBJ::HelperMethodFrame_1OBJ+0x14
0012e0c8  7a11e152 mscorwks!RuntimeMethodHandle::InvokeMethodFast
0012e0e0  79e7bbf2 mscorwks!MethodDesc::CallDescr+0x1f
0012e124  79e7bbd0 mscorwks!MethodDesc::CallTargetWorker+0x20
```

```
0012e13c  79e802f4
mscorwks!MethodDescCallSite::CallWithValueTypes_RetArgSlot+0x18

0012e150  7a11df2d mscorwks!InvokeImpl+0x43f

0012e15c  79f55262 mscorwks!CLRVectoredExceptionHandlerShimX86

0012e16c  7a11dd7f mscorwks!InvokeImpl+0x28e

0012e188  7a11dc21 mscorwks!InvokeImpl+0xe5

0012e1a0  79e725a0 mscorwks!GCFrame::`vftable'

0012e1bc  79e725a0 mscorwks!GCFrame::`vftable'

0012e1d8  79e73aa0 mscorwks!CustomGCFrame::`vftable'

0012e1e0  7a05bf8e mscorwks!ReportPointersFromStruct

0012e1ec  79e73aa0 mscorwks!CustomGCFrame::`vftable'

0012e1f8  79f4d7d4 mscorwks!SecurityStackWalk::SpecialDemand+0x4e

0012e208  79e82f7e mscorwks!SecurityTransparent::IsMethodTransparent+0x27

0012e27c  7a3353c6 mscorwks!GetManagedNameForTypeInfo+0x294b7

0012e2ec  79f1554a mscorwks!CanAccess+0x235

0012e300  79e725a0 mscorwks!GCFrame::`vftable'

0012e308  79e74e5c mscorwks!HelperMethodFrame::LazyInit+0x17

0012e310  79e70000 mscorwks!_imp__GetKernelObjectSecurity <PERF>
(mscorwks+0x0)

0012e314  7a11e152 mscorwks!RuntimeMethodHandle::InvokeMethodFast

0012e320  79e7cb94
mscorwks!HelperMethodFrame_1OBJ::HelperMethodFrame_1OBJ+0x14

0012e324  7a11e152 mscorwks!RuntimeMethodHandle::InvokeMethodFast

0012e344  7a11e212 mscorwks!RuntimeMethodHandle::InvokeMethodFast+0xbd

0012e378  79f396a5 mscorwks!RuntimeTypeHandle::IsInstanceOfType+0x26

0012e3a0  7a11e176 mscorwks!RuntimeMethodHandle::InvokeMethodFast+0x24

0012e3a8  79e71a30 mscorwks!HelperMethodFrame_1OBJ::`vftable'

0012e3b0  79f4daf4 mscorwks!ReflectionInvocation::PerformSecurityCheck+0xe7

0012e3c4  7a11e152 mscorwks!RuntimeMethodHandle::InvokeMethodFast

0012e3f8  7a335438 mscorwks!GetManagedNameForTypeInfo+0x294ea

0012e56c  79e73f5e mscorwks!JIT_MonExitWorker+0xb

0012e614  79e7be1b mscorwks!CallDescrWorker+0x33

0012e618  79e830d5
mscorwks!MemberLoader::GetDescFromMemberDefOrRefThrowing+0x62

0012e624  79e7bd9b mscorwks!CallDescrWorkerWithHandler+0xa3
```

```
0012e640  79f54466 mscorwks!COMPlusFrameHandler
0012e694  79f55eb6 mscorwks!_except_handler4
0012e6a4  79e7bce8 mscorwks!MethodDesc::CallDescr+0x19c
0012e6d4  79e7b6e8 mscorwks!MetaSig::MetaSig+0x38
0012e6e0  79e7bc6a mscorwks!MethodDesc::CallDescr+0xaf
0012e6ec  79e7bc7a mscorwks!MethodDesc::CallDescr+0xbb
.shell: Process exited
```

.cmdtree

This is a command that creates a debugger window with hyperlinks that can execute debugging commands. So we can click on each hyperlink and the command corresponding to the hyperlink is automatically called.

Here are the steps:

a) Create a text file, **CMDTREE.TXT**, with debugging commands, using the example below as a template. We can modify sections between {} the way we want:

```
windbg ANSI Command Tree 1.0
title {"Common Commands"}
body
{"Common Commands"}
 {"Information"}
  {"Time of dump"} {".time"}
  {"Process being debugged"} {"|"}
  {"Dump Location"} {"||"}
  {"Create server on port 9999"} {".server tcp:port=9999"}
  {"Show remote connections"} {".clients"}
  {"Process Environment Block"} {"!peb"}
 {"Logging"}
  {"Open Log"} {".logopen /t /u /d"}
  {"Close Log"} {".logclose"}
 {"Modules"}
  {"All Modules"} {"lm D sm"}
  {"Loaded Modules"} {"lmo D sm"}
  {"Loaded Modules (verbose)"} {"lmvo D sm"}
  {"Modules w/o symbols"} {"lme D sm"}
 {"Stacks"}
  {"Set frame length to 2000"} {".kframes 2000"}
```

```
  {"Dump current stack w/ DML"} {"kpM 1000"}
  {"Dump stacks without private info"} {"knL 1000"}
  {"Dump stacks with all parameters"} {"kPn 1000"}
  {"Dump stacks (distance from last frame)"} {"kf 1000"}
  {"Dump stacks with Frame Pointer Omission"} {"kvn 1000"}
  {"Dump all stack"} {"~*kbn 1000"}
  {"Dump unique stacks"} {"!uniqstack -pn"}
  {"Thread environment block"} {"!teb"}
  {"Move to next frame"} {".f+"}
  {"Move to previous frame"} {".f-"}
 {"Memory"}
  {"Dump heaps"} {"!heap -a"}
 {"Automated Task"}
  {"!analyze"} {"!analyze -v"}
  {"Locks"} {"!ntsdexts.locks"}
  {"CPU time for User and Kernel Mode"} {"!runaway 7"}
 {"Managed"}
  {"Load sos"} {".loadby sos mscorwks"}
  {"clrstack"} {"!clrstack"}
  {"Threads"} {"!threads"}
  {"Stack Objects"} {"!dso"}
  {"Exceptions"} {"!dae"}
```

b) Save the text file in the same folder where WinDbg is installed, for example, C:\Program Files\Debugging Tools for Windows:

c) Open a dump file, load the symbols, and then use this command:

```
.cmdtree CMDTREE.TXT
```

d) The command above will create a new WinDbg window with our commands. We can double click one item from the tree view window to execute the command.

Pseudo-registers

WinDbg has a set of internal pseudo-registers that we can use as variables or as a means to get specific information. Some examples include $exp (the last evaluated expression), $ra (the current return address, $ip (the value of EIP or RIP), $p (the value of the last d* command output), $proc and $thread (the addresses of the current _EPROCESS and _ETHREAD), $peb and $teb (the addresses of the current _PEB and _TEB), $tpid and $tid *the values of the current PID and TID). Additionally there are 20 user-defined registers $t0 - $t19.

To improve performance we should always use @ before the register or pseudo-register, for example:

`r @$t0 = @$t0 + 0n10` is faster than `r $t0 + $t0 + 0n10`

`r @ecx = @eax + 0x10` is faster than `r ecx = eax + 0x10`

To assign a new value to a register or pseudo-register or to do a mathematical operation, use the **r** command. Also, to display a register / pseudo-register value, the **r** command is cleaner than **?**. Use **??** when we want to know the type. Here are some examples to illustrate the differentce:

```
0:015> r @$t0 = 5

0:015> ?? @$t0
unsigned int64 5

0:015> r @$t0
$t0=00000005

0:015> ? @$t0
Evaluate expression: 5 = 00000005
```

It's very common to use registers or pseudo-registers with the **poi** command that dereferences an address like ***** dereference operator in C and C++:

```
0:010> r
eax=002590b8    ebx=00000000    ecx=39f366a1    edx=00000000    esi=00422600
edi=00000000
eip=77225cb4 esp=034dfcd0 ebp=034dfd34 iopl=0      nv up ei pl nz ac po cy
cs=001b  ss=0023  ds=0023  es=0023  fs=003b  gs=0000          efl=00000213
ntdll!KiFastSystemCallRet:
77225cb4 c3              ret

0:010> dd @ebp L1
034dfd34  034dfd5c

0:010> dd poi(@ebp) L1
034dfd5c  034dfdc8
```

.if and j

The **.if** and **j** commands are used to conditionally execute a command or series of commands in breakpoints and scripts. **.if** is very similar to **if** from C and C++:

```
.if (Cond) { Cmds } .elsif (Cond) { Cmds } .else { Cmds }
```

j does the same thing but uses a very different syntax:

```
j Expression 'Cmd1' ; 'Cmd2'
```

Generally, we prefer to use **.if** because we think it's more intuitive and it looks like C/C++. Some examples:

```
0:015> j (@ecx = 7) '.echo Condition is TRUE' ; '.echo Condition
is FALSE'

Condition is FALSE
```

```
0:015> .if (@ecx = 7) { .echo Condition is TRUE } .else  { .echo
Condition is FALSE }

Condition is FALSE
```

Let's suppose we need a breakpoint that performs some action when the breakpoint is hit over 10 times. We can create the equivalent of the command below using conditional commands:

```
bp mtgdi!CBallThread::SingleStep 10
```

```
0:015> r @$t0 = 0
```

```
0:015> bp mtgdi!CBallThread::SingleStep "r @$t0 = @$t0 + 1;.if
(@$t0 > 0n10){.echo More than 10 times...}.else{ gc }"
```

or with **j** command:

```
0:015> r @$t0 = 0

0:015> bp mtgdi!CBallThread::SingleStep " r @$t0 = @$t0 + 1; j
(@$t0 > 0n10) '.echo More than ten times...'; 'gc'  "
```

ln

ln is a very useful command. It stands for "**l**ist **n**earest". We provide an address as an argument, and it gives us the closest symbol that matches the address. Of course, we have to use the right symbols!

Here is the syntax:

```
ln [address]
```

Examples:

```
0:015> kL
ChildEBP RetAddr
03a0fccc 77225460 ntdll!KiFastSystemCallRet
03a0fcd0 771fffd9 ntdll!NtWaitForSingleObject+0xc
03a0fd34 771ff09e ntdll!RtlpWaitOnCriticalSection+0x155
03a0fd5c 00414ee7 ntdll!RtlEnterCriticalSection+0x152
03a0fdc8 00414834 mtgdi!CBallThread::SingleStep+0x147
03a0fe20 00414d8c mtgdi!CGDIThread::InitInstance+0x44
03a0fe78 5a3dd973 mtgdi!CBallThread::InitInstance+0x2c
03a0ff40 5a1fdfd3 mfc90d!_AfxThreadEntry+0x303
03a0ff7c 5a1fdf69 MSVCR90D!_callthreadstartex+0x53
03a0ff88 76fdb957 MSVCR90D!_threadstartex+0x89

0:015> ln 00414834
c:\downloads\mtgdi\threads.cpp(65)+0x10
(004147f0)   mtgdi!CGDIThread::InitInstance+0x44   |  (00414860)
mtgdi!CGDIThread::Delete
```

Tip: We can easily see if we have a stack corruption. If the stack is corrupt the **eip** register points to an invalid address and not to the next instruction. Thus, to validate if this is the case, use:

```
ln @eip
```

Normal stack (**eip** matches a valid symbol):

```
0:015> ln @eip
 (77225cb4)   ntdll!KiFastSystemCallRet   |  (77225cc0)
ntdll!_KiIntSystemCall@0
```

Corrupt stack (**eip** has no matching symbol):

```
0:015> ln @eip
```

(empty output here, it means the debugger couldn't resolve the **eip** address. If we use symbols it is a strong indication of a corrupt stack)

Logging and History

Using the pair of commands **.logopen** and **.logclose** we can save a log file that has all output from the debugger. Let's see some examples:

.logopen [filename]

```
0:015> .logopen c:\downloads\test.log

Opened log file 'c:\downloads\test.log'


0:015> kbn

 # ChildEBP RetAddr  Args to Child

00 03a0fd34 771ff09e 00000000 00000000 03810a90 ntdll!KiFastSystemCallRet

01 03a0fd5c 00414ee7 00422600 00000000 00000000 ntdll!RtlAddAccessAllowedAce+0x52

02 03a0fdc8 00414834 00000000 00000000 03810a90 mtgdi!CBallThread::SingleStep+0x147
[c:\downloads\mtgdi\threads.cpp @ 180]

03 03a0fe20 00414d8c 00000000 00000000 03810a90 mtgdi!CGDIThread::InitInstance+0x44
[c:\downloads\mtgdi\threads.cpp @ 65]

04 03a0fe78 5a3dd973 e9dcbc9f 00000000 00000000 mtgdi!CBallThread::InitInstance+0x2c
[c:\downloads\mtgdi\threads.cpp @ 156]

05 03a0ff40 5a1fdfd3 0012f7dc e9dcb579 00000000 mfc90d!_AfxThreadEntry+0x303

06 03a0ff7c 5a1fdf69 03810ce0 03a0ff94 76fdb957 MSVCR90D!_beginthreadex+0x243

07 03a0ff88 76fdb957 03810ce0 03a0ffd4 772072a9 MSVCR90D!_beginthreadex+0x1d9

08 03a0ff94 772072a9 03810a90 7ef14522 00000000 kernel32!BaseThreadInitThunk+0x12

09 03a0ffd4 7720727c 5a1fdee0 03810a90 00000000
ntdll!RtlIsCurrentThreadAttachExempt+0x63

0a 03a0ffec 00000000 5a1fdee0 03810a90 00000000
ntdll!RtlIsCurrentThreadAttachExempt+0x36


0:015> .logclose

Closing open log file c:\downloads\test.log
```

.logopen /d

```
0:015> .logopen /d

Opened log file '_Local_.log'
```

(AA) .loadby *Loads an extension from module path 0n161 0xA1 1010 0001*

```
.logopen /t
```

```
0:015> .logopen /t
Opened log file 'dbgeng_2568_2009-05-15_20-43-50-311.log'
```

Now let's suppose we want to save just the commands we typed. To do that we should use:

```
.write_cmd_hist [filename]
```

Tip: With this command we can learn from debugging sessions performed by other engineers! Remember, when using this command the history is cumulative as we can see from the screenshots below:

```
windbg> .write_cmd_hist c:\debuggers\cmd_hist.log
Wrote command history to 'c:\debuggers\cmd_hist.log'
```

```
0:015> kbn
 # ChildEBP RetAddr  Args to Child
WARNING: Stack unwind information not available. Following frames may be wrong.
00 03a0fd34 771ff09e 00000000 00000000 03810a90 ntdll!KiFastSystemCallRet
01 03a0fd5c 00414ee7 00422600 00000000 00000000 ntdll!RtlAddAccessAllowedAce+0x52
02 03a0fdc8 00414834 00000000 00000000 03810a90 mtgdi!CBallThread::SingleStep+0x147
[c:\downloads\mtgdi\threads.cpp @ 180]
03 03a0fe20 00414d8c 00000000 00000000 03810a90 mtgdi!CGDIThread::InitInstance+0x44
[c:\downloads\mtgdi\threads.cpp @ 65]
04 03a0fe78 5a3dd973 e9dcbc9f 00000000 00000000 mtgdi!CBallThread::InitInstance+0x2c
[c:\downloads\mtgdi\threads.cpp @ 156]
05 03a0ff40 5a1fdfd3 0012f7dc e9dcb579 00000000 mfc90d!_AfxThreadEntry+0x303
06 03a0ff7c 5a1fdf69 03810ce0 03a0ff94 76fdb957 MSVCR90D!_beginthreadex+0x243
07 03a0ff88 76fdb957 03810ce0 03a0ffd4 772072a9 MSVCR90D!_beginthreadex+0x1d9
08 03a0ff94 772072a9 03810a90 7ef14522 00000000 kernel32!BaseThreadInitThunk+0x12
09 03a0ffd4 7720727c 5a1fdee0 03810a90 00000000
ntdll!RtlIsCurrentThreadAttachExempt+0x63
0a 03a0ffec 00000000 5a1fdee0 03810a90 00000000
ntdll!RtlIsCurrentThreadAttachExempt+0x36
```

```
0:015> r
eax=ffffffa0 ebx=00000000 ecx=ffffffa0 edx=00000002 esi=00422600 edi=00000000
eip=77225cb4 esp=03a0fcd0 ebp=03a0fd34 iopl=0         nv up ei pl nz ac po cy
cs=001b  ss=0023  ds=0023  es=0023  fs=003b  gs=0000             efl=00000213
ntdll!KiFastSystemCallRet:
77225cb4 c3               ret
```

Now, if we open just created cmd_hist.log file we should see the commands above and any other commands we used during this debugging session.

!uniqstack

This command is not well known. As the name says, this command shows all distinct stacks. It works pretty much like **k** command and its variations; however, it doesn't show repeated call stacks that have the same call sequence.

This is helpful when we are debugging an application that has many threads and we don't want to see repeated stacks, just one call stack pattern. The following command variant shows full parameters and frame numbers:

!uniqstack -pn

```
0:015> !uniqstack -pn
Processing 27 threads, please wait

.  0  Id: 168c.780 Suspend: 1 Teb: 7ffdf000 Unfrozen
      Start: mtgdi!ILT+2340(_WinMainCRTStartup) (00411929)
      Priority: 0  Priority class: 32  Affinity: 3
 # ChildEBP RetAddr
WARNING: Stack unwind information not available. Following frames may be wrong.
00 0012fe30 5a3ddaa3 ntdll!KiFastSystemCallRet
01 0012fe5c 5a3df13e mfc90d!AfxInternalPumpMessage+0x23
02 0012fe68 5a3de90d mfc90d!CWinThread::PumpMessage+0xe
03 0012fe84 5a3e1179 mfc90d!CWinThread::Run+0x8d
04 0012fe98 5a36648f mfc90d!CWinApp::Run+0x59
05 0012febc 0041903a mfc90d!AfxWinMain+0xef
06 0012fed4 00416a18 mtgdi!WinMain(struct HINSTANCE__ * hInstance = 0x00400000, struct HINSTANCE__ * hPrevInstance = 0x00000000, char * lpCmdLine = 0x00622994 "", int nCmdShow = 10)+0x1a
```

```
07 0012ff80 0041677f mtgdi!__tmainCRTStartup(void)+0x288

08 0012ff88 76fdb957 mtgdi!WinMainCRTStartup(void)+0xf

09 0012ff94 772072a9 kernel32!BaseThreadInitThunk+0x12

0a 0012ffd4 7720727c ntdll!RtlIsCurrentThreadAttachExempt+0x63

0b 0012ffec 00000000 ntdll!RtlIsCurrentThreadAttachExempt+0x36


.  1  Id: 168c.1e94 Suspend: 1 Teb: 7ffde000 Unfrozen

      Start: ntdll!RtlUserThreadStart (77225c98)

      Priority: -15  Priority class: 32  Affinity: 3

 # ChildEBP RetAddr

WARNING: Stack unwind information not available. Following frames
may be wrong.

00 026ffd34 771ff09e ntdll!KiFastSystemCallRet

01 026ffd5c 00414ee7 ntdll!RtlAddAccessAllowedAce+0x52

02 026ffdc8 00414834 mtgdi!CBallThread::SingleStep(void)+0x147
[c:\downloads\mtgdi\threads.cpp @ 180]

03 026ffe20 00414d8c mtgdi!CGDIThread::InitInstance(void)+0x44
[c:\downloads\mtgdi\threads.cpp @ 65]

04 026ffe78 5a3dd973 mtgdi!CBallThread::InitInstance(void)+0x2c
[c:\downloads\mtgdi\threads.cpp @ 156]

05 026fff40 5a1fdfd3 mfc90d!_AfxThreadEntry+0x303

06 026fff7c 5a1fdf69 MSVCR90D!_beginthreadex+0x243

07 026fff88 76fdb957 MSVCR90D!_beginthreadex+0x1d9

08 026fff94 772072a9 kernel32!BaseThreadInitThunk+0x12

09 026fffd4 7720727c ntdll!RtlIsCurrentThreadAttachExempt+0x63

0a 026fffec 00000000 ntdll!RtlIsCurrentThreadAttachExempt+0x36
```

```
. 14  Id: 168c.1ac0 Suspend: 1 Teb: 7ffad000 Unfrozen

      Start: ntdll!RtlUserThreadStart (77225c98)

      Priority: -15  Priority class: 32  Affinity: 3

 # ChildEBP RetAddr

00 0380fcdc 5a3488c2
mfc90d!CThreadLocal<_AFX_THREAD_STATE>::operator->

01 0380fcf4 5a3489fd mfc90d!AfxGetModuleState+0x12

02 0380fd04 5a3afe2c mfc90d!AfxGetModuleThreadState+0xd

03 0380fd34 5a3afeff mfc90d!afxMapHGDIOBJ+0x2c

04 0380fd48 5a3ad461 mfc90d!CGdiObject::FromHandle+0xf

05 0380fd5c 00414f24 mfc90d!CDC::SelectObject+0x81

06 0380fdc8 00414834 mtgdi!CBallThread::SingleStep(void)+0x184
[c:\downloads\mtgdi\threads.cpp @ 191]

07 0380fe20 00414d8c mtgdi!CGDIThread::InitInstance(void)+0x44
[c:\downloads\mtgdi\threads.cpp @ 65]

08 0380fe78 5a3dd973 mtgdi!CBallThread::InitInstance(void)+0x2c
[c:\downloads\mtgdi\threads.cpp @ 156]

09 0380ff40 5a1fdfd3 mfc90d!_AfxThreadEntry+0x303

0a 0380ff7c 5a1fdf69 MSVCR90D!_beginthreadex+0x243

0b 0380ff88 76fdb957 MSVCR90D!_beginthreadex+0x1d9

WARNING: Stack unwind information not available. Following frames
may be wrong.

0c 0380ff94 772072a9 kernel32!BaseThreadInitThunk+0x12

0d 0380ffd4 7720727c ntdll!RtlIsCurrentThreadAttachExempt+0x63

0e 0380ffec 00000000 ntdll!RtlIsCurrentThreadAttachExempt+0x36
```

0n166 0xA6 1010 0110 ***!ubl*** *Lists user-space breakpoints* ***(KL)***

```
. 26  Id: 168c.20e4 Suspend: 1 Teb: 7ffa1000 Unfrozen

      Start: ntdll!RtlUserThreadStart (77225c98)

      Priority: 0  Priority class: 32  Affinity: 3

 # ChildEBP RetAddr

WARNING: Stack unwind information not available. Following frames
may be wrong.

00 0450ff88 76fdb957 ntdll!DbgBreakPoint

01 0450ff94 772072a9 kernel32!BaseThreadInitThunk+0x12

02 0450ffd4 7720727c ntdll!RtlIsCurrentThreadAttachExempt+0x63

03 0450ffec 00000000 ntdll!RtlIsCurrentThreadAttachExempt+0x36


Total threads: 27

Duplicate callstacks: 23 (windbg thread #s follow):

2, 3, 4, 5, 6, 7, 8, 9, 10, 11, 12, 13, 15, 16, 17, 18, 19, 20,
21, 22, 23, 24, 25
```

Breakpoints: bp, bm, ba, bu

When doing live debugging we use breakpoints. A simple *breakpoint* is easy to use. However, when we are in the trenches we might need to use advanced *breakpoints* that save us a lot of manual work.

For example, we may need to use a *breakpoint* that works only one time and changes the assembly code, thus changing the execution flow of our application. Or we may want to have a *breakpoint* that logs specific information to a file and then continues the execution. We can even call a script from our breakpoint. With breakpoints there's no limit to creativity!

Example of a basic breakpoint using a function symbol:

```
0:015> bp mtgdi!CGDIThread::InitInstance

0:015> bl
 0 e 004147f0     0001 (0001)  0:****
mtgdi!CGDIThread::InitInstance
```

Example of a basic breakpoint using an address:

```
0:015> bp 00414d60

0:015> bl
 0 e 00414d60     0001 (0001)  0:****
mtgdi!CBallThread::InitInstance
```

Example of a breakpoint based on a pattern:

```
0:015> bm mtgdi!CGDIThread*
  2: 004147b0 @!"mtgdi!CGDIThread::`scalar deleting destructor'"
  3: 00414860 @!"mtgdi!CGDIThread::Delete"
  4: 004149a0 @!"mtgdi!CGDIThread::KillThread"
  5: 00414680 @!"mtgdi!CGDIThread::GetThisMessageMap"
  6: 004147f0 @!"mtgdi!CGDIThread::InitInstance"
  7: 004148f0 @!"mtgdi!CGDIThread::~CGDIThread"
  8: 00414600 @!"mtgdi!CGDIThread::_GetBaseClass"
  9: 00414640 @!"mtgdi!CGDIThread::GetRuntimeClass"
 10: 00414620 @!"mtgdi!CGDIThread::GetThisClass"
 11: 004146a0 @!"mtgdi!CGDIThread::CGDIThread"
 12: 00414a60 @!"mtgdi!CGDIThread::UpdateBorder"
 13: 00414660 @!"mtgdi!CGDIThread::GetMessageMap"
```

Example of a *one shot* breakpoint. It's deleted after the first hit. We can see it using **bl** command:

```
bp /1 mtgdi!CRectThread::InitInstance
```

Example of a breakpoint using the call stack limit:

```
0:015> bp /c 6 mtgdi!CBallThread::InitInstance
```

```
0:015> bl

 0 e 00414d60     0001 (0001)  0:****
mtgdi!CBallThread::InitInstance

     Call stack shallower than: 00000006
```

Example of a breakpoint using *commands*:

```
bp mtgdi!CBallThread::InitInstance ".echo CALL STACK; kpn 1000;
.echo REGISTERS; r; .sleep 0n5000; gc"
```

Example of breaking on access (a write at 4-byte location):

```
ba w4 (0x02ed52b0 + 0x080)
```

Exampe of counting how many times a breakpoint was hit:

```
0:015> r @$t0 = 0

0:015> bp <address/symbol> "r @$t0 = @$t0 + 1; .echo Number of
times the breakpoint was hit; ? @$t0; gc"

0:015> g
```

dt

This command is used almost all the time whenever we need to get the fields and type for a structure or a class. For example, we may have a ***this*** pointer and use **dt** to get its fields and type. It is a simple command with interesting variations that we should be aware of, because it's an important armory when hunting nasty bugs.

The simplest **dt** form displays a type without using instance information. In other words, we don't need to provide the address where the object is located, just its type, for example:

```
0:015> dt  CBallThread
mtgdi!CBallThread
   +0x000 __VFN_table : Ptr32
   =00400000 classCObject     : CRuntimeClass
   =00400000 classCCmdTarget  : CRuntimeClass
   =00400000 _commandEntries  : [0] AFX_OLECMDMAP_ENTRY
   =00400000 commandMap       : AFX_OLECMDMAP
   =00400000 _dispatchEntries : [0] AFX_DISPMAP_ENTRY
   =00400000 _dispatchEntryCount : Uint4B
   =00400000 _dwStockPropMask : Uint4B
   =00400000 dispatchMap      : AFX_DISPMAP
   =00400000 _connectionEntries : [0] AFX_CONNECTIONMAP_ENTRY
   =00400000 connectionMap    : AFX_CONNECTIONMAP
   =00400000 _interfaceEntries : [0] AFX_INTERFACEMAP_ENTRY
   =00400000 interfaceMap     : AFX_INTERFACEMAP
   =00400000 _eventsinkEntries : [0] AFX_EVENTSINKMAP_ENTRY
   =00400000 _eventsinkEntryCount : Uint4B
   =00400000 eventsinkMap     : AFX_EVENTSINKMAP
   +0x004 m_dwRef           : Int4B
   +0x008 m_pOuterUnknown   : Ptr32 IUnknown
   +0x00c m_xInnerUnknown   : Uint4B
```

```
+0x010 m_xDispatch      : CCmdTarget::XDispatch
+0x014 m_bResultExpected : Int4B
+0x018 m_xConnPtContainer : CCmdTarget::XConnPtContainer
+0x01c m_pModuleState   : Ptr32 AFX_MODULE_STATE
=00400000 classCWinThread  : CRuntimeClass
+0x020 m_pMainWnd       : Ptr32 CWnd
+0x024 m_pActiveWnd     : Ptr32 CWnd
+0x028 m_bAutoDelete    : Int4B
+0x02c m_hThread        : Ptr32 Void
+0x030 m_nThreadID      : Uint4B
+0x034 m_pThreadParams  : Ptr32 Void
+0x038 m_pfnThreadProc  : Ptr32     unsigned int
+0x03c m_lpfnOleTermOrFreeLib : Ptr32     void
+0x040 m_pMessageFilter : Ptr32 COleMessageFilter
=0041f6b0 CGDIThread::classCGDIThread : CRuntimeClass
+0x044 m_rectBorder     : CRect
+0x054 m_hDC            : Ptr32 HDC__
+0x058 m_dc             : CDC
+0x068 m_hEventKill     : Ptr32 Void
+0x06c m_hEventDead     : Ptr32 Void
=00422618 CGDIThread::m_hAnotherDead : Ptr32 Void
=00422600 CGDIThread::m_csGDILock : _RTL_CRITICAL_SECTION
=0041f770 CBallThread::classCBallThread : CRuntimeClass
+0x070 m_rectPosition   : CRect
+0x080 m_ptVelocity     : CPoint
+0x088 m_hBrush         : Ptr32 HBRUSH__
+0x08c m_brush          : CBrush
```

The second variation uses the address of an object and shows details of the specific instance, like:

dt <symbol> <address> ← We can invert the order

```
0:015> dt  CBallThread  0x038109c0

mtgdi!CBallThread
   +0x000 __VFN_table : 0x0041f88c
   =00400000 classCObject     : CRuntimeClass
   =00400000 classCCmdTarget  : CRuntimeClass
   =00400000 _commandEntries  : [0] AFX_OLECMDMAP_ENTRY
   =00400000 commandMap       : AFX_OLECMDMAP
   =00400000 _dispatchEntries : [0] AFX_DISPMAP_ENTRY
   =00400000 _dispatchEntryCount : 0x905a4d
   =00400000 _dwStockPropMask : 0x905a4d
   =00400000 dispatchMap      : AFX_DISPMAP
   =00400000 _connectionEntries : [0] AFX_CONNECTIONMAP_ENTRY
   =00400000 connectionMap    : AFX_CONNECTIONMAP
   =00400000 _interfaceEntries : [0] AFX_INTERFACEMAP_ENTRY
   =00400000 interfaceMap     : AFX_INTERFACEMAP
   =00400000 _eventsinkEntries : [0] AFX_EVENTSINKMAP_ENTRY
   =00400000 _eventsinkEntryCount : 0x905a4d
   =00400000 eventsinkMap     : AFX_EVENTSINKMAP
   +0x004 m_dwRef           : 1
   +0x008 m_pOuterUnknown   : (null)
   +0x00c m_xInnerUnknown   : 0
   +0x010 m_xDispatch       : CCmdTarget::XDispatch
   +0x014 m_bResultExpected : 1
   +0x018 m_xConnPtContainer : CCmdTarget::XConnPtContainer
   +0x01c m_pModuleState    : 0x00628a28 AFX_MODULE_STATE
   =00400000 classCWinThread  : CRuntimeClass
   +0x020 m_pMainWnd        : 0x001a6190 CWnd
   +0x024 m_pActiveWnd      : (null)
   +0x028 m_bAutoDelete     : 0
   +0x02c m_hThread         : 0x000001c8
   +0x030 m_nThreadID       : 0x2004
   +0x034 m_pThreadParams   : (null)
   +0x038 m_pfnThreadProc   : (null)
```

```
+0x03c m_lpfnOleTermOrFreeLib : (null)
+0x040 m_pMessageFilter : (null)
=0041f6b0 CGDIThread::classCGDIThread : CRuntimeClass
+0x044 m_rectBorder     : CRect
+0x054 m_hDC            : 0xf0011110 HDC__
+0x058 m_dc             : CDC
+0x068 m_hEventKill     : 0x000001ac
+0x06c m_hEventDead     : 0x000001bc
=00422618 CGDIThread::m_hAnotherDead : 0x0000007c
=00422600 CGDIThread::m_csGDILock : _RTL_CRITICAL_SECTION
=0041f770 CBallThread::classCBallThread : CRuntimeClass
+0x070 m_rectPosition   : CRect
+0x080 m_ptVelocity     : CPoint
+0x088 m_hBrush         : 0xb21021d5 HBRUSH__
+0x08c m_brush          : Cbrush
```

This time we have not only the type and its fields but also the values of each field. If we want full details we can display all fields recursively. If a displayed structure contains substructures, they are expanded recursively too:

```
0:015> dt  CBallThread  0x038109c0 -b
mtgdi!CBallThread
   +0x000 __VFN_table : 0x0041f88c
   =00400000 classCObject     : CRuntimeClass
   =00400000 classCCmdTarget  : CRuntimeClass
   =00400000 _commandEntries  :
    [00] AFX_OLECMDMAP_ENTRY
   =00400000 commandMap       : AFX_OLECMDMAP
   =00400000 _dispatchEntries :
    [00] AFX_DISPMAP_ENTRY
   =00400000 _dispatchEntryCount : 0x905a4d
```

```
=00400000 _dwStockPropMask : 0x905a4d
=00400000 dispatchMap      : AFX_DISPMAP
=00400000 _connectionEntries :
 [00] AFX_CONNECTIONMAP_ENTRY
=00400000 connectionMap    : AFX_CONNECTIONMAP
=00400000 _interfaceEntries :
 [00] AFX_INTERFACEMAP_ENTRY
=00400000 interfaceMap     : AFX_INTERFACEMAP
=00400000 _eventsinkEntries :
 [00] AFX_EVENTSINKMAP_ENTRY
=00400000 _eventsinkEntryCount : 0x905a4d
=00400000 eventsinkMap     : AFX_EVENTSINKMAP
+0x004 m_dwRef          : 1
+0x008 m_pOuterUnknown  : (null)
+0x00c m_xInnerUnknown  : 0
+0x010 m_xDispatch      : CCmdTarget::XDispatch
   +0x000 m_vtbl           : 0
+0x014 m_bResultExpected : 1
+0x018 m_xConnPtContainer : CCmdTarget::XConnPtContainer
   +0x000 m_vtbl           : 0
+0x01c m_pModuleState   : 0x00628a28
=00400000 classCWinThread  : CRuntimeClass
+0x020 m_pMainWnd       : 0x001a6190
+0x024 m_pActiveWnd     : (null)
+0x028 m_bAutoDelete    : 0
+0x02c m_hThread        : 0x000001c8
+0x030 m_nThreadID      : 0x2004
+0x034 m_pThreadParams  : (null)
+0x038 m_pfnThreadProc  : (null)
+0x03c m_lpfnOleTermOrFreeLib : (null)
+0x040 m_pMessageFilter : (null)
=0041f6b0 CGDIThread::classCGDIThread : CRuntimeClass
+0x044 m_rectBorder     : CRect
   +0x000 left             : 0
```

```
      +0x004 top               : 0
      +0x008 right             : 1060
      +0x00c bottom            : 596
   +0x054 m_hDC             : 0xf0011110
   +0x058 m_dc              : CDC
      +0x000 __VFN_table : 0x5a2fe734
      =00400000 classCObject     : CRuntimeClass
      =00400000 classCDC         : CRuntimeClass
      +0x004 m_hDC             : 0xf0011110
      +0x008 m_hAttribDC       : 0xf0011110
      +0x00c m_bPrinting       : 0
   +0x068 m_hEventKill      : 0x000001ac
   +0x06c m_hEventDead      : 0x000001bc
   =00422618 CGDIThread::m_hAnotherDead : 0x0000007c
   =00422600 CGDIThread::m_csGDILock : _RTL_CRITICAL_SECTION
   =0041f770 CBallThread::classCBallThread : CRuntimeClass
   +0x070 m_rectPosition   : CRect
      +0x000 left              : 921
      +0x004 top               : 474
      +0x008 right             : 966
      +0x00c bottom            : 519
   +0x080 m_ptVelocity     : CPoint
      +0x000 x                 : -11
      +0x004 y                 : -6
   +0x088 m_hBrush          : 0xb21021d5
   +0x08c m_brush           : CBrush
      +0x000 __VFN_table : 0x5a2feb2c
      =00400000 classCObject     : CRuntimeClass
      =00400000 classCGdiObject  : CRuntimeClass
      +0x004 m_hObject         : 0xb21021d5
      =00400000 classCBrush      : CRuntimeClass
```

Suppose we have a linked list with more than 100 nodes. For this case we may want to control how many nodes we display. To do this we use this command:

dt <symbol> <address> -rn ← n is the depth, a number between 1 and 9.

```
0:015> dt  CBallThread  0x038109c0 -r2
mtgdi!CBallThread
   +0x000 __VFN_table : 0x0041f88c
   =00400000 classCObject     : CRuntimeClass
      +0x000 m_lpszClassName  : 0x00905a4d  "???"
      +0x004 m_nObjectSize    : 3
      +0x008 m_wSchema        : 4
      +0x00c m_pfnCreateObject : 0x0000ffff       CObject*  +ffff
      +0x010 m_pfnGetBaseClass : 0x000000b8       CRuntimeClass*  +b8
      +0x014 m_pNextClass     : (null)
      +0x018 m_pClassInit     : 0x00000040 AFX_CLASSINIT
   =00400000 classCCmdTarget  : CRuntimeClass
      +0x000 m_lpszClassName  : 0x00905a4d  "???"
      +0x004 m_nObjectSize    : 3
      +0x008 m_wSchema        : 4
      +0x00c m_pfnCreateObject : 0x0000ffff       CObject*  +ffff
      +0x010 m_pfnGetBaseClass : 0x000000b8       CRuntimeClass*  +b8
      +0x014 m_pNextClass     : (null)
      +0x018 m_pClassInit     : 0x00000040 AFX_CLASSINIT
   =00400000 _commandEntries  : [0] AFX_OLECMDMAP_ENTRY
      +0x000 pguid            : 0x00905a4d _GUID {cb02f1ca-0a83-f4ca-0208-
840acafa02ce}
         +0x000 Data1            : 0xcb02f1ca
         +0x004 Data2            : 0xa83
         +0x006 Data3            : 0xf4ca
         +0x008 Data4            : [8]  "???"
```

(AA) .netuse *Adds a network share connection* *0n177 0xB1 1011 0001*

```
      +0x004 cmdID            : 3
      +0x008 nID              : 4
   =00400000 commandMap       : AFX_OLECMDMAP
      +0x000 pfnGetBaseMap    : 0x00905a4d        AFX_OLECMDMAP*  +905a4d
      +0x004 lpEntries        : 0x00000003 AFX_OLECMDMAP_ENTRY
         +0x000 pguid            : ????
         +0x004 cmdID            : ??
         +0x008 nID              : ??
   =00400000 _dispatchEntries : [0] AFX_DISPMAP_ENTRY
      +0x000 lpszName         : 0x00905a4d  "???"
      +0x004 lDispID          : 3
      +0x008 lpszParams       : 0x00000004  "--- memory read error at
address 0x00000004 ---"
      +0x00c vt               : 0xffff
      +0x010 pfn              : 0x000000b8        void  +b8
      +0x014 pfnSet           : (null)
      +0x018 nPropOffset      : 0x40
      +0x01c flags            : 0 ( afxDispCustom )
   =00400000 _dispatchEntryCount : 0x905a4d
   =00400000 _dwStockPropMask : 0x905a4d
   =00400000 dispatchMap      : AFX_DISPMAP
      +0x000 pfnGetBaseMap    : 0x00905a4d        AFX_DISPMAP*  +905a4d
      +0x004 lpEntries        : 0x00000003 AFX_DISPMAP_ENTRY
         +0x000 lpszName         : ????
         +0x004 lDispID          : ??
         +0x008 lpszParams       : ????
         +0x00c vt               : ??
         +0x010 pfn              : ????
         +0x014 pfnSet           : ????
         +0x018 nPropOffset      : ??
         +0x01c flags            : ??
      +0x008 lpEntryCount     : 0x00000004  -> ??
      +0x00c lpStockPropMask  : 0x0000ffff  -> ??
   =00400000 _connectionEntries : [0] AFX_CONNECTIONMAP_ENTRY
```

0n178 0xB2 1011 0010 ***!tls*** *Shows a thread local storage slot* ***(AA)***

```
      +0x000 piid              : 0x00905a4d
      +0x004 nOffset           : 3
   =00400000 connectionMap     : AFX_CONNECTIONMAP
      +0x000 pfnGetBaseMap     : 0x00905a4d        AFX_CONNECTIONMAP*
+905a4d
      +0x004 pEntry            : 0x00000003 AFX_CONNECTIONMAP_ENTRY
         +0x000 piid              : ????
         +0x004 nOffset           : ??
   =00400000 _interfaceEntries : [0] AFX_INTERFACEMAP_ENTRY
      +0x000 piid              : 0x00905a4d
      +0x004 nOffset           : 3
   =00400000 interfaceMap      : AFX_INTERFACEMAP
      +0x000 pfnGetBaseMap     : 0x00905a4d        AFX_INTERFACEMAP*  +905a4d
      +0x004 pEntry            : 0x00000003 AFX_INTERFACEMAP_ENTRY
         +0x000 piid              : ????
         +0x004 nOffset           : ??
   =00400000 _eventsinkEntries : [0] AFX_EVENTSINKMAP_ENTRY
      +0x000 dispEntry         : AFX_DISPMAP_ENTRY
         +0x000 lpszName          : 0x00905a4d  "???"
         +0x004 lDispID           : 3
         +0x008 lpszParams        : 0x00000004  "--- memory read error at
address 0x00000004 ---"
         +0x00c vt                : 0xffff
         +0x010 pfn               : 0x000000b8          void  +b8
         +0x014 pfnSet            : (null)
         +0x018 nPropOffset       : 0x40
         +0x01c flags             : 0 ( afxDispCustom )
      +0x020 nCtrlIDFirst      : 0
      +0x024 nCtrlIDLast       : 0
   =00400000 _eventsinkEntryCount : 0x905a4d
   =00400000 eventsinkMap      : AFX_EVENTSINKMAP
      +0x000 pfnGetBaseMap     : 0x00905a4d        AFX_EVENTSINKMAP*  +905a4d
      +0x004 lpEntries         : 0x00000003 AFX_EVENTSINKMAP_ENTRY
         +0x000 dispEntry         : AFX_DISPMAP_ENTRY
         +0x020 nCtrlIDFirst      : ??
```

```
      +0x024 nCtrlIDLast      : ??
   +0x008 lpEntryCount     : 0x00000004  -> ??
+0x004 m_dwRef           : 1
+0x008 m_pOuterUnknown   : (null)
+0x00c m_xInnerUnknown   : 0
+0x010 m_xDispatch       : CCmdTarget::XDispatch
   +0x000 m_vtbl           : 0
+0x014 m_bResultExpected : 1
+0x018 m_xConnPtContainer : CCmdTarget::XConnPtContainer
   +0x000 m_vtbl           : 0
+0x01c m_pModuleState    : 0x00628a28 AFX_MODULE_STATE
   +0x000 __VFN_table : 0x5a2f3a34
   +0x004 m_pCurrentWinApp : 0x00422528 CWinApp
      +0x000 __VFN_table : 0x0041ec5c
      =00400000 classCObject     : CRuntimeClass
      =00400000 classCCmdTarget  : CRuntimeClass
      =00400000 _commandEntries  : [0] AFX_OLECMDMAP_ENTRY
      =00400000 commandMap       : AFX_OLECMDMAP
      =00400000 _dispatchEntries : [0] AFX_DISPMAP_ENTRY
      =00400000 _dispatchEntryCount : 0x905a4d
      =00400000 _dwStockPropMask : 0x905a4d
      =00400000 dispatchMap      : AFX_DISPMAP
      =00400000 _connectionEntries : [0] AFX_CONNECTIONMAP_ENTRY
      =00400000 connectionMap    : AFX_CONNECTIONMAP
      =00400000 _interfaceEntries : [0] AFX_INTERFACEMAP_ENTRY
      =00400000 interfaceMap     : AFX_INTERFACEMAP
      =00400000 _eventsinkEntries : [0] AFX_EVENTSINKMAP_ENTRY
      =00400000 _eventsinkEntryCount : 0x905a4d
      =00400000 eventsinkMap     : AFX_EVENTSINKMAP
      +0x004 m_dwRef           : 1
      +0x008 m_pOuterUnknown   : (null)
      +0x00c m_xInnerUnknown   : 0
      +0x010 m_xDispatch       : CCmdTarget::XDispatch
      +0x014 m_bResultExpected : 1
```

0n180 0xB4 1011 0100 **!timer** *Shows system timers* ***(KA)***

```
   +0x018 m_xConnPtContainer : CCmdTarget::XConnPtContainer
   +0x01c m_pModuleState   : 0x00628a28 AFX_MODULE_STATE
   =00400000 classCWinThread  : CRuntimeClass
   +0x020 m_pMainWnd       : 0x001a5d28 CWnd
   +0x024 m_pActiveWnd     : (null)
   +0x028 m_bAutoDelete    : 1
   +0x02c m_hThread        : 0xfffffffe
   +0x030 m_nThreadID      : 0x780
   +0x034 m_pThreadParams  : (null)
   +0x038 m_pfnThreadProc  : (null)
   +0x03c m_lpfnOleTermOrFreeLib : (null)
   +0x040 m_pMessageFilter : (null)
   =00400000 classCWinApp     : CRuntimeClass
   +0x044 m_hInstance      : 0x00400000 HINSTANCE__
   +0x048 m_lpCmdLine      : 0x00622994  ""
   +0x04c m_nCmdShow       : -1
   +0x050 m_pszAppName     : 0x001a5930  "Multithread GDI (no
threads)"
   +0x054 m_pszRegistryKey : (null)
   +0x058 m_pDocManager    : 0x001a5b80 CDocManager
   +0x05c m_bHelpMode      : 0
   +0x060 m_pszExeName     : 0x001a58e8  "MtGdi"
   +0x064 m_pszHelpFilePath : 0x001a5990  "C:\development\My
Tools\Book\mtgdi\Debug\MtGdi.HLP"
   +0x068 m_pszProfileName : 0x001a5a00  "MtGdi.INI"
   +0x06c m_eHelpType      : 0 ( afxWinHelp )
   +0x070 m_hDevMode       : (null)
   +0x074 m_hDevNames      : (null)
   +0x078 m_dwPromptContext : 0
   +0x07c m_hLangResourceDLL : (null)
   +0x080 m_nWaitCursorCount : 0
   +0x084 m_hcurWaitCursorRestore : (null)
   +0x088 m_pRecentFileList : (null)
   +0x08c m_pCmdInfo       : (null)
   +0x090 m_atomApp        : 0
```

(AA) .noversion *Disables ver. check for extensions* *0n181 0xB5 1011 0101*

```
         +0x092 m_atomSystemTopic : 0
         +0x094 m_nNumPreviewPages : 0
         +0x098 m_nSafetyPoolSize : 0x200
         +0x09c m_lpfnDaoTerm    : (null)
         +0x0a0 m_dwPolicies     : 0
      +0x008 m_hCurrentInstanceHandle : 0x00400000 HINSTANCE__
         +0x000 unused            : 9460301
      +0x00c m_hCurrentResourceHandle : 0x00400000 HINSTANCE__
         +0x000 unused            : 9460301
      +0x010 m_lpszCurrentAppName : 0x001a5930  "Multithread GDI (no
threads)"
      +0x014 m_bDLL            : 0 ''
      +0x015 m_bSystem         : 0 ''
      +0x016 m_bReserved       : [2]  ""
      +0x018 m_fRegisteredClasses : 8
      +0x01c m_pClassInit      : (null)
      +0x020 m_classList       : CTypedSimpleList<CRuntimeClass *>
         +0x000 m_pHead           : (null)
         +0x004 m_nNextOffset     : 0x14
      +0x028 m_pFactoryInit    : (null)
      +0x02c m_factoryList     : CTypedSimpleList<COleObjectFactory *>
         +0x000 m_pHead           : (null)
         +0x004 m_nNextOffset     : 0x20
      +0x034 m_nObjectCount    : 0
      +0x038 m_bUserCtrl       : 1
      +0x03c m_strUnregisterList :
ATL::CStringT<char,StrTraitMFC_DLL<char,ATL::ChTraitsCRT<char> > >
         +0x000 m_pszData         : 0x001a46d0  ""
      +0x040 m_pfnAfxWndProc   : 0x5a348800        long
mfc90d!AfxWndProcBase+0
      +0x044 m_dwVersion       : 0x900
      +0x048 m_pfnFilterToolTipMessage : (null)
      +0x04c m_libraryList     : CTypedSimpleList<CDynLinkLibrary *>
         +0x000 m_pHead           : 0x001a4640
         +0x004 m_nNextOffset     : 0x3c
```

```
      +0x054 m_appLangDLL      : 0x72940000 HINSTANCE__
         +0x000 unused            : 9460301
      +0x058 m_pOccManager     : (null)
      +0x05c m_lockList        : CTypedSimpleList<COleControlLock *>
         +0x000 m_pHead           : (null)
         +0x004 m_nNextOffset     : 0x18
      +0x064 m_pDaoState       : (null)
      +0x068 m_typeLibCache    : CTypeLibCache
         +0x000 m_pTypeLibID      : (null)
         +0x004 m_lcid            : 0xffffffff
         +0x008 m_ptlib           : (null)
         +0x00c m_guidInfo        : _GUID {00000000-0000-0000-0000-
000000000000}
         +0x01c m_ptinfo          : (null)
         +0x020 m_cRef            : 0
      +0x08c m_pTypeLibCacheMap : (null)
      +0x090 m_thread          : CThreadLocal<AFX_MODULE_THREAD_STATE>
         +0x000 m_nSlot           : 3
      +0x094 m_pDllIsolationWrappers : 0x001a5710  -> 0x00628ae8
CDllIsolationWrapperBase
         +0x000 __VFN_table : 0x5a2f3a3c
         +0x004 m_hModule         : (null)
         +0x008 m_bFreeLib        : 0
         +0x00c m_strModuleName   :
ATL::CStringT<char,StrTraitMFC_DLL<char,ATL::ChTraitsCRT<char> > >
      +0x098 m_bSetAmbientActCtx : 1
      +0x09c m_hActCtx         : 0x00629f2c
      +0x0a0 m_bInitNetworkAddressControl : 0
      +0x0a4 m_bInitNetworkAddressControlCalled : 0
   =00400000 classCWinThread   : CRuntimeClass
      +0x000 m_lpszClassName   : 0x00905a4d  "???"
      +0x004 m_nObjectSize     : 3
      +0x008 m_wSchema         : 4
      +0x00c m_pfnCreateObject : 0x0000ffff        CObject*  +ffff
      +0x010 m_pfnGetBaseClass : 0x000000b8        CRuntimeClass*  +b8
```

(UL) .ocommand *Enables commands from target 0n183 0xB7 1011 0111*

```
    +0x014 m_pNextClass     : (null)
    +0x018 m_pClassInit     : 0x00000040 AFX_CLASSINIT
  +0x020 m_pMainWnd       : 0x001a6190 CWnd
    +0x000 __VFN_table : 0x0041f23c
    =00400000 classCObject     : CRuntimeClass
      +0x000 m_lpszClassName  : 0x00905a4d  "???"
      +0x004 m_nObjectSize    : 3
      +0x008 m_wSchema        : 4
      +0x00c m_pfnCreateObject : 0x0000ffff          CObject*  +ffff
      +0x010 m_pfnGetBaseClass : 0x000000b8          CRuntimeClass*  +b8
      +0x014 m_pNextClass     : (null)
      +0x018 m_pClassInit     : 0x00000040 AFX_CLASSINIT
    =00400000 classCCmdTarget  : CRuntimeClass
      +0x000 m_lpszClassName  : 0x00905a4d  "???"
      +0x004 m_nObjectSize    : 3
      +0x008 m_wSchema        : 4
      +0x00c m_pfnCreateObject : 0x0000ffff          CObject*  +ffff
      +0x010 m_pfnGetBaseClass : 0x000000b8          CRuntimeClass*  +b8
      +0x014 m_pNextClass     : (null)
      +0x018 m_pClassInit     : 0x00000040 AFX_CLASSINIT
    =00400000 _commandEntries  : [0] AFX_OLECMDMAP_ENTRY
      +0x000 pguid            : 0x00905a4d _GUID {cb02f1ca-0a83-f4ca-
0208-840acafa02ce}
      +0x004 cmdID            : 3
      +0x008 nID              : 4
    =00400000 commandMap       : AFX_OLECMDMAP
      +0x000 pfnGetBaseMap    : 0x00905a4d          AFX_OLECMDMAP*
+905a4d
      +0x004 lpEntries        : 0x00000003 AFX_OLECMDMAP_ENTRY
    =00400000 _dispatchEntries : [0] AFX_DISPMAP_ENTRY
      +0x000 lpszName         : 0x00905a4d  "???"
      +0x004 lDispID          : 3
      +0x008 lpszParams       : 0x00000004  "--- memory read error at
address 0x00000004 ---"
      +0x00c vt               : 0xffff
```

0n184 0xB8 1011 1000 ***!teb*** *Shows formatted thread environment block* ***(UA)***

```
        +0x010 pfn              : 0x000000b8         void  +b8
        +0x014 pfnSet           : (null)
        +0x018 nPropOffset      : 0x40
        +0x01c flags            : 0 ( afxDispCustom )
      =00400000 _dispatchEntryCount : 0x905a4d
      =00400000 _dwStockPropMask : 0x905a4d
      =00400000 dispatchMap      : AFX_DISPMAP
        +0x000 pfnGetBaseMap    : 0x00905a4d         AFX_DISPMAP*
+905a4d
        +0x004 lpEntries        : 0x00000003 AFX_DISPMAP_ENTRY
        +0x008 lpEntryCount     : 0x00000004  -> ??
        +0x00c lpStockPropMask  : 0x0000ffff  -> ??
      =00400000 _connectionEntries : [0] AFX_CONNECTIONMAP_ENTRY
        +0x000 piid             : 0x00905a4d
        +0x004 nOffset          : 3
      =00400000 connectionMap    : AFX_CONNECTIONMAP
        +0x000 pfnGetBaseMap    : 0x00905a4d         AFX_CONNECTIONMAP*
+905a4d
        +0x004 pEntry           : 0x00000003 AFX_CONNECTIONMAP_ENTRY
      =00400000 _interfaceEntries : [0] AFX_INTERFACEMAP_ENTRY
        +0x000 piid             : 0x00905a4d
        +0x004 nOffset          : 3
      =00400000 interfaceMap     : AFX_INTERFACEMAP
        +0x000 pfnGetBaseMap    : 0x00905a4d         AFX_INTERFACEMAP*
+905a4d
        +0x004 pEntry           : 0x00000003 AFX_INTERFACEMAP_ENTRY
      =00400000 _eventsinkEntries : [0] AFX_EVENTSINKMAP_ENTRY
        +0x000 dispEntry        : AFX_DISPMAP_ENTRY
        +0x020 nCtrlIDFirst     : 0
        +0x024 nCtrlIDLast      : 0
      =00400000 _eventsinkEntryCount : 0x905a4d
      =00400000 eventsinkMap     : AFX_EVENTSINKMAP
        +0x000 pfnGetBaseMap    : 0x00905a4d         AFX_EVENTSINKMAP*
+905a4d
        +0x004 lpEntries        : 0x00000003 AFX_EVENTSINKMAP_ENTRY
```

(AA) .ofilter *Filters debugging output from target* *0n185 0xB9 1011 1001*

```
      +0x008 lpEntryCount     : 0x00000004  -> ??
   +0x004 m_dwRef          : 1
   +0x008 m_pOuterUnknown  : (null)
   +0x00c m_xInnerUnknown  : 0
   +0x010 m_xDispatch      : CCmdTarget::XDispatch
      +0x000 m_vtbl           : 0
   +0x014 m_bResultExpected : 1
   +0x018 m_xConnPtContainer : CCmdTarget::XConnPtContainer
      +0x000 m_vtbl           : 0
   +0x01c m_pModuleState   : 0x00628a28 AFX_MODULE_STATE
      +0x000 __VFN_table : 0x5a2f3a34
      +0x004 m_pCurrentWinApp : 0x00422528 CWinApp
      +0x008 m_hCurrentInstanceHandle : 0x00400000 HINSTANCE__
      +0x00c m_hCurrentResourceHandle : 0x00400000 HINSTANCE__
      +0x010 m_lpszCurrentAppName : 0x001a5930  "Multithread GDI (no
threads)"
      +0x014 m_bDLL           : 0 ''
      +0x015 m_bSystem        : 0 ''
      +0x016 m_bReserved      : [2]  ""
      +0x018 m_fRegisteredClasses : 8
      +0x01c m_pClassInit     : (null)
      +0x020 m_classList      : CTypedSimpleList<CRuntimeClass *>
      +0x028 m_pFactoryInit   : (null)
      +0x02c m_factoryList    : CTypedSimpleList<COleObjectFactory *>
      +0x034 m_nObjectCount   : 0
      +0x038 m_bUserCtrl      : 1
      +0x03c m_strUnregisterList :
ATL::CStringT<char,StrTraitMFC_DLL<char,ATL::ChTraitsCRT<char> > >
      +0x040 m_pfnAfxWndProc  : 0x5a348800           long
mfc90d!AfxWndProcBase+0
      +0x044 m_dwVersion      : 0x900
      +0x048 m_pfnFilterToolTipMessage : (null)
      +0x04c m_libraryList    : CTypedSimpleList<CDynLinkLibrary *>
      +0x054 m_appLangDLL     : 0x72940000 HINSTANCE__
      +0x058 m_pOccManager    : (null)
```

```
        +0x05c m_lockList        : CTypedSimpleList<COleControlLock *>
        +0x064 m_pDaoState       : (null)
        +0x068 m_typeLibCache    : CTypeLibCache
        +0x08c m_pTypeLibCacheMap : (null)
        +0x090 m_thread          : CThreadLocal<AFX_MODULE_THREAD_STATE>
        +0x094 m_pDllIsolationWrappers : 0x001a5710  -> 0x00628ae8
CDllIsolationWrapperBase
        +0x098 m_bSetAmbientActCtx : 1
        +0x09c m_hActCtx         : 0x00629f2c
        +0x0a0 m_bInitNetworkAddressControl : 0
        +0x0a4 m_bInitNetworkAddressControlCalled : 0
     =00400000 classCWnd         : CRuntimeClass
        +0x000 m_lpszClassName   : 0x00905a4d  "???"
        +0x004 m_nObjectSize     : 3
        +0x008 m_wSchema         : 4
        +0x00c m_pfnCreateObject : 0x0000ffff          CObject*  +ffff
        +0x010 m_pfnGetBaseClass : 0x000000b8          CRuntimeClass*  +b8
        +0x014 m_pNextClass      : (null)
        +0x018 m_pClassInit      : 0x00000040 AFX_CLASSINIT
     +0x020 m_hWnd            : 0x00100872 HWND__
        +0x000 unused            : ??
     =00400000 wndTop            : CWnd
        +0x000 __VFN_table : 0x00905a4d
        =00400000 classCObject     : CRuntimeClass
        =00400000 classCCmdTarget  : CRuntimeClass
        =00400000 _commandEntries  : [0] AFX_OLECMDMAP_ENTRY
        =00400000 commandMap       : AFX_OLECMDMAP
        =00400000 _dispatchEntries : [0] AFX_DISPMAP_ENTRY
        =00400000 _dispatchEntryCount : 0x905a4d
        =00400000 _dwStockPropMask : 0x905a4d
        =00400000 dispatchMap      : AFX_DISPMAP
        =00400000 _connectionEntries : [0] AFX_CONNECTIONMAP_ENTRY
        =00400000 connectionMap    : AFX_CONNECTIONMAP
        =00400000 _interfaceEntries : [0] AFX_INTERFACEMAP_ENTRY
```

```
=00400000 interfaceMap     : AFX_INTERFACEMAP
=00400000 _eventsinkEntries : [0] AFX_EVENTSINKMAP_ENTRY
=00400000 _eventsinkEntryCount : 0x905a4d
=00400000 eventsinkMap     : AFX_EVENTSINKMAP
+0x004 m_dwRef          : 3
+0x008 m_pOuterUnknown  : 0x00000004 IUnknown
+0x00c m_xInnerUnknown  : 0xffff
+0x010 m_xDispatch      : CCmdTarget::XDispatch
+0x014 m_bResultExpected : 0
+0x018 m_xConnPtContainer : CCmdTarget::XConnPtContainer
+0x01c m_pModuleState   : (null)
=00400000 classCWnd        : CRuntimeClass
+0x020 m_hWnd           : (null)
=00400000 wndTop           : CWnd
=00400000 wndBottom        : CWnd
=00400000 wndTopMost       : CWnd
=00400000 wndNoTopMost     : CWnd
+0x024 m_bEnableActiveAccessibility : 0
+0x028 m_pStdObject     : (null)
=00400000 m_pfnNotifyWinEvent : 0x00905a4d           void  +905a4d
+0x02c m_pProxy         : (null)
=00400000 _interfaceEntries : [0] AFX_INTERFACEMAP_ENTRY
=00400000 interfaceMap     : AFX_INTERFACEMAP
+0x030 m_xAccessible    : CWnd::XAccessible
+0x034 m_xAccessibleServer : CWnd::XAccessibleServer
+0x038 m_hWndOwner      : (null)
+0x03c m_nFlags         : 0xe8
+0x040 m_pfnSuper       : 0x0eba1f0e           long  +eba1f0e
=00400000 m_nMsgDragList   : 0x905a4d
+0x044 m_nModalResult   : -855002112
+0x048 m_pDropTarget    : 0x4c01b821 COleDropTarget
+0x04c m_pCtrlCont      : 0x685421cd COleControlContainer
+0x050 m_pCtrlSite      : 0x70207369 COleControlSite
=00400000 wndBottom        : CWnd
```

0n188 0xBC 1011 1100 ***!sysinfo*** *Shows BIOS and CPU information* ***(KA)***

```
+0x000 __VFN_table : 0x00905a4d
=00400000 classCObject     : CRuntimeClass
=00400000 classCCmdTarget  : CRuntimeClass
=00400000 _commandEntries  : [0] AFX_OLECMDMAP_ENTRY
=00400000 commandMap       : AFX_OLECMDMAP
=00400000 _dispatchEntries : [0] AFX_DISPMAP_ENTRY
=00400000 _dispatchEntryCount : 0x905a4d
=00400000 _dwStockPropMask : 0x905a4d
=00400000 dispatchMap      : AFX_DISPMAP
=00400000 _connectionEntries : [0] AFX_CONNECTIONMAP_ENTRY
=00400000 connectionMap    : AFX_CONNECTIONMAP
=00400000 _interfaceEntries : [0] AFX_INTERFACEMAP_ENTRY
=00400000 interfaceMap     : AFX_INTERFACEMAP
=00400000 _eventsinkEntries : [0] AFX_EVENTSINKMAP_ENTRY
=00400000 _eventsinkEntryCount : 0x905a4d
=00400000 eventsinkMap     : AFX_EVENTSINKMAP
+0x004 m_dwRef          : 3
+0x008 m_pOuterUnknown  : 0x00000004 IUnknown
+0x00c m_xInnerUnknown  : 0xffff
+0x010 m_xDispatch      : CCmdTarget::XDispatch
+0x014 m_bResultExpected : 0
+0x018 m_xConnPtContainer : CCmdTarget::XConnPtContainer
+0x01c m_pModuleState   : (null)
=00400000 classCWnd        : CRuntimeClass
+0x020 m_hWnd           : (null)
=00400000 wndTop           : CWnd
=00400000 wndBottom        : CWnd
=00400000 wndTopMost       : CWnd
=00400000 wndNoTopMost     : CWnd
+0x024 m_bEnableActiveAccessibility : 0
+0x028 m_pStdObject     : (null)
=00400000 m_pfnNotifyWinEvent : 0x00905a4d          void  +905a4d
+0x02c m_pProxy         : (null)
=00400000 _interfaceEntries : [0] AFX_INTERFACEMAP_ENTRY
```

```
   =00400000 interfaceMap     : AFX_INTERFACEMAP
   +0x030 m_xAccessible    : CWnd::XAccessible
   +0x034 m_xAccessibleServer : CWnd::XAccessibleServer
   +0x038 m_hWndOwner      : (null)
   +0x03c m_nFlags         : 0xe8
   +0x040 m_pfnSuper       : 0x0eba1f0e         long  +eba1f0e
   =00400000 m_nMsgDragList   : 0x905a4d
   +0x044 m_nModalResult   : -855002112
   +0x048 m_pDropTarget    : 0x4c01b821 COleDropTarget
   +0x04c m_pCtrlCont      : 0x685421cd COleControlContainer
   +0x050 m_pCtrlSite      : 0x70207369 COleControlSite
=00400000 wndTopMost       : CWnd
   +0x000 __VFN_table : 0x00905a4d
   =00400000 classCObject     : CRuntimeClass
   =00400000 classCCmdTarget  : CRuntimeClass
   =00400000 _commandEntries  : [0] AFX_OLECMDMAP_ENTRY
   =00400000 commandMap       : AFX_OLECMDMAP
   =00400000 _dispatchEntries : [0] AFX_DISPMAP_ENTRY
   =00400000 _dispatchEntryCount : 0x905a4d
   =00400000 _dwStockPropMask : 0x905a4d
   =00400000 dispatchMap      : AFX_DISPMAP
   =00400000 _connectionEntries : [0] AFX_CONNECTIONMAP_ENTRY
   =00400000 connectionMap    : AFX_CONNECTIONMAP
   =00400000 _interfaceEntries : [0] AFX_INTERFACEMAP_ENTRY
   =00400000 interfaceMap     : AFX_INTERFACEMAP
   =00400000 _eventsinkEntries : [0] AFX_EVENTSINKMAP_ENTRY
   =00400000 _eventsinkEntryCount : 0x905a4d
   =00400000 eventsinkMap     : AFX_EVENTSINKMAP
   +0x004 m_dwRef          : 3
   +0x008 m_pOuterUnknown  : 0x00000004 IUnknown
   +0x00c m_xInnerUnknown  : 0xffff
   +0x010 m_xDispatch      : CCmdTarget::XDispatch
   +0x014 m_bResultExpected : 0
   +0x018 m_xConnPtContainer : CCmdTarget::XConnPtContainer
```

```
+0x01c m_pModuleState   : (null)
=00400000 classCWnd        : CRuntimeClass
+0x020 m_hWnd           : (null)
=00400000 wndTop           : CWnd
=00400000 wndBottom        : CWnd
=00400000 wndTopMost       : CWnd
=00400000 wndNoTopMost     : CWnd
+0x024 m_bEnableActiveAccessibility : 0
+0x028 m_pStdObject     : (null)
=00400000 m_pfnNotifyWinEvent : 0x00905a4d           void  +905a4d
+0x02c m_pProxy         : (null)
=00400000 _interfaceEntries : [0] AFX_INTERFACEMAP_ENTRY
=00400000 interfaceMap     : AFX_INTERFACEMAP
+0x030 m_xAccessible    : CWnd::XAccessible
+0x034 m_xAccessibleServer : CWnd::XAccessibleServer
+0x038 m_hWndOwner      : (null)
+0x03c m_nFlags         : 0xe8
+0x040 m_pfnSuper       : 0x0eba1f0e           long  +eba1f0e
=00400000 m_nMsgDragList   : 0x905a4d
+0x044 m_nModalResult   : -855002112
+0x048 m_pDropTarget    : 0x4c01b821 COleDropTarget
+0x04c m_pCtrlCont      : 0x685421cd COleControlContainer
+0x050 m_pCtrlSite      : 0x70207369 COleControlSite
=00400000 wndNoTopMost     : CWnd
+0x000 __VFN_table : 0x00905a4d
=00400000 classCObject     : CRuntimeClass
=00400000 classCCmdTarget  : CRuntimeClass
=00400000 _commandEntries  : [0] AFX_OLECMDMAP_ENTRY
=00400000 commandMap       : AFX_OLECMDMAP
=00400000 _dispatchEntries : [0] AFX_DISPMAP_ENTRY
=00400000 _dispatchEntryCount : 0x905a4d
=00400000 _dwStockPropMask : 0x905a4d
=00400000 dispatchMap      : AFX_DISPMAP
=00400000 _connectionEntries : [0] AFX_CONNECTIONMAP_ENTRY
```

***(AA)* .outmask** *Sets the output mask* *0n191 0xBF 1011 1111*

```
=00400000 connectionMap    : AFX_CONNECTIONMAP
=00400000 _interfaceEntries : [0] AFX_INTERFACEMAP_ENTRY
=00400000 interfaceMap     : AFX_INTERFACEMAP
=00400000 _eventsinkEntries : [0] AFX_EVENTSINKMAP_ENTRY
=00400000 _eventsinkEntryCount : 0x905a4d
=00400000 eventsinkMap     : AFX_EVENTSINKMAP
+0x004 m_dwRef          : 3
+0x008 m_pOuterUnknown  : 0x00000004 IUnknown
+0x00c m_xInnerUnknown  : 0xffff
+0x010 m_xDispatch      : CCmdTarget::XDispatch
+0x014 m_bResultExpected : 0
+0x018 m_xConnPtContainer : CCmdTarget::XConnPtContainer
+0x01c m_pModuleState   : (null)
=00400000 classCWnd        : CRuntimeClass
+0x020 m_hWnd           : (null)
=00400000 wndTop           : CWnd
=00400000 wndBottom        : CWnd
=00400000 wndTopMost       : CWnd
=00400000 wndNoTopMost     : CWnd
+0x024 m_bEnableActiveAccessibility : 0
+0x028 m_pStdObject     : (null)
=00400000 m_pfnNotifyWinEvent : 0x00905a4d          void  +905a4d
+0x02c m_pProxy         : (null)
=00400000 _interfaceEntries : [0] AFX_INTERFACEMAP_ENTRY
=00400000 interfaceMap     : AFX_INTERFACEMAP
+0x030 m_xAccessible    : CWnd::XAccessible
+0x034 m_xAccessibleServer : CWnd::XAccessibleServer
+0x038 m_hWndOwner      : (null)
+0x03c m_nFlags         : 0xe8
+0x040 m_pfnSuper       : 0x0eba1f0e           long  +eba1f0e
=00400000 m_nMsgDragList   : 0x905a4d
+0x044 m_nModalResult   : -855002112
+0x048 m_pDropTarget    : 0x4c01b821 COleDropTarget
+0x04c m_pCtrlCont      : 0x685421cd COleControlContainer
```

```
        +0x050 m_pCtrlSite      : 0x70207369 COleControlSite
      +0x024 m_bEnableActiveAccessibility : 0
      +0x028 m_pStdObject     : (null)
      =00400000 m_pfnNotifyWinEvent : 0x00905a4d        void  +905a4d
      +0x02c m_pProxy         : (null)
      =00400000 _interfaceEntries : [0] AFX_INTERFACEMAP_ENTRY
        +0x000 piid             : 0x00905a4d
        +0x004 nOffset          : 3
      =00400000 interfaceMap     : AFX_INTERFACEMAP
        +0x000 pfnGetBaseMap    : 0x00905a4d           AFX_INTERFACEMAP*
+905a4d
        +0x004 pEntry           : 0x00000003 AFX_INTERFACEMAP_ENTRY
      +0x030 m_xAccessible    : CWnd::XAccessible
        +0x000 __VFN_table : 0x5a2f3f74
      +0x034 m_xAccessibleServer : CWnd::XAccessibleServer
        +0x000 __VFN_table : 0x5a2f3fe8
      +0x038 m_hWndOwner      : (null)
      +0x03c m_nFlags         : 0
      +0x040 m_pfnSuper       : 0x75f2d060        long
USER32!DefWindowProcA+0
      =00400000 m_nMsgDragList   : 0x905a4d
      +0x044 m_nModalResult   : 0
      +0x048 m_pDropTarget    : (null)
      +0x04c m_pCtrlCont      : (null)
      +0x050 m_pCtrlSite      : (null)
   +0x024 m_pActiveWnd      : (null)
   +0x028 m_bAutoDelete     : 0
   +0x02c m_hThread         : 0x000001c8
   +0x030 m_nThreadID       : 0x2004
   +0x034 m_pThreadParams   : (null)
   +0x038 m_pfnThreadProc   : (null)
   +0x03c m_lpfnOleTermOrFreeLib : (null)
   +0x040 m_pMessageFilter : (null)
   =0041f6b0 CGDIThread::classCGDIThread : CRuntimeClass
      +0x000 m_lpszClassName  : 0x0041f6a0  "CGDIThread"
```

(KL) .pagein *Pages in specified memory address* *0n193 0xC1 1100 0001*

```
      +0x004 m_nObjectSize    : 112
      +0x008 m_wSchema        : 0xffff
      +0x00c m_pfnCreateObject : (null)
      +0x010 m_pfnGetBaseClass : 0x00411c3a       CRuntimeClass*
mtgdi!ILT+3125(?_GetBaseClassCGDIThreadKGPAUCRuntimeClassXZ)+0
      +0x014 m_pNextClass     : (null)
      +0x018 m_pClassInit     : (null)
   +0x044 m_rectBorder     : CRect
      +0x000 left             : 0
      +0x004 top              : 0
      +0x008 right            : 1060
      +0x00c bottom           : 596
   +0x054 m_hDC            : 0xf0011110 HDC__
      +0x000 unused           : ??
   +0x058 m_dc             : CDC
      +0x000 __VFN_table : 0x5a2fe734
      =00400000 classCObject     : CRuntimeClass
         +0x000 m_lpszClassName  : 0x00905a4d  "???"
         +0x004 m_nObjectSize    : 3
         +0x008 m_wSchema        : 4
         +0x00c m_pfnCreateObject : 0x0000ffff          CObject*  +ffff
         +0x010 m_pfnGetBaseClass : 0x000000b8          CRuntimeClass*  +b8
         +0x014 m_pNextClass     : (null)
         +0x018 m_pClassInit     : 0x00000040 AFX_CLASSINIT
      =00400000 classCDC         : CRuntimeClass
         +0x000 m_lpszClassName  : 0x00905a4d  "???"
         +0x004 m_nObjectSize    : 3
         +0x008 m_wSchema        : 4
         +0x00c m_pfnCreateObject : 0x0000ffff          CObject*  +ffff
         +0x010 m_pfnGetBaseClass : 0x000000b8          CRuntimeClass*  +b8
         +0x014 m_pNextClass     : (null)
         +0x018 m_pClassInit     : 0x00000040 AFX_CLASSINIT
      +0x004 m_hDC            : 0xf0011110 HDC__
         +0x000 unused           : ??
```

0n194 0xC2 1100 0010 ***!swd*** *Shows software watchdog timer state* ***(KA)***

```
      +0x008 m_hAttribDC      : 0xf0011110 HDC__
         +0x000 unused           : ??
      +0x00c m_bPrinting      : 0
   +0x068 m_hEventKill     : 0x000001ac
   +0x06c m_hEventDead     : 0x000001bc
   =00422618 CGDIThread::m_hAnotherDead : 0x0000007c
   =00422600 CGDIThread::m_csGDILock : _RTL_CRITICAL_SECTION
      +0x000 DebugInfo        : 0x0062a098 _RTL_CRITICAL_SECTION_DEBUG
         +0x000 Type             : 0
         +0x002 CreatorBackTraceIndex : 0
         +0x004 CriticalSection  : 0x00422600 _RTL_CRITICAL_SECTION
         +0x008 ProcessLocksList : _LIST_ENTRY [ 0x62a310 - 0x6299e8 ]
         +0x010 EntryCount       : 0
         +0x014 ContentionCount  : 0x1113d
         +0x018 Flags            : 0
         +0x01c CreatorBackTraceIndexHigh : 0
         +0x01e SpareWORD        : 0xbaad
      +0x004 LockCount        : -98
      +0x008 RecursionCount   : 1
      +0x00c OwningThread     : 0x00001ac0
      +0x010 LockSemaphore    : 0x000000e8
      +0x014 SpinCount        : 0
   =0041f770 CBallThread::classCBallThread : CRuntimeClass
      +0x000 m_lpszClassName  : 0x0041f690  "CBallThread"
      +0x004 m_nObjectSize    : 148
      +0x008 m_wSchema        : 0xffff
      +0x00c m_pfnCreateObject : (null)
      +0x010 m_pfnGetBaseClass : 0x00411a41        CRuntimeClass*
mtgdi!ILT+2620(?_GetBaseClassCBallThreadKGPAUCRuntimeClassXZ)+0
      +0x014 m_pNextClass     : (null)
      +0x018 m_pClassInit     : (null)
   +0x070 m_rectPosition   : CRect
      +0x000 left             : 921
      +0x004 top              : 474
```

(AA) .pcmd *Sets command to execute on prompt* *0n195 0xC3 1100 0011*

```
   +0x008 right             : 966
   +0x00c bottom            : 519
+0x080 m_ptVelocity      : CPoint
   +0x000 x                 : -11
   +0x004 y                 : -6
+0x088 m_hBrush          : 0xb21021d5 HBRUSH__
   +0x000 unused            : ??
+0x08c m_brush           : CBrush
   +0x000 __VFN_table : 0x5a2feb2c
   =00400000 classCObject     : CRuntimeClass
      +0x000 m_lpszClassName  : 0x00905a4d  "???"
      +0x004 m_nObjectSize    : 3
      +0x008 m_wSchema        : 4
      +0x00c m_pfnCreateObject : 0x0000ffff          CObject*  +ffff
      +0x010 m_pfnGetBaseClass : 0x000000b8          CRuntimeClass*  +b8
      +0x014 m_pNextClass     : (null)
      +0x018 m_pClassInit     : 0x00000040 AFX_CLASSINIT
   =00400000 classCGdiObject  : CRuntimeClass
      +0x000 m_lpszClassName  : 0x00905a4d  "???"
      +0x004 m_nObjectSize    : 3
      +0x008 m_wSchema        : 4
      +0x00c m_pfnCreateObject : 0x0000ffff          CObject*  +ffff
      +0x010 m_pfnGetBaseClass : 0x000000b8          CRuntimeClass*  +b8
      +0x014 m_pNextClass     : (null)
      +0x018 m_pClassInit     : 0x00000040 AFX_CLASSINIT
   +0x004 m_hObject        : 0xb21021d5
   =00400000 classCBrush      : CRuntimeClass
      +0x000 m_lpszClassName  : 0x00905a4d  "???"
      +0x004 m_nObjectSize    : 3
      +0x008 m_wSchema        : 4
      +0x00c m_pfnCreateObject : 0x0000ffff          CObject*  +ffff
      +0x010 m_pfnGetBaseClass : 0x000000b8          CRuntimeClass*  +b8
      +0x014 m_pNextClass     : (null)
      +0x018 m_pClassInit     : 0x00000040 AFX_CLASSINIT
```

For a linked list we can specify the name that links the linked list, for example, a pointer that points to the next node by using the following command:

dt <symbol> <address> -l *fieldname*

```
0:015> dt CBallThread 0x3a0fdc4 -l m_pMainWnd
mtgdi!CBallThread
m_pMainWnd at 0x3a0fdc4
---------------------------------------------
   +0x000 __VFN_table : 0x038109c0
   =00400000 classCObject     : CRuntimeClass
   =00400000 classCCmdTarget  : CRuntimeClass
   =00400000 _commandEntries  : [0] AFX_OLECMDMAP_ENTRY
   =00400000 commandMap       : AFX_OLECMDMAP
   =00400000 _dispatchEntries : [0] AFX_DISPMAP_ENTRY
   =00400000 _dispatchEntryCount : 0x905a4d
   =00400000 _dwStockPropMask : 0x905a4d
   =00400000 dispatchMap      : AFX_DISPMAP
   =00400000 _connectionEntries : [0] AFX_CONNECTIONMAP_ENTRY
   =00400000 connectionMap    : AFX_CONNECTIONMAP
   =00400000 _interfaceEntries : [0] AFX_INTERFACEMAP_ENTRY
   =00400000 interfaceMap     : AFX_INTERFACEMAP
   =00400000 _eventsinkEntries : [0] AFX_EVENTSINKMAP_ENTRY
   =00400000 _eventsinkEntryCount : 0x905a4d
   =00400000 eventsinkMap     : AFX_EVENTSINKMAP
   +0x004 m_dwRef           : 60882464
   +0x008 m_pOuterUnknown   : 0x00414834 IUnknown
   +0x00c m_xInnerUnknown   : 0
   +0x010 m_xDispatch       : CCmdTarget::XDispatch
   +0x014 m_bResultExpected : 58788496
   +0x018 m_xConnPtContainer : CCmdTarget::XConnPtContainer
   +0x01c m_pModuleState    : 0x03a0fdf0 AFX_MODULE_STATE
   =00400000 classCWinThread  : CRuntimeClass
```

```
    +0x020 m_pMainWnd        : 0x5a331107 CWnd
    +0x024 m_pActiveWnd      : 0x00000001 CWnd
    +0x028 m_bAutoDelete     : 0
    +0x02c m_hThread         : 0x03a0fe04
    +0x030 m_nThreadID       : 0x5a366062
    +0x034 m_pThreadParams   : 0x00000001
    +0x038 m_pfnThreadProc   : 0x03810b00     unsigned int  +3810b00
    +0x03c m_lpfnOleTermOrFreeLib : 0x00000001     void  +1
    +0x040 m_pMessageFilter : 0x03a0fe1c COleMessageFilter
    =0041f6b0 CGDIThread::classCGDIThread : CRuntimeClass
    +0x044 m_rectBorder      : CRect
    +0x054 m_hDC             : 0x03810b00 HDC__
    +0x058 m_dc              : CDC
    +0x068 m_hEventKill      : (null)
    +0x06c m_hEventDead      : 0x03810a90
    =00422618 CGDIThread::m_hAnotherDead : 0x0000007c
    =00422600 CGDIThread::m_csGDILock : _RTL_CRITICAL_SECTION
    =0041f770 CBallThread::classCBallThread : CRuntimeClass
    +0x070 m_rectPosition    : CRect
    +0x080 m_ptVelocity      : CPoint
    +0x088 m_hBrush          : 0x03a0ff34 HBRUSH__
    +0x08c m_brush           : CBrush

m_pMainWnd at 0x5a331107
---------------------------------------------
    +0x000 __VFN_table : 0xeb04c483
    =00400000 classCObject      : CRuntimeClass
    =00400000 classCCmdTarget   : CRuntimeClass
    =00400000 _commandEntries   : [0] AFX_OLECMDMAP_ENTRY
    =00400000 commandMap        : AFX_OLECMDMAP
    =00400000 _dispatchEntries : [0] AFX_DISPMAP_ENTRY
    =00400000 _dispatchEntryCount : 0x905a4d
    =00400000 _dwStockPropMask : 0x905a4d
    =00400000 dispatchMap       : AFX_DISPMAP
```

0n198 0xC6 1100 0110 ***!stl*** *Dumps STL variables like vector and list* ***(AA)***

```
=00400000 _connectionEntries : [0] AFX_CONNECTIONMAP_ENTRY
=00400000 connectionMap    : AFX_CONNECTIONMAP
=00400000 _interfaceEntries : [0] AFX_INTERFACEMAP_ENTRY
=00400000 interfaceMap     : AFX_INTERFACEMAP
=00400000 _eventsinkEntries : [0] AFX_EVENTSINKMAP_ENTRY
=00400000 _eventsinkEntryCount : 0x905a4d
=00400000 eventsinkMap     : AFX_EVENTSINKMAP
+0x004 m_dwRef           : -62026992
+0x008 m_pOuterUnknown   : 0x51fee183 IUnknown
+0x00c m_xInnerUnknown   : 0x179c15ff
+0x010 m_xDispatch       : CCmdTarget::XDispatch
+0x014 m_bResultExpected : -62551292
+0x018 m_xConnPtContainer : CCmdTarget::XConnPtContainer
+0x01c m_pModuleState    : 0x04c25de5 AFX_MODULE_STATE
=00400000 classCWinThread  : CRuntimeClass
+0x020 m_pMainWnd        : 0xcccccc00 CWnd
+0x024 m_pActiveWnd      : 0xcccccccc CWnd
+0x028 m_bAutoDelete     : 1442810828
+0x02c m_hThread         : 0x458bec8b
+0x030 m_nThreadID       : 0x15ff5008
+0x034 m_pThreadParams   : 0x5a2f1780
+0x038 m_pfnThreadProc   : 0x5d04c483     unsigned int  +5d04c483
+0x03c m_lpfnOleTermOrFreeLib : 0xcc0004c2     void  +cc0004c2
+0x040 m_pMessageFilter : 0xcccccccc COleMessageFilter
=0041f6b0 CGDIThread::classCGDIThread : CRuntimeClass
+0x044 m_rectBorder      : CRect
+0x054 m_hDC             : 0xccccc35d HDC__
+0x058 m_dc              : CDC
+0x068 m_hEventKill      : 0x55ff8bcc
+0x06c m_hEventDead      : 0x006aec8b
=00422618 CGDIThread::m_hAnotherDead : 0x0000007c
=00422600 CGDIThread::m_csGDILock : _RTL_CRITICAL_SECTION
=0041f770 CBallThread::classCBallThread : CRuntimeClass
+0x070 m_rectPosition    : CRect
```

(KA) .process *Specifies process for process context* *0n199 0xC7 1100 0111*

```
   +0x080 m_ptVelocity     : CPoint
   +0x088 m_hBrush         : 0xcc000cc2 HBRUSH__
   +0x08c m_brush          : CBrush

m_pMainWnd at 0xcccccc00
---------------------------------------------
   +0x000 __VFN_table : ????
   =00400000 classCObject     : CRuntimeClass
   =00400000 classCCmdTarget  : CRuntimeClass
   =00400000 _commandEntries  : [0] AFX_OLECMDMAP_ENTRY
   =00400000 commandMap       : AFX_OLECMDMAP
   =00400000 _dispatchEntries : [0] AFX_DISPMAP_ENTRY
   =00400000 _dispatchEntryCount : 0x905a4d
   =00400000 _dwStockPropMask : 0x905a4d
   =00400000 dispatchMap      : AFX_DISPMAP
   =00400000 _connectionEntries : [0] AFX_CONNECTIONMAP_ENTRY
   =00400000 connectionMap    : AFX_CONNECTIONMAP
   =00400000 _interfaceEntries : [0] AFX_INTERFACEMAP_ENTRY
   =00400000 interfaceMap     : AFX_INTERFACEMAP
   =00400000 _eventsinkEntries : [0] AFX_EVENTSINKMAP_ENTRY
   =00400000 _eventsinkEntryCount : 0x905a4d
   =00400000 eventsinkMap     : AFX_EVENTSINKMAP
   +0x004 m_dwRef          : ??
   +0x008 m_pOuterUnknown  : ????
   +0x00c m_xInnerUnknown  : ??
   +0x010 m_xDispatch      : CCmdTarget::XDispatch
   +0x014 m_bResultExpected : ??
   +0x018 m_xConnPtContainer : CCmdTarget::XConnPtContainer
   +0x01c m_pModuleState   : ????
   =00400000 classCWinThread  : CRuntimeClass
   +0x020 m_pMainWnd       : ????
   +0x024 m_pActiveWnd     : ????
   +0x028 m_bAutoDelete    : ??
   +0x02c m_hThread        : ????
```

```
   +0x030 m_nThreadID      : ??
   +0x034 m_pThreadParams  : ????
   +0x038 m_pfnThreadProc  : ????
   +0x03c m_lpfnOleTermOrFreeLib : ????
   +0x040 m_pMessageFilter : ????
   =0041f6b0 CGDIThread::classCGDIThread : CRuntimeClass
   +0x044 m_rectBorder     : CRect
   +0x054 m_hDC            : ????
   +0x058 m_dc             : CDC
   +0x068 m_hEventKill     : ????
   +0x06c m_hEventDead     : ????
   =00422618 CGDIThread::m_hAnotherDead : 0x0000007c
   =00422600 CGDIThread::m_csGDILock : _RTL_CRITICAL_SECTION
   =0041f770 CBallThread::classCBallThread : CRuntimeClass
   +0x070 m_rectPosition   : CRect
   +0x080 m_ptVelocity     : CPoint
   +0x088 m_hBrush         : ????
   +0x08c m_brush          : CBrush
```

Finally the sniper shot! The following command provides the verbose output that gives us additional information such as the total size of a structure or a class and the number of elements with all symbols:

dt <symbol> <address> -v

```
0:015> dt CBallThread 0x3a0fdc4 -v
mtgdi!CBallThread
class CBallThread, 18 elements, 0x94 bytes
   +0x000 __BaseClass class CGDIThread, 24 elements, 0x70 bytes
   +0x000 __BaseClass class CWinThread, 44 elements, 0x44 bytes
   +0x000 __BaseClass class CCmdTarget, 97 elements, 0x20 bytes
   +0x000 __BaseClass class CObject, 22 elements, 0x4 bytes
```

```
+0x000 __VFN_table : 0x038109c0 5 entries
 [00] mtgdi!CBallThread::`vftable'
<function> GetRuntimeClass     CRuntimeClass* ( void )+3a0fdc4
<function> ~CObject     void ( void )+3a0fdc4
<function> operator new     void* (
      unsigned int,
      char*,
      int)+3a0fdc4
<function> operator new     void* (
      unsigned int,
      void*)+3a0fdc4
<function> operator new     void* (
      unsigned int)+3a0fdc4
<function> operator delete     void (
      void*,
      char*,
      int)+3a0fdc4
<function> operator delete     void (
      void*,
      void*)+3a0fdc4
<function> operator delete     void (
      void*)+3a0fdc4
<function> CObject     void (
      CObject*)+3a0fdc4
<function> CObject     void ( void )+3a0fdc4
<function> operator=     void (
      CObject*)+3a0fdc4
<function> IsSerializable     int ( void )+3a0fdc4
<function> IsKindOf     int (
      CRuntimeClass*)+3a0fdc4
<function> Serialize     void (
      CArchive*)+3a0fdc4
<function> AssertValid     void ( void )+3a0fdc4
<function> Dump     void (
```

```
        CDumpContext*)+3a0fdc4
   =00400000 classCObject     : struct CRuntimeClass, 15 elements, 0x1c
bytes
   <function> _GetBaseClass     CRuntimeClass* ( void )+3a0fdc4
   <function> GetThisClass     CRuntimeClass* ( void )+3a0fdc4
   <function> __local_vftable_ctor_closure     void ( void )+3a0fdc4
   <function> __vecDelDtor     void* (
        unsigned int)+3a0fdc4
   <function> _GetBaseClass     CRuntimeClass* ( void )+3a0fdc4
   =00400000 classCCmdTarget  : struct CRuntimeClass, 15 elements, 0x1c
bytes
   <function> GetThisClass     CRuntimeClass* ( void )+3a0fdc4
   <function> GetRuntimeClass     CRuntimeClass* ( void )+3a0fdc4
   <function> CCmdTarget     void (
        CCmdTarget*)+3a0fdc4
   <function> CCmdTarget     void ( void )+3a0fdc4
   <function> GetIDispatch     IDispatch* (
        int)+3a0fdc4
   <function> FromIDispatch     CCmdTarget* (
        IDispatch*)+3a0fdc4
   <function> IsResultExpected     int ( void )+3a0fdc4
   <function> EnableAutomation     void ( void )+3a0fdc4
   <function> EnableConnections     void ( void )+3a0fdc4
   <function> BeginWaitCursor     void ( void )+3a0fdc4
   <function> EndWaitCursor     void ( void )+3a0fdc4
   <function> RestoreWaitCursor     void ( void )+3a0fdc4
   <function> EnumOleVerbs     int (
        IEnumOLEVERB**)+3a0fdc4
   <function> DoOleVerb     int (
        long,
        tagMSG*,
        HWND__*,
        tagRECT*)+3a0fdc4
   <function> OnCmdMsg     int (
        unsigned int,
```

```
        int,
        void*,
        AFX_CMDHANDLERINFO*)+3a0fdc4
  <function> OnFinalRelease     void ( void )+3a0fdc4
  <function> IsInvokeAllowed     int (
        long)+3a0fdc4
  <function> EnableTypeLib     void ( void )+3a0fdc4
  <function> GetTypeInfoOfGuid     HRESULT (
        unsigned long,
        _GUID*,
        ITypeInfo**)+3a0fdc4
  <function> GetDispatchIID     int (
        _GUID*)+3a0fdc4
  <function> GetTypeInfoCount     unsigned int ( void )+3a0fdc4
  <function> GetTypeLibCache     CTypeLibCache* ( void )+3a0fdc4
  <function> GetTypeLib     HRESULT (
        unsigned long,
        ITypeLib**)+3a0fdc4
  <function> ~CCmdTarget     void ( void )+3a0fdc4
  <function> Dump     void (
        CDumpContext*)+3a0fdc4
  <function> AssertValid     void ( void )+3a0fdc4
  <function> GetNotSupported     void ( void )+3a0fdc4
  <function> SetNotSupported     void ( void )+3a0fdc4
  <function> GetRoutingView     CView* ( void )+3a0fdc4
  <function> GetRoutingFrame     CFrameWnd* ( void )+3a0fdc4
  <function> GetRoutingView_     CView* ( void )+3a0fdc4
  <function> GetRoutingFrame_     CFrameWnd* ( void )+3a0fdc4
  <function> GetThisMessageMap     AFX_MSGMAP* ( void )+3a0fdc4
  <function> GetMessageMap     AFX_MSGMAP* ( void )+3a0fdc4
  =00400000 _commandEntries  : [0] struct AFX_OLECMDMAP_ENTRY, 3 elements,
0xc bytes
  =00400000 commandMap       : struct AFX_OLECMDMAP, 2 elements, 0x8 bytes
  <function> GetThisCommandMap     AFX_OLECMDMAP* ( void )+3a0fdc4
```

0n204 0xCC 1100 1100 ***!srb*** *Shows SCSI Request Block* ***(KA)***

```
   <function> GetCommandMap     AFX_OLECMDMAP* ( void )+3a0fdc4
   =00400000 _dispatchEntries : [0] struct AFX_DISPMAP_ENTRY, 8 elements, 
0x20 bytes
   =00400000 _dispatchEntryCount : 0x905a4d
   =00400000 _dwStockPropMask : 0x905a4d
   =00400000 dispatchMap      : struct AFX_DISPMAP, 4 elements, 0x10 bytes
   <function> GetThisDispatchMap     AFX_DISPMAP* ( void )+3a0fdc4
   <function> GetDispatchMap     AFX_DISPMAP* ( void )+3a0fdc4
   =00400000 _connectionEntries : [0] struct AFX_CONNECTIONMAP_ENTRY, 2 
elements, 0x8 bytes
   =00400000 connectionMap    : struct AFX_CONNECTIONMAP, 2 elements, 0x8 
bytes
   <function> GetThisConnectionMap     AFX_CONNECTIONMAP* ( void )+3a0fdc4
   <function> GetConnectionMap     AFX_CONNECTIONMAP* ( void )+3a0fdc4
   =00400000 _interfaceEntries : [0] struct AFX_INTERFACEMAP_ENTRY, 2 
elements, 0x8 bytes
   =00400000 interfaceMap     : struct AFX_INTERFACEMAP, 2 elements, 0x8 
bytes
   <function> GetThisInterfaceMap     AFX_INTERFACEMAP* ( void )+3a0fdc4
   <function> GetInterfaceMap     AFX_INTERFACEMAP* ( void )+3a0fdc4
   =00400000 _eventsinkEntries : [0] struct AFX_EVENTSINKMAP_ENTRY, 3 
elements, 0x28 bytes
   =00400000 _eventsinkEntryCount : 0x905a4d
   =00400000 eventsinkMap     : struct AFX_EVENTSINKMAP, 3 elements, 0xc 
bytes
   <function> GetThisEventSinkMap     AFX_EVENTSINKMAP* ( void )+3a0fdc4
   <function> GetEventSinkMap     AFX_EVENTSINKMAP* ( void )+3a0fdc4
   +0x004 m_dwRef          : 60882464
   +0x008 m_pOuterUnknown  : 0x00414834 struct IUnknown, 7 elements, 0x4 
bytes
   +0x00c m_xInnerUnknown  : 0
   <function> EnableAggregation     void ( void )+3a0fdc4
   <function> ExternalDisconnect     void ( void )+3a0fdc4
   <function> GetControllingUnknown     IUnknown* ( void )+3a0fdc4
   <function> InternalQueryInterface     unsigned long (
         void*,
         void**)+3a0fdc4
```

(AA) .readmem *Copies binary data from a file* *0n205 0xCD 1100 1101*

```
   <function> InternalAddRef     unsigned long ( void )+3a0fdc4
   <function> InternalRelease     unsigned long ( void )+3a0fdc4
   <function> ExternalQueryInterface     unsigned long (
         void*,
         void**)+3a0fdc4
   <function> ExternalAddRef     unsigned long ( void )+3a0fdc4
   <function> ExternalRelease     unsigned long ( void )+3a0fdc4
   <function> GetInterface     IUnknown* (
         void*)+3a0fdc4
   <function> QueryAggregates     IUnknown* (
         void*)+3a0fdc4
   <function> OnCreateAggregates     int ( void )+3a0fdc4
   <function> GetInterfaceHook     IUnknown* (
         void*)+3a0fdc4
struct XDispatch, 1 elements, 0x4 bytes
   +0x010 m_xDispatch      : struct CCmdTarget::XDispatch, 1 elements, 0x4
bytes
   +0x014 m_bResultExpected : 58788496
   <function> GetStandardProp     void (
         AFX_DISPMAP_ENTRY*,
         tagVARIANT*,
         unsigned int*)+3a0fdc4
   <function> SetStandardProp     long (
         AFX_DISPMAP_ENTRY*,
         tagDISPPARAMS*,
         unsigned int*)+3a0fdc4
   <function> GetEntryCount     unsigned int (
         AFX_DISPMAP*)+3a0fdc4
   <function> GetDispEntry     AFX_DISPMAP_ENTRY* (
         long)+3a0fdc4
   <function> MemberIDFromName     long (
         AFX_DISPMAP*,
         char*)+3a0fdc4
   <function> GetStackSize     unsigned int (
```

```
        unsigned char*,
        unsigned short)+3a0fdc4
   <function> PushStackArgs     long (
        unsigned char*,
        unsigned char*,
        void*,
        unsigned short,
        tagDISPPARAMS*,
        unsigned int*,
        tagVARIANT*,
        CVariantBoolConverter*)+3a0fdc4
   <function> CallMemberFunc     long (
        AFX_DISPMAP_ENTRY*,
        unsigned short,
        tagVARIANT*,
        tagDISPPARAMS*,
        unsigned int*)+3a0fdc4
   <function> OnEvent     int (
        unsigned int,
        AFX_EVENT*,
        AFX_CMDHANDLERINFO*)+3a0fdc4
   <function> GetEventSinkEntry     AFX_EVENTSINKMAP_ENTRY* (
        unsigned int,
        AFX_EVENT*)+3a0fdc4
struct XConnPtContainer, 1 elements, 0x4 bytes
   +0x018 m_xConnPtContainer : struct CCmdTarget::XConnPtContainer, 1
elements, 0x4 bytes
   +0x01c m_pModuleState   : 0x03a0fdf0 class AFX_MODULE_STATE, 38 elements,
0xa8 bytes
   <function> GetExtraConnectionPoints     int (
        CPtrArray*)+3a0fdc4
   <function> GetConnectionHook     IConnectionPoint* (
        _GUID*)+3a0fdc4
   <function> operator=     CCmdTarget* (
        CCmdTarget*)+3a0fdc4
```

(KL) .reboot *Restarts the target* *0n207 0xCF 1100 1111*

```
   <function> __local_vftable_ctor_closure     void ( void )+3a0fdc4
   <function> __vecDelDtor     void* (
         unsigned int)+3a0fdc4
   <function> _GetBaseClass     CRuntimeClass* ( void )+3a0fdc4
   =00400000 classCWinThread  : struct CRuntimeClass, 15 elements, 0x1c
bytes
   <function> GetThisClass     CRuntimeClass* ( void )+3a0fdc4
   <function> GetRuntimeClass     CRuntimeClass* ( void )+3a0fdc4
   <function> CWinThread     void (
         CWinThread*)+3a0fdc4
   <function> CWinThread     void (
         <function>*,
         void*)+3a0fdc4
   <function> CWinThread     void ( void )+3a0fdc4
   <function> CreateThread     int (
         unsigned long,
         unsigned int,
         _SECURITY_ATTRIBUTES*)+3a0fdc4
   +0x020 m_pMainWnd       : 0x5a331107 class CWnd, 510 elements, 0x54 bytes
   +0x024 m_pActiveWnd     : 0x00000001 class CWnd, 510 elements, 0x54 bytes
   +0x028 m_bAutoDelete    : 0
   +0x02c m_hThread        : 0x03a0fe04
   <function> operator void *     void* ( void )+3a0fdc4
   +0x030 m_nThreadID      : 0x5a366062
   <function> GetThreadPriority     int ( void )+3a0fdc4
   <function> SetThreadPriority     int (
         int)+3a0fdc4
   <function> SuspendThread     unsigned long ( void )+3a0fdc4
   <function> ResumeThread     unsigned long ( void )+3a0fdc4
   <function> PostThreadMessageA     int (
         unsigned int,
         unsigned int,
         long)+3a0fdc4
   <function> InitInstance     int ( void )+3a0fdc4
```

0n208 0xD0 1101 0000 ***!spoolused*** *Shows session pool usage* ***(KA)***

```
    <function> Run     int ( void )+3a0fdc4
    <function> PreTranslateMessage     int (
          tagMSG*)+3a0fdc4
    <function> PumpMessage     int ( void )+3a0fdc4
    <function> OnIdle     int (
          long)+3a0fdc4
    <function> IsIdleMessage     int (
          tagMSG*)+3a0fdc4
    <function> ExitInstance     int ( void )+3a0fdc4
    <function> ProcessWndProcException     long (
          CException*,
          tagMSG*)+3a0fdc4
    <function> ProcessMessageFilter     int (
          int,
          tagMSG*)+3a0fdc4
    <function> GetMainWnd     CWnd* ( void )+3a0fdc4
    <function> ~CWinThread     void ( void )+3a0fdc4
    <function> AssertValid     void ( void )+3a0fdc4
    <function> Dump     void (
          CDumpContext*)+3a0fdc4
    <function> CommonConstruct     void ( void )+3a0fdc4
    <function> Delete     void ( void )+3a0fdc4
    +0x034 m_pThreadParams  : 0x00000001
    +0x038 m_pfnThreadProc  : 0x03810b00     unsigned int  +3810b00
    +0x03c m_lpfnOleTermOrFreeLib : 0x00000001     void  +1
    +0x040 m_pMessageFilter : 0x03a0fe1c class COleMessageFilter, 36
elements, 0x44 bytes
    <function> DispatchThreadMessageEx     int (
          tagMSG*)+3a0fdc4
    <function> DispatchThreadMessage     void (
          tagMSG*)+3a0fdc4
    <function> operator=     CWinThread* (
          CWinThread*)+3a0fdc4
    <function> __local_vftable_ctor_closure     void ( void )+3a0fdc4
```

(AL) .record_branches *Enables recording (x64)* *0n209 0xD1 1101 0001*

```
   <function> __vecDelDtor     void* (
         unsigned int)+3a0fdc4
   <function> CGDIThread::_GetBaseClass     CRuntimeClass* ( void )+3a0fdc4
   =0041f6b0 CGDIThread::classCGDIThread : struct CRuntimeClass, 15
elements, 0x1c bytes
   <function> CGDIThread::GetThisClass     CRuntimeClass* ( void )+3a0fdc4
   <function> CGDIThread::GetRuntimeClass     CRuntimeClass* ( void
)+3a0fdc4
   <function> CGDIThread     void (
         CGDIThread*)+3a0fdc4
   <function> CGDIThread::CGDIThread     void (
         CWnd*,
         HDC__*)+3a0fdc4
   +0x044 m_rectBorder     : class CRect, 65 elements, 0x10 bytes
   +0x054 m_hDC            : 0x03810b00 struct HDC__, 1 elements, 0x4 bytes
   +0x058 m_dc             : class CDC, 277 elements, 0x10 bytes
   +0x068 m_hEventKill     : (null)
   +0x06c m_hEventDead     : 0x03810a90
   =00422618 CGDIThread::m_hAnotherDead : 0x0000007c
   =00422600 CGDIThread::m_csGDILock : struct _RTL_CRITICAL_SECTION, 6
elements, 0x18 bytes
   <function> CGDIThread::KillThread     void ( void )+3a0fdc4
   <function> CGDIThread::UpdateBorder     void ( void )+3a0fdc4
   <function> SingleStep     void ( void )+3a0fdc4
   <function> CGDIThread::~CGDIThread     void ( void )+3a0fdc4
   <function> CGDIThread::Delete     void ( void )+3a0fdc4
   <function> CGDIThread::InitInstance     int ( void )+3a0fdc4
   <function> CGDIThread::GetThisMessageMap     AFX_MSGMAP* ( void )+3a0fdc4
   <function> CGDIThread::GetMessageMap     AFX_MSGMAP* ( void )+3a0fdc4
   <function> operator=     CGDIThread* (
         CGDIThread*)+3a0fdc4
   <function> __vecDelDtor     void* (
         unsigned int)+3a0fdc4
   <function> CBallThread::_GetBaseClass     CRuntimeClass* ( void )+3a0fdc4
```

```
   =0041f770 CBallThread::classCBallThread : struct CRuntimeClass, 15
elements, 0x1c bytes

   <function> CBallThread::GetThisClass     CRuntimeClass* ( void )+3a0fdc4

   <function> CBallThread::GetRuntimeClass     CRuntimeClass* ( void
)+3a0fdc4

   <function> CBallThread     void (

         CBallThread*)+3a0fdc4

   <function> CBallThread::CBallThread     void (

         CWnd*,

         HDC__*,

         CPoint,

         CPoint,

         CSize,

         unsigned long)+3a0fdc4

   +0x070 m_rectPosition   : class CRect, 65 elements, 0x10 bytes

   +0x080 m_ptVelocity     : class CPoint, 23 elements, 0x8 bytes

   +0x088 m_hBrush         : 0x03a0ff34 struct HBRUSH__, 1 elements, 0x4
bytes

   +0x08c m_brush          : class CBrush, 25 elements, 0x8 bytes

   <function> CBallThread::InitInstance     int ( void )+3a0fdc4

   <function> CBallThread::SingleStep     void ( void )+3a0fdc4

   <function> CBallThread::~CBallThread     void ( void )+3a0fdc4

   <function> CBallThread::GetThisMessageMap     AFX_MSGMAP* ( void
)+3a0fdc4

   <function> CBallThread::GetMessageMap     AFX_MSGMAP* ( void )+3a0fdc4

   <function> operator=     CBallThread* (

         CBallThread*)+3a0fdc4

   <function> __vecDelDtor     void* (

         unsigned int)+3a0fdc4
```

Tip: we should not forget to load symbols. Without them we won't be able to use **dt** command.

lm*

Usually, when we get used to a command we don't try to explore its variations and sometimes one of these variations may give us the information we're looking for. Let's start getting all the basic information from all modules with **lm** command.

Tip: The end address of a module is not inclusive. For example, if the start address is F88AA000 and the end address is F88AB000, then to dump all module bytes we should use the following command: `db F88AA000 F88AB000-1`.

Displaying all modules:

```
0:015> lm

start    end        module name

00400000 00427000   mtgdi    C (private pdb symbols)  C:\development\My Tools\Book\mtgdi\Debug\mtgdi.pdb

5a1c0000 5a2e3000   MSVCR90D   (pdb symbols)
c:\publicsymbols\msvcr90d.i386.pdb\BF45F5CC5B814A7E9519AC19D1F729471\msvcr90d.i386.pdb

5a2f0000 5a536000   mfc90d     (pdb symbols)
c:\publicsymbols\mfc90d.i386.pdb\D8C4518B1AE74FADB4EA98EBA12EF063e\mfc90d.i386.pdb

72940000 7294c000   MFC90ENU   (no symbols)

74690000 746cf000   uxtheme    (pdb symbols)
c:\publicsymbols\UxTheme.pdb\D6B5A4E899AF4946BA6E4611D58409C02\UxTheme.pdb

746d0000 7486e000   comctl32   (export symbols)
C:\Windows\WinSxS\x86_microsoft.windows.common-controls_6595b64144ccf1df_6.0.6002.16670_none_5cbe9ee0088446b4\comctl32.dll

74c50000 74c55000   MSIMG32    (pdb symbols)
c:\publicsymbols\msimg32.pdb\F3CCF1CDEF724758A292CC67212D6C0C2\msimg32.pdb

75a80000 75b48000   MSCTF      (export symbols)
C:\Windows\system32\MSCTF.dll

75d40000 75dea000   msvcrt     (export symbols)
C:\Windows\system32\msvcrt.dll

75f20000 75fbd000   USER32     (export symbols)
C:\Windows\system32\USER32.dll
```

```
76bf0000 76c6d000   USP10      (export symbols)
C:\Windows\system32\USP10.dll

76c70000 76cfd000   OLEAUT32   (pdb symbols)
c:\publicsymbols\oleaut32.pdb\DDDA4738DBC94A3CB5523186E8E021502\oleaut32.pdb

76d00000 76d58000   SHLWAPI    (export symbols)
C:\Windows\system32\SHLWAPI.dll

76d60000 76dab000   GDI32      (export symbols)
C:\Windows\system32\GDI32.dll

76db0000 76e34000   CLBCatQ    (pdb symbols)
c:\publicsymbols\CLBCatQ.pdb\9E0BF37E9B7B468BA033F0003A14A3A32\CLBCatQ.pdb

76ec0000 76f83000   RPCRT4     (export symbols)
C:\Windows\system32\RPCRT4.dll

76f90000 7706c000   kernel32   (export symbols)
C:\Windows\system32\kernel32.dll

77070000 771b4000   ole32      (export symbols)
C:\Windows\system32\ole32.dll

771c0000 772e7000   ntdll      (export symbols)
C:\Windows\system32\ntdll.dll

772f0000 7730e000   IMM32      (export symbols)
C:\Windows\system32\IMM32.DLL

77340000 77349000   LPK        (pdb symbols)
c:\publicsymbols\lpk.pdb\EE7B434B5C904EF2AACEA045AD88806A2\lpk.pdb

77350000 77416000   ADVAPI32   (export symbols)
C:\Windows\system32\ADVAPI32.dll
```

Displaying only the loaded modules:

```
0:015> lmo

start    end        module name

00400000 00427000   mtgdi    C (private pdb symbols)  C:\development\My
Tools\Book\mtgdi\Debug\mtgdi.pdb

5a1c0000 5a2e3000   MSVCR90D   (pdb symbols)
c:\publicsymbols\msvcr90d.i386.pdb\BF45F5CC5B814A7E9519AC19D1F729471\msvcr90
d.i386.pdb

5a2f0000 5a536000   mfc90d     (pdb symbols)
c:\publicsymbols\mfc90d.i386.pdb\D8C4518B1AE74FADB4EA98EBA12EF063e\mfc90d.i3
86.pdb

72940000 7294c000   MFC90ENU   (no symbols)
```

```
74690000 746cf000   uxtheme    (pdb symbols)
c:\publicsymbols\UxTheme.pdb\D6B5A4E899AF4946BA6E4611D58409C02\UxTheme.pdb

746d0000 7486e000   comctl32   (export symbols)
C:\Windows\WinSxS\x86_microsoft.windows.common-
controls_6595b64144ccf1df_6.0.6002.16670_none_5cbe9ee0088446b4\comctl32.dll

74c50000 74c55000   MSIMG32    (pdb symbols)
c:\publicsymbols\msimg32.pdb\F3CCF1CDEF724758A292CC67212D6C0C2\msimg32.pdb

75a80000 75b48000   MSCTF      (export symbols)
C:\Windows\system32\MSCTF.dll

75d40000 75dea000   msvcrt     (export symbols)
C:\Windows\system32\msvcrt.dll

75f20000 75fbd000   USER32     (export symbols)
C:\Windows\system32\USER32.dll

76bf0000 76c6d000   USP10      (export symbols)
C:\Windows\system32\USP10.dll

76c70000 76cfd000   OLEAUT32   (pdb symbols)
c:\publicsymbols\oleaut32.pdb\DDDA4738DBC94A3CB5523186E8E021502\oleaut32.pdb

76d00000 76d58000   SHLWAPI    (export symbols)
C:\Windows\system32\SHLWAPI.dll

76d60000 76dab000   GDI32      (export symbols)
C:\Windows\system32\GDI32.dll

76db0000 76e34000   CLBCatQ    (pdb symbols)
c:\publicsymbols\CLBCatQ.pdb\9E0BF37E9B7B468BA033F0003A14A3A32\CLBCatQ.pdb

76ec0000 76f83000   RPCRT4     (export symbols)
C:\Windows\system32\RPCRT4.dll

76f90000 7706c000   kernel32   (export symbols)
C:\Windows\system32\kernel32.dll

77070000 771b4000   ole32      (export symbols)
C:\Windows\system32\ole32.dll

771c0000 772e7000   ntdll      (export symbols)
C:\Windows\system32\ntdll.dll

772f0000 7730e000   IMM32      (export symbols)
C:\Windows\system32\IMM32.DLL

77340000 77349000   LPK        (pdb symbols)
c:\publicsymbols\lpk.pdb\EE7B434B5C904EF2AACEA045AD88806A2\lpk.pdb

77350000 77416000   ADVAPI32   (export symbols)
C:\Windows\system32\ADVAPI32.dll
```

Displaying details for all modules:

```
0:015> lmv
start    end        module name
00400000 00427000   mtgdi    C (private pdb symbols)  C:\development\My
Tools\Book\mtgdi\Debug\mtgdi.pdb
    Loaded symbol image file: C:\development\My
Tools\Book\mtgdi\Debug\MtGdi.exe
    Image path: mtgdi.exe
    Image name: mtgdi.exe
    Timestamp:        Sat Jul 12 00:17:20 2008 (48785A80)
    CheckSum:         00000000
    ImageSize:        00027000
    File version:     1.0.0.1
    Product version:  1.0.0.1
    File flags:       1 (Mask 3F) Debug
    File OS:          4 Unknown Win32
    File type:        1.0 App
    File date:        00000000.00000000
    Translations:     0409.04b0
    ProductName:      MTGDI Application
    InternalName:     MTGDI
    OriginalFilename: MTGDI.EXE
    ProductVersion:   1, 0, 0, 1
    FileVersion:      1, 0, 0, 1
    FileDescription:  MTGDI MFC Application
    LegalCopyright:   © Microsoft Corporation.  All rights reserved.
5a1c0000 5a2e3000   MSVCR90D   (pdb symbols)
c:\publicsymbols\msvcr90d.i386.pdb\BF45F5CC5B814A7E9519AC19D1F729471\msvcr90
d.i386.pdb
    Loaded symbol image file:
C:\Windows\WinSxS\x86_microsoft.vc90.debugcrt_1fc8b3b9a1e18e3b_9.0.21022.8_n
one_96748342450f6aa2\MSVCR90D.dll
    Image path:
C:\Windows\WinSxS\x86_microsoft.vc90.debugcrt_1fc8b3b9a1e18e3b_9.0.21022.8_n
one_96748342450f6aa2\MSVCR90D.dll
```

(AA) .remote_exit *Exits a a debugging client* *0n215 0xD7 1101 0111*

```
    Image name: MSVCR90D.dll
    Timestamp:        Tue Nov 06 20:23:45 2007 (47313DD1)
    CheckSum:         0012A47D
    ImageSize:        00123000
    File version:     9.0.21022.8
    Product version:  9.0.21022.8
    File flags:       1 (Mask 3F) Debug
    File OS:          40004 NT Win32
    File type:        2.0 Dll
    File date:        00000000.00000000
    Translations:     0409.04b0
    CompanyName:      Microsoft Corporation
    ProductName:      Microsoft® Visual Studio® 2008
    InternalName:     MSVCR90D.DLL
    OriginalFilename: MSVCR90D.DLL
    ProductVersion:   9.00.21022.8
    FileVersion:      9.00.21022.8
    FileDescription:  Microsoft® C Runtime Library
    LegalCopyright:   © Microsoft Corporation.  All rights reserved.
5a2f0000 5a536000   mfc90d     (pdb symbols)
c:\publicsymbols\mfc90d.i386.pdb\D8C4518B1AE74FADB4EA98EBA12EF063e\mfc90d.i3
86.pdb
    Loaded symbol image file:
C:\Windows\WinSxS\x86_microsoft.vc90.debugmfc_1fc8b3b9a1e18e3b_9.0.21022.8_n
one_9b54853441e399d5\mfc90d.dll
    Image path:
C:\Windows\WinSxS\x86_microsoft.vc90.debugmfc_1fc8b3b9a1e18e3b_9.0.21022.8_n
one_9b54853441e399d5\mfc90d.dll
    Image name: mfc90d.dll
    Timestamp:        Tue Nov 06 22:49:38 2007 (47316002)
    CheckSum:         00252C7C
    ImageSize:        00246000
    File version:     9.0.21022.8
    Product version:  9.0.21022.8
    File flags:       1 (Mask 3F) Debug
    File OS:          4 Unknown Win32
```

```
    File type:        2.0 Dll
    File date:        00000000.00000000
    Translations:     0409.04b0
    CompanyName:      Microsoft Corporation
    ProductName:      Microsoft® Visual Studio® 2008
    InternalName:     MFC90D.DLL
    OriginalFilename: MFC90D.DLL
    ProductVersion:   9.00.21022.08
    FileVersion:      9.00.21022.08
    FileDescription:  MFCDLL Shared Library - Debug Version
    LegalCopyright:   © Microsoft Corporation.  All rights reserved.
72940000 7294c000   MFC90ENU   (no symbols)
    Loaded symbol image file:
C:\Windows\WinSxS\x86_microsoft.vc90.mfcloc_1fc8b3b9a1e18e3b_9.0.21022.8_non
e_b59bae9d65014b98\MFC90ENU.DLL
    Image path:
C:\Windows\WinSxS\x86_microsoft.vc90.mfcloc_1fc8b3b9a1e18e3b_9.0.21022.8_non
e_b59bae9d65014b98\MFC90ENU.DLL
    Image name: MFC90ENU.DLL
    Timestamp:        Tue Nov 06 22:50:02 2007 (4731601A)
    CheckSum:         0000DCB9
    ImageSize:        0000C000
    File version:     9.0.21022.8
    Product version:  9.0.21022.8
    File flags:       0 (Mask 3F)
    File OS:          4 Unknown Win32
    File type:        2.0 Dll
    File date:        00000000.00000000
    Translations:     0409.04b0
    CompanyName:      Microsoft Corporation
    ProductName:      Microsoft® Visual Studio® 2008
    InternalName:     MFC90ENU.DLL
    OriginalFilename: MFC90ENU.DLL
    ProductVersion:   9.00.21022.08
    FileVersion:      9.00.21022.08
```

(KA) .restart *Restarts the kernel connection (KD)* *0n217 0xD9 1101 1001*

```
    FileDescription:  MFC Language Specific Resources
    LegalCopyright:   © Microsoft Corporation.  All rights reserved.
74690000 746cf000   uxtheme    (pdb symbols)
c:\publicsymbols\UxTheme.pdb\D6B5A4E899AF4946BA6E4611D58409C02\UxTheme.pdb
    Loaded symbol image file: C:\Windows\system32\uxtheme.dll
    Image path: C:\Windows\system32\uxtheme.dll
    Image name: uxtheme.dll
    Timestamp:        Fri Jan 18 23:32:10 2008 (4791A77A)
    CheckSum:         0004868F
    ImageSize:        0003F000
    File version:     6.0.6001.18000
    Product version:  6.0.6001.18000
    File flags:       0 (Mask 3F)
    File OS:          40004 NT Win32
    File type:        2.0 Dll
    File date:        00000000.00000000
    Translations:     0409.04b0
    CompanyName:      Microsoft Corporation
    ProductName:      Microsoft® Windows® Operating System
    InternalName:     UxTheme.dll
    OriginalFilename: UxTheme.dll
    ProductVersion:   6.0.6001.18000
    FileVersion:      6.0.6001.18000 (longhorn_rtm.080118-1840)
    FileDescription:  Microsoft UxTheme Library
    LegalCopyright:   © Microsoft Corporation. All rights reserved
```

0n218 0xDA 1101 1010 **!session** *Shows user sessions* ***(KA)***

Displaying details for a specific module:

```
0:015> lmv m mtgdi
start    end        module name
00400000 00427000   mtgdi    C (private pdb symbols)  C:\development\My Tools\Book\mtgdi\Debug\mtgdi.pdb
    Loaded symbol image file: C:\development\My Tools\Book\mtgdi\Debug\MtGdi.exe
    Image path: mtgdi.exe
    Image name: mtgdi.exe
    Timestamp:        Sat Jul 12 00:17:20 2008 (48785A80)
    CheckSum:         00000000
    ImageSize:        00027000
    File version:     1.0.0.1
    Product version:  1.0.0.1
    File flags:       1 (Mask 3F) Debug
    File OS:          4 Unknown Win32
    File type:        1.0 App
    File date:        00000000.00000000
    Translations:     0409.04b0
    ProductName:      MTGDI Application
    InternalName:     MTGDI
    OriginalFilename: MTGDI.EXE
    ProductVersion:   1, 0, 0, 1
    FileVersion:      1, 0, 0, 1
    FileDescription:  MTGDI MFC Application
    LegalCopyright:   © Microsoft Corporation.  All rights reserved.
```

Tip: Use this command whenever we see an offset from the call stack that doesn't look normal.

The stack below was manually crafted, just to use as an example:

```
053ffd4c 7731b071 ntdll!KiFastSystemCallRet
053ffd74 004153e7 ntdll!RtlPcToFileHeader+0x45
053ffe38 0041528c mtgdi!CGDIThread+0xed900
053ffe90 5796d973 mtgdi!CRectThread+0xed973
053fff58 6aacdfd3 mfc90d+0x3c
053fff94 6aacdf69 MSVCR90D!beginthreadex+0x1F
053fffa0 76e63833 MSVCR90D!beginthreadex+0x1a
053fffac 7731a9bd kernel32!BaseThreadInitThunk+3b
053fffec 00000000 ntdll!LdrInitializeThunk
```

Whenever we see a long offset, like above, it means we have no symbols or there's a problem and the symbols don't match, so we cannot trust the names of method calls! Usually, when we don't have symbols, it is because we have a third-party component, so we use **lmv m** command to get information like its version and the company name.

Displaying only modules that have some sort of a symbol problem, for example, no symbols or modules whose symbol status is **export:**

```
0:015> lme

start    end        module name

00400000 00427000   mtgdi    C (private pdb symbols)  C:\development\My Tools\Book\mtgdi\Debug\mtgdi.pdb

72940000 7294c000   MFC90ENU   (no symbols)

746d0000 7486e000   comctl32   (export symbols)
C:\Windows\WinSxS\x86_microsoft.windows.common-controls_6595b64144ccf1df_6.0.6002.16670_none_5cbe9ee0088446b4\comctl32.dll

75a80000 75b48000   MSCTF      (export symbols)
C:\Windows\system32\MSCTF.dll

75d40000 75dea000   msvcrt     (export symbols)
C:\Windows\system32\msvcrt.dll

75f20000 75fbd000   USER32     (export symbols)
C:\Windows\system32\USER32.dll

76bf0000 76c6d000   USP10      (export symbols)
C:\Windows\system32\USP10.dll

76d00000 76d58000   SHLWAPI    (export symbols)
C:\Windows\system32\SHLWAPI.dll
```

```
76d60000 76dab000   GDI32      (export symbols)
C:\Windows\system32\GDI32.dll

76ec0000 76f83000   RPCRT4     (export symbols)
C:\Windows\system32\RPCRT4.dll

76f90000 7706c000   kernel32   (export symbols)
C:\Windows\system32\kernel32.dll

77070000 771b4000   ole32      (export symbols)
C:\Windows\system32\ole32.dll

771c0000 772e7000   ntdll      (export symbols)
C:\Windows\system32\ntdll.dll

772f0000 7730e000   IMM32      (export symbols)
C:\Windows\system32\IMM32.DLL

77350000 77416000   ADVAPI32   (export symbols)
C:\Windows\system32\ADVAPI32.dll
```

Using **lm** output in a **.foreach** loop:

```
0:015> lm1m

mtgdi

MSVCR90D

mfc90d

MFC90ENU

uxtheme

comctl32

MSIMG32

MSCTF

msvcrt

USER32

USP10

OLEAUT32

SHLWAPI

GDI32

CLBCatQ

RPCRT4

kernel32

ole32
```

(UL) .scroll_prefs *Sets source scrolling prefs* *0n221 0xDD 1101 1101*

```
ntdll

IMM32

LPK

ADVAPI32
```

Displaying modules based on a pattern:

```
0:015> lm m m*

start    end        module name

00400000 00427000   mtgdi    C (private pdb symbols)  C:\development\My
Tools\Book\mtgdi\Debug\mtgdi.pdb

5a1c0000 5a2e3000   MSVCR90D   (pdb symbols)
c:\publicsymbols\msvcr90d.i386.pdb\BF45F5CC5B814A7E9519AC19D1F729471\msvcr90
d.i386.pdb

5a2f0000 5a536000   mfc90d     (pdb symbols)
c:\publicsymbols\mfc90d.i386.pdb\D8C4518B1AE74FADB4EA98EBA12EF063e\mfc90d.i3
86.pdb

72940000 7294c000   MFC90ENU   (no symbols)

74c50000 74c55000   MSIMG32    (pdb symbols)
c:\publicsymbols\msimg32.pdb\F3CCF1CDEF724758A292CC67212D6C0C2\msimg32.pdb

75a80000 75b48000   MSCTF      (export symbols)
C:\Windows\system32\MSCTF.dll

75d40000 75dea000   msvcrt     (export symbols)
C:\Windows\system32\msvcrt.dll
```

Displaying modules based on an address:

```
0:015> lm a 00400000

start    end        module name

00400000 00427000   mtgdi    C (private pdb symbols)  C:\development\My
Tools\Book\mtgdi\Debug\mtgdi.pdb
```

An **lm** variation using **DML**. We can click on hyperlinks and get more information, including module functions and data:

```
0:015> lmD

start    end        module name

00400000 00427000   mtgdi    C (private pdb symbols)  C:\development\My
Tools\Book\mtgdi\Debug\mtgdi.pdb

5a1c0000 5a2e3000   MSVCR90D   (pdb symbols)
c:\publicsymbols\msvcr90d.i386.pdb\BF45F5CC5B814A7E9519AC19D1F729471\msvcr90
d.i386.pdb

5a2f0000 5a536000   mfc90d     (pdb symbols)
c:\publicsymbols\mfc90d.i386.pdb\D8C4518B1AE74FADB4EA98EBA12EF063e\mfc90d.i3
86.pdb

72940000 7294c000   MFC90ENU   (no symbols)

74690000 746cf000   uxtheme    (pdb symbols)
c:\publicsymbols\UxTheme.pdb\D6B5A4E899AF4946BA6E4611D58409C02\UxTheme.pdb

746d0000 7486e000   comctl32   (export symbols)
C:\Windows\WinSxS\x86_microsoft.windows.common-
controls_6595b64144ccf1df_6.0.6002.16670_none_5cbe9ee0088446b4\comctl32.dll

74c50000 74c55000   MSIMG32    (pdb symbols)
c:\publicsymbols\msimg32.pdb\F3CCF1CDEF724758A292CC67212D6C0C2\msimg32.pdb

75a80000 75b48000   MSCTF      (export symbols)
C:\Windows\system32\MSCTF.dll

75d40000 75dea000   msvcrt     (export symbols)
C:\Windows\system32\msvcrt.dll

75f20000 75fbd000   USER32     (export symbols)
C:\Windows\system32\USER32.dll

76bf0000 76c6d000   USP10      (export symbols)
C:\Windows\system32\USP10.dll

76c70000 76cfd000   OLEAUT32   (pdb symbols)
c:\publicsymbols\oleaut32.pdb\DDDA4738DBC94A3CB5523186E8E021502\oleaut32.pdb

76d00000 76d58000   SHLWAPI    (export symbols)
C:\Windows\system32\SHLWAPI.dll

76d60000 76dab000   GDI32      (export symbols)
C:\Windows\system32\GDI32.dll

76db0000 76e34000   CLBCatQ    (pdb symbols)
c:\publicsymbols\CLBCatQ.pdb\9E0BF37E9B7B468BA033F0003A14A3A32\CLBCatQ.pdb

76ec0000 76f83000   RPCRT4     (export symbols)
C:\Windows\system32\RPCRT4.dll

76f90000 7706c000   kernel32   (export symbols)
C:\Windows\system32\kernel32.dll

77070000 771b4000   ole32      (export symbols)
C:\Windows\system32\ole32.dll
```

```
771c0000 772e7000   ntdll      (export symbols)
C:\Windows\system32\ntdll.dll

772f0000 7730e000   IMM32      (export symbols)
C:\Windows\system32\IMM32.DLL

77340000 77349000   LPK        (pdb symbols)
c:\publicsymbols\lpk.pdb\EE7B434B5C904EF2AACEA045AD88806A2\lpk.pdb

77350000 77416000   ADVAPI32   (export symbols)
C:\Windows\system32\ADVAPI32.dll

0:015> lmDvmUSER32

Browse full module list

start    end        module name

75f20000 75fbd000   USER32     (export symbols)
C:\Windows\system32\USER32.dll

    Loaded symbol image file: C:\Windows\system32\USER32.dll

    Image path: C:\Windows\system32\USER32.dll

    Image name: USER32.dll

    Browse all global symbols  functions  data

    Timestamp:        Fri Jan 30 22:26:18 2009 (4983EF0A)

    CheckSum:         0009EE3F

    ImageSize:        0009D000

    File version:     6.0.6002.16670

    Product version:  6.0.6002.16670

    File flags:       0 (Mask 3F)

    File OS:          40004 NT Win32

    File type:        2.0 Dll

    File date:        00000000.00000000

    Translations:     0409.04b0

    CompanyName:      Microsoft Corporation

    ProductName:      Microsoft® Windows® Operating System

    InternalName:     user32

    OriginalFilename: user32

    ProductVersion:   6.0.6002.16670

    FileVersion:      6.0.6002.16670 (lh_sp2rc.090130-1715)

    FileDescription:  Multi-User Windows USER API Client DLL

    LegalCopyright:   © Microsoft Corporation. All rights reserved.
```

0n224 0xE0 1110 0000 ***!running*** *Shows running threads **(KA)***

!findstack

During our debugging session we may find ourselves trying to identify whether a specific symbol or module appears in one or more threads. There is more than one way to do that, and the simplest way is to use this command.

```
0:015> !findstack mfc90d!_AfxThreadEntry 2
Thread 001, 1 frame(s) match
        00 026ffd34 771ff09e ntdll!KiFastSystemCallRet
        01 026ffd5c 00414ee7 ntdll!RtlAddAccessAllowedAce+0x52
        02 026ffdc8 00414834 mtgdi!CBallThread::SingleStep+0x147
        03 026ffe20 00414d8c mtgdi!CGDIThread::InitInstance+0x44
        04 026ffe78 5a3dd973
mtgdi!CBallThread::InitInstance+0x2c
      * 05 026fff40 5a1fdfd3 mfc90d!_AfxThreadEntry+0x303
        06 026fff7c 5a1fdf69 MSVCR90D!_beginthreadex+0x243
        07 026fff88 76fdb957 MSVCR90D!_beginthreadex+0x1d9
        08 026fff94 772072a9 kernel32!BaseThreadInitThunk+0x12
        09 026fffd4 7720727c
ntdll!RtlIsCurrentThreadAttachExempt+0x63
        10 026fffec 00000000
ntdll!RtlIsCurrentThreadAttachExempt+0x36

Thread 002, 1 frame(s) match
        00 02c0fd34 771ff09e ntdll!KiFastSystemCallRet
        01 02c0fd5c 00414ee7 ntdll!RtlAddAccessAllowedAce+0x52
        02 02c0fdc8 00414834 mtgdi!CBallThread::SingleStep+0x147
        03 02c0fe20 00414d8c mtgdi!CGDIThread::InitInstance+0x44
        04 02c0fe78 5a3dd973
mtgdi!CBallThread::InitInstance+0x2c
      * 05 02c0ff40 5a1fdfd3 mfc90d!_AfxThreadEntry+0x303
```

```
        06 02c0ff7c 5a1fdf69 MSVCR90D!_beginthreadex+0x243
        07 02c0ff88 76fdb957 MSVCR90D!_beginthreadex+0x1d9
        08 02c0ff94 772072a9 kernel32!BaseThreadInitThunk+0x12
        09 02c0ffd4 7720727c
ntdll!RtlIsCurrentThreadAttachExempt+0x63
        10 02c0ffec 00000000
ntdll!RtlIsCurrentThreadAttachExempt+0x36

Thread 003, 1 frame(s) match
        00 02d0fd34 771ff09e ntdll!KiFastSystemCallRet
        01 02d0fd5c 00414ee7 ntdll!RtlAddAccessAllowedAce+0x52
        02 02d0fdc8 00414834 mtgdi!CBallThread::SingleStep+0x147
        03 02d0fe20 00414d8c mtgdi!CGDIThread::InitInstance+0x44
        04 02d0fe78 5a3dd973
mtgdi!CBallThread::InitInstance+0x2c
      * 05 02d0ff40 5a1fdfd3 mfc90d!_AfxThreadEntry+0x303
        06 02d0ff7c 5a1fdf69 MSVCR90D!_beginthreadex+0x243
        07 02d0ff88 76fdb957 MSVCR90D!_beginthreadex+0x1d9
        08 02d0ff94 772072a9 kernel32!BaseThreadInitThunk+0x12
        09 02d0ffd4 7720727c
ntdll!RtlIsCurrentThreadAttachExempt+0x63
        10 02d0ffec 00000000
ntdll!RtlIsCurrentThreadAttachExempt+0x36

Thread 004, 1 frame(s) match
        00 02e0fd34 771ff09e ntdll!KiFastSystemCallRet
        01 02e0fd5c 00414ee7 ntdll!RtlAddAccessAllowedAce+0x52
        02 02e0fdc8 00414834 mtgdi!CBallThread::SingleStep+0x147
        03 02e0fe20 00414d8c mtgdi!CGDIThread::InitInstance+0x44
        04 02e0fe78 5a3dd973
mtgdi!CBallThread::InitInstance+0x2c
      * 05 02e0ff40 5a1fdfd3 mfc90d!_AfxThreadEntry+0x303
        06 02e0ff7c 5a1fdf69 MSVCR90D!_beginthreadex+0x243
```

```
07 02e0ff88 76fdb957 MSVCR90D!_beginthreadex+0x1d9

08 02e0ff94 772072a9 kernel32!BaseThreadInitThunk+0x12

09 02e0ffd4 7720727c
ntdll!RtlIsCurrentThreadAttachExempt+0x63

10 02e0ffec 00000000
ntdll!RtlIsCurrentThreadAttachExempt+0x36
```

s

Very often we find ourselves scanning the stack or the entire virtual memory of a process to find information that may be strings, DWORDS, bytes or chars. To accomplish this we use the **s** command.

These are some possible variations.

Dumping all ASCII strings:

```
s -sa initialAddress finalAddress
```

Dumping all Unicode strings that match a pattern:

```
s -u  initialAddress finalAddress "string"
```

Displaying just the address where the strings that match the argument are located:

```
s -[1]a initialAddress finalAddress "stringToSearchFor"
```

Displaying all ASCII strings from the current call stack:

```
0:015> s -sa poi(@$teb+0x8) poi(@$teb+0x4)
03a0f0e5  "I w"
03a0f119  "I w"
03a0f11d  "n w"
03a0f299  "+ w"
03a0f2a4  "O+ w"
03a0f2b9  "+ w8"
03a0f2de  "1S0"
03a0f2e5  ", w"
03a0f2f5  ") w8"
03a0f325  "- wd"
03a0f346  " wd"
03a0f3b0  "x@(wJ"
```

```
03a0f3b6  " w@"
03a0f453  "~x@(wx@(w"
03a0f46e  " wU"
03a0f472  " wx@(w"
03a0f48a  " wx@(w"
03a0f59d  "H w"
03a0f5a1  "H w&O"
03a0f5be  " w4"
03a0f5d1  "H ww"
03a0f620  "X(b"
03a0f677  "v7k"
03a0f792  ""wJ"
03a0f7a6  ""wvB"
03a0f816  "#w@k"
03a0f83a  "#w "
03a0f862  ""wx"
03a0f8e3  "P8k"
03a0f926  ""wX"
03a0f942  ""w@"
03a0f971  ""'w"
03a0f9a1  "+'w0"
03a0f9a9  "*'w"
03a0f9bd  "+'w"
03a0f9e5  "*'w"
03a0f9f6  ""w&@"
03a0fa45  ""'w"
03a0fa75  "+'w"
03a0fa7d  "*'w"
```

(AA) .servers *Shows the list of debugging servers 0n229 0xE5 1110 0101*

```
03a0fad6  ""wX"
03a0faf2  ""w@"
03a0fb5d  "[-Z"
03a0fba1  "2)Z"
03a0fbb2  "(Z4"
03a0fbbd  "7/Z"
03a0fbd2  "(Z4"
03a0fbe1  "7/Z"
03a0fbfa  "(Z4"
03a0fc09  "7/Z"
03a0fcce  "5Z`T"w"
03a0fd17  "vI6"
03a0fda3  "v?Z"
03a0fdcc  "4HA"
03a0fdf4  "b`6Z"
03a0fe53  "v?Z"
03a0fe63  "v`A"wk"
03a0fe94  "(%B"
03a0feb4  "(%B"
03a0fed0  ",>/Z"
03a0ff00  "t?/Z"
03a0ff05  "?/Z"
03a0ff5c  "hC-Z"
03a0ff71  "2)Z"
03a0ff99  "r w"
03a0ffd8  "|r w"
```

Displaying all UNICODE strings from the current call stack:

```
0:015> s -su poi(@$teb+0x8) poi(@$teb+0x4)
03a0f0e4  "闎眠髳绱"
03a0f108  "ᒪ∩ᓑ眛"
03a0f118  "闎眠潀眠"
03a0f132  "∩è@"
03a0f13a  "∩ᖷ眭"
03a0f142  "@ᑝ眭نى∩ᕑ眭"
03a0f2e2  "∩□眠"
03a0f318  "퀸 翻 뫰 翱"
03a0f322  "∩□眠"
03a0f396  "∩ᗫ眠"
03a0f3ae  "∩矏眨ᑫ眠@"
03a0f450  "亢绱矏眨矏眨"
03a0f45e  "∩ᓭ眠"
03a0f46a  "∩ọ眠ᕕ眠矏眨"
03a0f486  "∩ọ眠矏眨"
03a0f59a  "∩酞眠醗眠伦绱"
03a0f5aa  "∩ọ眠"
03a0f5c2  "∩ᓑ眛蓋"
03a0f5e2  "眠鴓绱"
03a0f636  "∩ᓑ眛藏"
03a0f646  "眠ụ眠"
03a0f662  "∩艋眭"
03a0f672  "∩鰀眭欷"
```

```
03a0f6a2  "ℿ裂 盹ə僘"
03a0f6b6  "畔鮔畔暯"
03a0f6c0  "ںℿنℿ"
03a0f6d2  "娜ㄱℿ"
03a0f6e6  "Ì滑ℿ"
03a0f702  "Ì鸞ℿ"
03a0f764  "وو ﬞ"
03a0f78e  "ℿ錀晉J"
03a0f7a2  "眠錡晉雙绱"
03a0f7f8  "甖昳殨"
03a0f814  "甖昳款"
03a0f82c  "鸞ℿ錀晉"
03a0f838  "昗昳鸞ℿ"
03a0f842  "眠錡晉朋绱"
```

There seems to be no meaningful UNICODE strings above.

Displaying all occurrences of ASCII strings that appear within the process virtual memory:

```
0:015> s -sa 0 0FFFFFFF
00010131  "b(w"
00126c96  ""wG"
00126caa  ""wr"
00126dd5  ""'w"
00126e05  "+'w0"
00126e0d  "*'w"
00126e49  "*'w"
00127022  ""w,"
```

```
0012706d  """'w"
00130255  "_P8"
00160bde  "rKt"
00160c55  "\a*L"
00161e60  "GsHd("
00161e88  "GsHd("
00161eb0  "GsHd("
00161ed8  "GsHd("
00170131  "i(w"
00171180  "COMReg.ClassesInternal"
00171197  "COMReg.LegacyClassesInternal"
001718b6  "                              "
00171934  "                            "
0017194d  "          "
00171996  "abcdefghijklmnopqrstuvwxyz"
001719b6  "ABCDEFGHIJKLMNOPQRSTUVWXYZ"
00171b18  "ALLUSERSPROFILE=C:\ProgramData"
00171b37  "APPDATA=C:\Users\user\AppData"
00171b57  "\Roaming"
```

Searching for a specific ASCII string on a current call stack:

```
s -a poi(@$teb+0x8) poi(@$teb+0x4) "RtlDecodePointer"
```

Searching for a specific DWORD on a current call stack:

```
s -d poi(@$teb+0x8) poi(@$teb+0x4) 7783b7ee
```

Tip: Sometimes we need to use the addresses returned from the **s** command. For example, we may want to use a loop that scans the returned addresses. These are just the commands to return the addresses:

```
s -[1]d poi(@$teb+0x8) poi(@$teb+0x4) 7783b7ee

s -[1]a poi(@$teb+0x8) poi(@$teb+0x4) "RtlDecodePointer"
```

Notice the **–[1]**. This is used to return only the addresses that match the query.

```
0:015> s -[1]a 0 0FFFFFFF "ab"
0x00171996
0x001a1c76
0x0027099d
0x00270a9d
0x003c4594
0x003c4688
0x003c469b
0x003c4923
0x003c492e
0x003c493a
0x003c4c89
0x003c4c9c
0x00852de2
0x0086a95d
0x0086aa65
0x00884126
0x0088b362
0x008b555a
0x008d0b2b
0x008df249
0x008df267
0x008e9ebd
0x008e9ee1
```

```
0x008f310e

0x008f4db3

0x008fa0e6

0x009a531a

0x009ac899

0x009d741a

0x009f1166

0x009fae44

0x00a13793

0x00aa3ff4
```

Scripting

We should use WinDbg scripting when we need to create a very specific small script. If we want to build a rather complex script we can use PowerDbg, which is a tool that uses PowerShell to interact with WinDbg debugger. Now we explain the most used commands and scripting techniques.

Declaring Variables

Variables are created as aliases not as real variables. We're going to use the term "variable", but in fact we're talking about aliases.

Aliases are very flexible. We can, for instance, create an alias that has a block of commands.

Here is the way to create variables:

```
as [alias type] <alias Name> <value>
```

Example:

```
as ${/v:ScriptName} myscripts\\test_script.txt
```

The example creates an alias ScriptName that represents the path. Notice that we're using **${/v:}**. If we don't use **${/v:}**, we'll have problems to delete the alias.

To simplify things follow this template when creating "variables":

```
as [alias type] ${/v:<alias name>} <alias value>
```

Freeing Variables (aliases)

The way to delete "variables" is:

```
ad ${/v:<variable name>}
```

Example:

```
ad ${/v:ScriptName}
```

Executing Scripts

The most common way to call a script is:

```
$$><path\scriptName
```

Example:

```
$$><myscripts\GET_PERFMON.txt
```

If our script accepts arguments we must provide them using this format:

```
$$>a<path\scriptName argument1 argument2 argument3 …
```

Example:

```
$$>a<myscripts\GET_HEADERS.txt kernel32
```

We can even use recursive calls and make a script call itself.

Identifying Arguments

If our script accepts arguments, we should verify if a user provided the arguments:

```
.if(${/d:$arg1})
{
    $$ Do something...
}
```

${/d:} evaluates the expression to one or zero. **arg1** refers to the first argument, **arg2** to the second, and so on.

32/64 bits Compatibility

Most of the time we don't need to write two scripts. The technique is based on **$ptrsize** pseudo-register (the size of a pointer).

Example snippet from a real script:

```
r @$t1 = poi(@$t0) + @$ptrsize;
.printf "\n.NET GC Counters\n\n";
.printf "GenCollection 0                = 0n%d\n", poi(@$t1);
.printf "GenCollection 1                = 0n%d\n", poi(@$t1+@$ptrsize);
.printf "GenCollection 2                = 0n%d\n",
poi(@$t1+@$ptrsize*2);
.printf "PromotedMemory                 = 0n%d\n",
poi(@$t1+@$ptrsize*3);
.printf "PromotedMemory 1               = 0n%d\n",
poi(@$t1+@$ptrsize*4);
```

Another example:

```
!do poi(${obj}+(4*@$ptrsize))
```

DML – Debug Markup Language

With DML we can create hyperlinks that execute commands. This can be done via a variation of the **.printf** command:

```
.printf /D
```

Note: to learn more about DML, refer to DML.DOC that comes with Debugging Tools for Windows.

Example:

```
.printf /D "<link cmd=\"dps @$csp poi(@$teb+0x4);ad
${/v:ScriptName}; $$><${ScriptName}\"><b>Symbols</b></link>\n\n"
```

Tip: Between **<link cmd=\"   \"></link>** we can use an alias defined before the DML line. This alias can be a block of code, for example:

```
.block
{
    $$ Creating an alias for a block of code!
    as ${/v:OracleCommand} .block
    {
        !DumpObj poi(@$t0+0x14)
        !DumpObj @$t0
        !GCRoot @$t0
    }
}

.foreach(obj {!dumpheap -short -type
System.Data.OracleClient.OracleCommand } )
{
    .printf /D "<link cmd=\"r @$t0 = ${obj}; ${OracleCommand}
;\"><b>%mu</b></link>\n\n", poi(${obj}+0x14)+0xc
}
```

.printf is very similar to the **printf**() function from C and C++ programming languages.

Pseudo-Registers as Variables

Most of the time, we want to use some kind of a counter in our script or save the address of an object or a structure field. To do that we can use pseudo-registers.

Readability May Hurt Your Script

If we have a command line like this:

```
!do poi(@$t0+(4*@$ptrsize))
```

and we decide to improve the readability by adding a few spaces we may end up having an error. For example, this line fails with an error "Incorrect argument: + (4 * @$ptrsize))":

```
!do poi(@$t0 + (4 * @$ptrsize))
```

!chksym/!itoldyouso

These are two debugger extensions that are used to see the PDB file that matches a specific module. At the time of this writing !itoldyouso is not documented. The output of both commands is identical.

Example:

```
0:025> !chksym ntdll

ntdll.dll
    Timestamp: 49EEA706
  SizeOfImage: 180000
          pdb: wntdll.pdb
      pdb sig: E06BEA15-5E97-48BE-A818-E2D0DD2FED95
          age: 2

Loaded pdb is
c:\publicsymbols\wntdll.pdb\E06BEA155E9748BEA818E2D0DD2FED952\wntd
ll.pdb

wntdll.pdb
      pdb sig: E06BEA15-5E97-48BE-A818-E2D0DD2FED95
          age: 2

MATCH: wntdll.pdb and ntdll.dll

0:025> !itoldyouso ntdll

ntdll.dll
    Timestamp: 49EEA706
  SizeOfImage: 180000
          pdb: wntdll.pdb
```

```
      pdb sig: E06BEA15-5E97-48BE-A818-E2D0DD2FED95
          age: 2

Loaded pdb is
c:\publicsymbols\wntdll.pdb\E06BEA155E9748BEA818E2D0DD2FED952\wntd
ll.pdb

wntdll.pdb
      pdb sig: E06BEA15-5E97-48BE-A818-E2D0DD2FED95
          age: 2

MATCH: wntdll.pdb and ntdll.dll

0:025> !chksym mtgdi

mtgdi.exe
    Timestamp: 48785A80
  SizeOfImage: 27000
          pdb: c:\DOWNLOADS\mtgdi\Debug\mtgdi.pdb
      pdb sig: EC1B3DB2-25C1-4337-8676-DFB3C5B1C8C9
          age: 3

Loaded pdb is C:\development\My Tools\Book\mtgdi\Debug\mtgdi.pdb

mtgdi.pdb
      pdb sig: EC1B3DB2-25C1-4337-8676-DFB3C5B1C8C9
          age: 3

MATCH: mtgdi.pdb and mtgdi.exe

0:025> !itoldyouso mtgdi
```

```
mtgdi.exe
    Timestamp: 48785A80
  SizeOfImage: 27000
          pdb: c:\DOWNLOADS\mtgdi\Debug\mtgdi.pdb
      pdb sig: EC1B3DB2-25C1-4337-8676-DFB3C5B1C8C9
          age: 3

Loaded pdb is C:\development\My Tools\Book\mtgdi\Debug\mtgdi.pdb

mtgdi.pdb
      pdb sig: EC1B3DB2-25C1-4337-8676-DFB3C5B1C8C9
          age: 3

MATCH: mtgdi.pdb and mtgdi.exe
```

# #

Sometimes we need to look for patterns of disassembled code. We can browse the disassembled code and manually look for a specific pattern or we can use **#** command to automate it.

To demonstrate this command in action let's use the simple Visual C++ application that recursively calculates a Fibonacci number:

```
#include "stdafx.h"

using namespace std;


// Recursive function

unsigned FiboRecursive(unsigned n, int nNum = 0)

{

        if(n <= 1)

        {

                return n;

        }


        return FiboRecursive(n - 1, 1) + FiboRecursive(n - 2, 2);

}


int _tmain(int argc, _TCHAR* argv[])

{

        cout << FiboRecursive(5) << endl;

        return 0;

}
```

Let's put a breakpoint at _tmain (**wmain**) function and then disassemble the code pointed to by **eip** register.

```
0:000> uf @eip

Fibo!wmain [c:\development\my tools\book\fibo\fibo\fibo.cpp @ 20]:

   20 00a71440 55              push    ebp

   20 00a71441 8bec            mov     ebp,esp

   20 00a71443 81ecc0000000    sub     esp,0C0h

   20 00a71449 53              push    ebx

   20 00a7144a 56              push    esi

   20 00a7144b 57              push    edi

   20 00a7144c 8dbd40ffffff    lea     edi,[ebp-0C0h]

   20 00a71452 b930000000      mov     ecx,30h

   20 00a71457 b8cccccccc      mov     eax,0CCCCCCCCh

   20 00a7145c f3ab            rep stos dword ptr es:[edi]

   21 00a7145e 8bf4            mov     esi,esp

   21 00a71460 a19882a700      mov     eax,dword ptr
[Fibo!_imp_?endlstdYAAAV?$basic_ostreamDU?$char_traitsDstd (00a78298)]

   21 00a71465 50              push    eax

   21 00a71466 6a00            push    0

   21 00a71468 6a05            push    5

   21 00a7146a e89bfbffff      call    Fibo!ILT+5(?FiboRecursiveYAIIHZ)
(00a7100a)

   21 00a7146f 83c408          add     esp,8

   21 00a71472 8bfc            mov     edi,esp

   21 00a71474 50              push    eax

   21 00a71475 8b0d9082a700    mov     ecx,dword ptr [Fibo!_imp_?coutstd
(00a78290)]

   21 00a7147b ff159482a700    call    dword ptr
[Fibo!_imp_??6?$basic_ostreamDU?$char_traitsDstdstdQAEAAV01IZ (00a78294)]

   21 00a71481 3bfc            cmp     edi,esp

   21 00a71483 e8d1fcffff      call    Fibo!ILT+340(__RTC_CheckEsp)
(00a71159)

   21 00a71488 8bc8            mov     ecx,eax
```

```
   21 00a7148a ff159c82a700     call     dword ptr
[Fibo!_imp_??6?$basic_ostreamDU?$char_traitsDstdstdQAEAAV01P6AAAV01AAV01ZZ
(00a7829c)]

   21 00a71490 3bf4             cmp      esi,esp

   21 00a71492 e8c2fcffff       call     Fibo!ILT+340(__RTC_CheckEsp)
(00a71159)

   23 00a71497 33c0             xor      eax,eax

   24 00a71499 5f               pop      edi

   24 00a7149a 5e               pop      esi

   24 00a7149b 5b               pop      ebx

   24 00a7149c 81c4c0000000     add      esp,0C0h

   24 00a714a2 3bec             cmp      ebp,esp

   24 00a714a4 e8b0fcffff       call     Fibo!ILT+340(__RTC_CheckEsp)
(00a71159)

   24 00a714a9 8be5             mov      esp,ebp

   24 00a714ab 5d               pop      ebp

   24 00a714ac c3               ret
```

Using the command below we're going to display the first occurrence of **ret** instruction:

```
0:000> # ret 00a71440

Fibo!wmain+0x6c [c:\development\my tools\book\fibo\fibo\fibo.cpp @ 24]:

00a714ac c3              ret
```

Let's look for another pattern:

```
0:000> # call*Fibo!ILT 00a71440

Fibo!wmain+0x2a [c:\development\my tools\book\fibo\fibo\fibo.cpp @ 21]:

00a7146a e89bfbffff      call    Fibo!ILT+5(?FiboRecursiveYAIIHZ) (00a7100a)
```

Now, let's look for **push** instructions in a specific module/executable:

```
0:000> lm
start    end        module name
00a60000 00a7b000   Fibo     C (private pdb symbols)  C:\development\My Tools\Book\Fibo\Debug\Fibo.pdb
67350000 67473000   MSVCR90D   (deferred)
690c0000 69197000   MSVCP90D   (private pdb symbols)  c:\publicsymbols\msvcp90d.i386.pdb\7B1C9137C0074A0E921BE874ADF944191\msvcp90d.i386.pdb
75e00000 75e44000   KERNELBASE   (deferred)
75eb0000 75fb0000   kernel32   (deferred)
776c0000 77840000   ntdll      (pdb symbols)  c:\publicsymbols\wntdll.pdb\E06BEA155E9748BEA818E2D0DD2FED952\wntdll.pdb

0:000> # push 00a60000
Fibo!__ImageBase+0x40:
00a60040 0e              push    cs
```

[This page is intentionally left blank]

Notes

(KA) .thread *Sets the current thread context* *0n255 0xFF 1111 1111*

CPSIA information can be obtained at www.ICGtesting.com
Printed in the USA
BVOW08s0924230814

363973BV00016B/258/P